THE LIZARD SPEAKS

The Lizard Speaks:
Essays on the Writings of
Frederick Manfred

Edited by
Nancy Owen Nelson

The Center for Western Studies

© 1998 by The Center for Western Studies

ALL RIGHTS RESERVED

The Prairie Plains Series Number 6

Published by The Center for Western Studies
Box 727, Augustana College
Sioux Falls, South Dakota 57197

    The Center for Western Studies is an archives, library, museum, publishing house, and educational agency concerned principally with collecting, preserving, and interpreting prehistoric, historic, and contemporary materials that document native and immigrant cultures of the northern prairie plains. The Center promotes understanding of the region through exhibits, publications, art shows, conferences, and academic programs. It is committed, ultimately, to defining the contribution of the region to American civilization. The Prairie Plains Series is dedicated to the publication at moderate prices of essential but limited-market titles.

Library of Congress Cataloging-in-Publication Data:

The lizard speaks: essays on the writings of Frederick Manfred / edited by
    Nancy Owen Nelson, 1946—
        p. cm. — (The Prairie plains series)
    Includes bibliographical references.
    ISBN 0-931170-67-2
        1. Manfred Frederick Feikema, 1912-   . 2. Authors, American—20th century. 3. Great Plains in literature. 4. West (U.S.) in literature. I. Title. II. Series

Printed in United States of America

PINE HILL PRESS, INC.
Freeman, S. Dak. 57029

Table of Contents

Introduction: Nancy Owen Nelson vii

I. FINDING A VOICE: THE EARLY WORKS

Arthur R. Huseboe, Introduction to *The Golden Bowl*,
50th Anniversary Edition 2

John R. Milton, Afterword to *The Golden Bowl* 11

Nancy Owen Nelson, Frederick Manfred and
the Anglo-Saxon Oral Tradition 16

Forrest M. Byrd, *This is the Year:* A Southern Perspective 30

Patricia Marie Murphy, Someday Hero 41

Lawrence I. Berkove, The Search for Wisdom:
The World's Wanderer Trilogy 54

II. FINDING A NAME: BUCKSKINS AND OTHER MATTERS

Mick McAllister, "Wolf That I Am . . .": Animal Symbology in
the Buckskin Man Tales 64

Larry R. Juchartz, From the Usable Past, Models for
Postmodern Readers: Student Responses and
Theoretical Approaches to *Lord Grizzly* 75

Richard Bailey, Gender, Power, and Knowing in
Conquering Horse. 97

Barbara Howard Meldrum, The Land, History, and the Self in
Fiction by Margaret Laurence and Frederick Manfred 108

Karol Brue Aeschlimann, Manfred's Use of Language in
Riders of Judgment 124

Sanford E. Marovitz, From Mythic American Visions
to a Shattered American Dream: Nature Expropriated
in the Buckskin Man Tales. 130

Delbert E. Wylder, Frederick Manfred: The Quest of the
Independent Writer 155

III. RETURNING TO SIOUXLAND: THE LATER NOVELS

Christy Rishoi, Seduction, Betrayal—and Redemption:
Flowers of Desire as a Modern Sentimental Novel. 172

Joseph M. Flora, Baseball as Passionate Preference in
No Fun on Sunday 180

IV. ASSESSING A LEGACY: NOTES OF APPRECIATION

Olga Klekner, Hypnotized by a Reptile: A Student's Account
of How the East Was Won by a Giant's Dusty Roar 198

Max Westbrook, "What would they do?"
The Narrative Integrity of Fred Manfred 208

Freya Manfred, "Love, Dad" 217

Books by Frederick Manfred 229

Introduction

The Metamorphosis of *The Lizard Speaks: Essays on the Writings of Frederick Manfred*

by Nancy Owen Nelson

In some of the most poetic writing of Frederick Manfred's career, he recreates the transformation of the Badlands from the Glacial Age to the 1930s. This passage from his 1944 novel *The Golden Bowl* describes the living and dying of dinosaur life in the midwestern plains:

> This great swamp wriggled with gargantuan life, with the oreodon, the brontosaurus, and tyrannosaurus rex. In it, savage-toothed triceratop struggled with wallowing dinosaur. The hollows and bogs and puddles were loud with the wrestling of treacherous reptiles. There were sounds made then, and echoes, that no man's ear has ever heard. Millions of the most monstrous bodies, caging but the very feeblest sorts of mental light, died every day for thousands of centuries. And filled the bottom of the huge swamp with their bones. (147-48)

This passage reveals two characteristics about Frederick Manfred's creative vision which have been evident from the beginnings of his career as an artist: first, his ability, through intuition, to recreate a sensory experience that "no man's ear has ever heard" (147): second, his innate connection to the primordial "lizard brain" which is the center of the creative process.

This creative theory is what binds together the essays in this collection. It is the aspect of Manfred's work which has distinguished it from the works of his peers over the past fifty years; it is, I believe, the element which gives power to his writing, leading Wallace Stegner in his Foreword to *Conversations with Frederick Manfred* (1974) to call him an "elemental force" (xvi) who "boils with imaginative vigor and a mighty gusto" and who "trusts his Old Lizard more than I would trust mine" (xiv) .

Throughout his writing life, Manfred has made clear his beliefs in the power of the intuition to evoke the creative voice.[1] One of his most striking examinations of this concept is in "Space, Yes: Time, No," a 1981 lecture at the University of South Dakota.[2] In a fascinating layman's discussion of quantum physics, Manfred presents his theory that the "IC [Interior Commentator] lives in the right hemisphere of our brain, where other voices also live, the kind of voices that once qualified a man to become a priest or soothsayer, or the voice at Delphi . . ." (85). Manfred explains this intuitive process as a result of the interaction of subatomic matter, which he names

> "Deon[s]" (after the Latin word "deo" meaning "god-like" and the Greek word "deon" or "deontos" meaning "that which is obligatory") . . . the superluminal communication with all other building blocks at all times. This would account for ESP, for premonition, prescience, intuition, hunches, etc. (94)

Thus, our creative energies are fed and enlightened by a process of interactive matter: "The deons in US are identical with deons OUT THERE. Deons know. They correspond with each other—if we let them" (95).

It is the driving force of his creativity that first drew me to Manfred's work: the poetic chapter prefaces in *The Chokecherry Tree* (1948), the poet/commentator's voice in *This is the Year* (1947), the lyrical beauty of the "poems" which begin and end *The Golden Bowl*. Pulled into his work by this poetic voice, I began to study how it related to Manfred's important theme of the land, and man's primordial connection to his sources.[3] My exploration led to the concept of this volume, *The Lizard Speaks*.

Manfred's theory of creativity is well-rooted in Western realism, according to Max Westbrook. In his essay "Conservative, Liberal, and Western: Three Modes of American Realism," published in *The South Dakota Review* in 1966, he argues that in the Western mode, the real is a part of the unconscious; the real "cannot be penetrated by the rational mind" (15). For the Western writer, the "inner self . . . is our contact with the universal" (18). In light of this interpretation of Western American literature, Westbrook illuminates what distinguishes Manfred's creative vision: a direct relationship between the subconscious elements (intuition, pri-

INTRODUCTION ix

mordial forces) and the creative process. This process is, in one way or another, the subject of each of the essays included in this volume.

The generic arrangement of the essays suggests Manfred's developing vision of voice, and place, and the ways in which these elements would figure into his creative process. Section One, "Finding a Voice: the Early Works," explores Manfred's efforts to define voice in the context of his home territory, Siouxland. The first two pieces, reprinted from editions of his first novel, *The Golden Bowl* (1944) provide background and analysis of the novel. Arthur Huseboe's Introduction to the 50th Anniversary edition examines the canvas of Manfred's fifty-year career, including his commitment to the regional realism of many of his novels. Manfred's voice, which he first identified in writing *Bowl*, continues to be his own distinctive expression, one which dominates the broad canon of his work. John R. Milton's Afterword to the same edition, thrice published with editions of *The Golden Bowl*, provides a biographical sketch and background on the seven drafts of the book, its critical reception, and (important to our purpose) the "visionary" nature of the experiences of Maury Grant, protagonist. Milton's essay analyzes the novel mythically, rooting it firmly in Manfred's use of the subconscious in the creative process.

The mythical aspect of Manfred's early voice is analyzed in my essay "Frederick Manfred and the Anglo-Saxon Oral Tradition," in which I explore the influence of Manfred's Anglo-Saxon roots on the creation of voice in *The Golden Bowl, This is the Year,* and *The Chokecherry Tree*; the poetic passages in these three novels reveal Manfred's function as "singer of tales," one who relies on the intuitive powers of the Lizard.[4] Likewise, Forrest M. Byrd, in *"This is the Year:* A Southern Perspective," suggests the deeper, more intuitive and primordial themes of the novel, analyzing "the overlooked" in *This is the Year.* Byrd contends that looking deeper into the otherwise "observant[ly] mute" protagonist reveals multiple layers of meaning which have gone unacknowledged and unappreciated by both critics and readers. Patricia M. Murphy in "Someday Hero" explores the Biblical roots of the ordinary heroism of Elof Lofblom in *The Chokecherry Tree*. The last essay dealing with the visionary quality of Manfred's early work is Lawrence I. Berkove's essay "The Search for Wisdom: The *World's Wanderer* Trilogy." While tracing Manfred's upbringing in the Calvinist tradition,

Berkove shows how Manfred's knowledge of the Bible shaped his literary effort in the trilogy. In particular, the book of Ecclesiastes directed protagonist Thurs Wraldson's "infinite search" for the "infinite truth." Ecclesiastes' "Preacher," who illustrates the "vanity" of searching for truth in man's mundane goods—"knowledge, righteousness, pleasure, and wealth"—provides a context for Thurs' search in the novels. Berkove's essay suggests to the Manfred reader a connection between the trilogy and *The Golden Bowl* (the title of which is derived from Ecclesiastes); both novels examine the Preacher's theme of the folly of earthly gains, and mankind's ultimate return to the earth.

The second section of this collection, "Finding a Name: Buckskins and Other Matters," examines some of Manfred's much-lauded Buckskin Man Tales in light of his creative theory. In the "middle period" (1954-1976) defined by the Buckskins and ending with *Green Earth*, Manfred moved outside of his immediate territory to write about the historical West. The publications of *Milk of Wolves* (1976) and *Green Earth* (1977) mark a turning back toward his own region and his own twentieth century.

In "Wolf that I Am: Animal Symbology in the Buckskin Man Tales," Mick McAllister reveals the wolf and bear symbolism in both novels as it aids the characters to discover their own kinship to the animal.[5] An essay which connects this animal theme to urban students is L. R. Juchartz' "From the Usable Past, Models for Postmodern Readers: Student Responses to *Lord Grizzly*." By examining specific student reactions taken from journals and essays, Juchartz studies the threefold impact of the novel on the contemporary urban student: the reader's personal identification with the novel, the novel as "stimulus for escape," and the novel as "guide to survival." Juchartz' analysis suggests the intuitive nature of *Lord Grizzly*, giving further credence to the Lizard concept.

Richard Bailey, in "Gender, Power, and Knowing in *Conquering Horse*," discusses the primordial feminine principle in that novel (1959), illustrating Manfred's redefinition of masculinity; in Conquering Horse's character lies the androgynous potential, the blending of the anima and animus. Certainly, this interpretation relates the role of the unconscious to Manfred's creativity. Barbara Meldrum's "The Land, History, and the Self in Fiction by Margaret Laurence and Frederick Manfred" explores Manfred's treatment of D. H. Lawrence's "American self" in *Milk of Wolves* and *Conquer-*

INTRODUCTION   xi

ing Horse. The primordial link of man to the land and animals illustrates the creative energy of the Lizard.

Karol Aeschlimann takes a look at how the language of another Buckskin Tale, *Riders of Judgment* (1957), illustrates Manfred's use of mythic language to evoke the "Old Lizard" in the experiences of the three Hammett brothers. This language, she argues, connects these men, as it does all of Manfred's characters, to their animal natures.

Sanford E. Marovitz' piece, "From Mythic American Visions to a Shattered American Dream," traces the gradual devolution throughout the Buckskins, chronologically considered, from the mythic "dream of paradise" depicted in the Native American world of *Conquering Horse* to the "chaos of nineteenth-century American reality" in *Riders of Judgment.*

Closing out the second section is Delbert Wylder's seminal essay "Frederick Manfred: The Quest of the Independent Writer," which reviews Manfred's career to 1979, focusing on the development of his distinctive narrative voice, a voice independent of the expectation of the current literary community. Wylder examines *Milk of Wolves*, *The Manly-Hearted Woman*, and *Green Earth*, finding the last one Manfred's "finest to date" because of its detail of everyday life.

The third section, "Returning to Siouxland: the Later Novels," considers two of Manfred's final three published novels produced in his later years—*Flowers of Desire* (1989) and *No Fun on Sunday* (1990)—and how they reveal Manfred's "return," in his last years, to writing about his own time and the territory of his birth. In these novels, as I have indicated elsewhere, Manfred explores a number of issues that have been central to his writing: "the quality of rural life in the Midwest, the importance of properly maintaining the land, the importance of family tradition, and the realities of human passion" ("Frederick Manfred," 695).

Christy Rishoi's essay, "Seduction, Betrayal—and Redemption: *Flowers of Desire* as a Modern Sentimental Novel," places Manfred's story about a young girl's loss of innocence in the context of a nineteenth-century form—the sentimental novel—while giving it a twentieth-century solution—Carla Simmons' personal salvation. Rishoi sees this work as distinctly different from Manfred's canon, an effort which, while not "flawless, . . . [is] no less a testament to the strongly individualized creative force he brought to all of his work."

The second essay in Section Three brings the reader back to the small communities and farms of Siouxland. Joseph Flora in "Baseball as Passionate Preference in *No Fun on Sunday*" examines baseball as a metaphor in Manfred's world: the gender game, and thus the novel, defines the gender roles of the society.

Certainly the small number of essays in this section reveals the open territory which the later Manfred works offer to readers and critics. In particular, the gender issue discussed by both Rishoi and Flora points us in an important direction which is explored in depth in his last published novel, *Of Lizards and Angels*.

The final section of *The Lizard Speaks* brings the book to an appropriate close by paying tribute to the legacy that Frederick Feikema Manfred has made to the American literary canon. Olga Klekner's "Hypnotized by a Reptile" illustrates how, as a non-native speaker and a college student, she came to appreciate the poetry and beauty of the English language through studying *The Golden Bowl*. Klekner attributes Manfred's poetic power to the primordial voice of the Lizard. Max Westbrook's "'What would they do?': The Narrative Integrity of Fred Manfred" gives emphasis to Manfred's discovery of the importance of sacrality in everyday life and the problems which his characters encounter when they ignore it. In Manfred's ability to enter into his characters' consciousnesses, he is able to create ones who are "stubborn and contrary, filled with abounding energy, and excited to be alive."

The section of tribute to Frederick Manfred ends with a piece which I believe is perhaps the most fitting tribute possible—from the writings of Manfred's daughter Freya Manfred. In the passages from her memoir-in-progress, "Love, Dad," she provides us with a first-hand account of living with Frederick Manfred, father and writer, and of the inseparable nature of these two sides of his consciousness. She tells of his daily writing regimen, that it "suffused our house and yard as if it were a kind of plant life, growing and changing and natural as weather. . ."; of how he taught his children the love of reading, the appreciation of the artist's struggle. Freya Manfred includes a letter of advice from her father about the writing life; she comments on his love of his craft: he was "tired, but happy. Writing was a gift and a blessing, and he was lucky." What better way to complete a volume of essays about an artist than with a tribute from his artist-daughter?

*****

The mystical nature of intuition in Manfred's work has been explored by other writers and critics before the publication of this collection. Robert C. Wright, in his book-length study of Manfred, writes an insightful chapter called "Coming to Terms with The Old Lizard" (140-58) . In studying Manfred's connections between mysticism and creativity, Wright states that "mysticism . . . is . . . a key to [Manfred's] creative style and energy" (140) . Manfred believes that civilization erodes our access to primordial knowledge and that we must strive to regain contact with the Old Lizard. His Lizard is "akin to instinct or to G. C. Jung's notion of the collective unconscious": we have lost our primordial wisdom, and one way to rediscover it is through dreams (Wright 143) .

Peter P. DeBoer, in his article "Frederick Feikema Manfred: Spiritual Naturalist," further explores the almost holy relationship between man and the land which permeates Manfred's works:

> He is concerned with the relationship of the human being to his environment. He insists that [quoting Manfred] "it's as if the land [Siouxland] has its own souls and it evolves its own souls. . . . I think you're given the nervous equipment to have a soul; that's all you're given at birth. After that your environment makes you whatever you are, makes your soul." (19)

For Martin Bucco, stated in *A Literary History of the American West* (1987), Manfred "favors historical realism overlaid with mythic patterns. . . . He loves sacred places, responds to dreams, listens to his own 'tone'" (1307). Rodney J. Mulder and John H. Timmerman, in *Frederick Manfred: a Bibliography and Publishing History*, further align Manfred's work with the mythic scope of Western literature, and they cite Mircea Eliade in *Myth and Reality*: "Such literature begins in the physical thing in order to seek the primordial thing; the real meaning behind the fact" (11). Mick McAllister, in the Foreword to Manfred's essay collection *Prime Fathers* (1989), describes Manfred as a "whole sexual creature . . . at peace with his anima rather than threatened by his feminine role" (x), and Joe Flora, in his Introduction to the Gregg Press edition of *Lord Grizzly,* cites the primordial connection of Hugh to "both the American Indian and the animal in his discovery of self" (xi). Further, Les Whipp, in his article on the autobiographical *The Wind Blows Free,* describes the poetic ecstasy which permeates much of Manfred's creative effort:

> . . . the artist responds to the mystical sounds of nature with aspirations of his own sounds, voice, creation. . . . he senses the creative process that . . . seems linked to the center of the earth . . . and . . . to the very beginnings of life on earth by the relic of the earliest ages. ("Frederick Manfred's *The Wind Blows Free,*" 125).

Indeed, the youthful Manfred saw in the South Dakota Badlands the divine beauty of the origins of all life and found his voice to tell his dust bowl tales in *The Golden Bowl;* in his life's work he continued to fulfill his dream of creating a kind of "Siouxland Saga" which would cover the broad sweep of the history of land, man, and animal in the midwestern plains of our continent. In Manfred's own words,

> In my work I want to be a voice speaking—telling how we are and how we were; that is how we grew up and these were our dreams and, too bad, we are going to die. This is holy work. I'm in it for keeps. (qtd. in Wright 148)

In pursuing his vision, Manfred reminds us all of our own indebtedness to that which connects us with all living forms—our intuitive, primordial selves. These essays will, I hope, provide Manfred readers and scholars with more evidence of his expression of "the sacrality of all life" (Westbrook 17).

*****

Works Cited

Bucco, Martin. "Epilogue: The Development of Western Literary Criticism." *A Literary History of the American West*. Fort Worth: Texas Christian UP, 1987. 1283-1316.

DeBoer, Peter P. "Frederick Feikema Manfred: Spiritual Naturalist." *Reformed Journal* (April, 1963) : 19-23.

Flora, Joseph. Introduction. *Lord Grizzly*. By Frederick Manfred. Boston: Gregg Press, 1980. v-xix.

Manfred, Frederick. *The Golden Bowl*. Brookings, South Dakota: South Dakota Humanities Foundation, 1992.

----. *Conversations with Frederick Manfred*. Mod. John R. Milton. Salt Lake City: U of Utah P, 1974.

---. "Space, Yes: Time: No." *Duke's Mixture*. Sioux Falls: The Center for Western Studies, 1994. 81-96.

McAllister, Mick. Foreword. *Prime Fathers*. Frederick Manfred. Salt Lake City: Howe Bros., 1988. ix-xiii.

Mulder, Rodney J. and John H. Timmerman. Introduction. *Frederick Manfred: a Bibliography and Publishing History*. Sioux Falls: The Center for Western Studies, 1981. 9-13.

Nelson, Nancy Owen. "Frederick Manfred." *Updating the Literary West*. Fort Worth: Texas Christian UP, 1997. 693-700.

Stegner, Wallace. Foreword. *Conversations with Frederick Manfred*. Mod. John R. Milton. Salt Lake City: U of Utah P, 1974. xi-xvi.

Westbrook, Max. "Conservative, Liberal, and Western: Three Modes of American Realism." *South Dakota Review*. 4.2 (Summer, 1966) : 3-19.

Whipp, Leslie. "Frederick Manfred's *The Wind Blows Free:* Autobiographical Mythology." *South Dakota Review*. 27.2 (Summer, 1989) : 100-128.

Wright, Robert C. *Frederick Manfred*. Boston: Twayne Publishers, 1979.

---. "The Myth of the Isolated Self in Manfred's Siouxland Novels." *Where the West Begins*. Ed. Arthur R. Huseboe and William Geyer. Sioux Falls, The Center for Western Studies, 1978. 110-118.

*****

Bibliographic Note[6]

For readers who wish to explore the Manfred canon in greater depth, there are a number of studies and editions that have been produced which will serve as guides to the exploration.

One of the first—or perhaps the first—critical writings on Manfred was John R. Milton's "Voice from Siouxland: Frederick Feikema Manfred," in *College English*, 19 (December 1957) : 104-111. Milton sets the stage for serious consideration of Manfred's work by providing an analysis of his first eight books. Another critic who brought attention to Manfred was publisher Alan Swallow, who in "The Mavericks" placed him among writers who had broken from the traditions of the eastern publishing establishment (*Critique: Studies in Modern Fiction*, 11 [1958-59]: 74-92) . By 1974, after several articles had been published on Manfred, Joseph M. Flora's Western Writers Series monograph, *Frederick Manfred* (Boise State University, Boise, Idaho, 1974), provided a useful critical perspective on his early novels, the Buckskin Man Tales, and his short fiction collected in *Arrow of Love* and *Apples of Paradise*. And Robert Wright's book *Frederick Manfred* (Boston: Twayne Publishers, 1979) presented the Manfred canon from biographical and literary perspectives.

Another valuable resource which provides insight into Manfred's creative vision is *The Selected Letters of Frederick Manfred: 1932-1954*, Lincoln: U of Nebraska P, 1989, ed. Arthur R. Huseboe and Nancy Owen Nelson. The letters reveal much about Manfred's college years and travels throughout the United States in the 1930s, his battle with tuberculosis, his marriage to his wife, Maryanna, and the birth of their children, and, throughout the correspondence, his developing vision of his writing craft; readers can follow the writer's thought processes behind the creation of such novels as *The Golden Bowl* and *Lord Grizzly*.

In addition, during the last decade of his life Manfred produced two volumes of essays which provide insights into his literary theory as well as the influential voices in his life. *Prime Fathers* (1989) contains essays on important men such as his father, Sinclair Lewis, and Hubert Humphrey, and the *Duke's Mixture* essays (1994) deal with a variety of topics related to his theories on writing and on the importance of place.

INTRODUCTION   xvii

Much remains to be read and explored. The posthumously published *The Frederick Manfred Reader* (Duluth: Holy Cow! Press, 1996) compiles thematically arranged excerpts from Manfred's work ranging from early publications such as *Boy Almighty* (1945), *This is the Year*, and *The Chokecherry Tree* through the later works such as *No Fun on Sunday* and *Of Lizards and Angels;* such an arrangement reinforces both the thematic unity and the universality of Frederick Manfred's work. Editor John Calvin Rezmerski illustrates Manfred's breadth and vision in the Introduction to the reader:

> . . . clarity of sensory experience was always important to Manfred's writing—as important as the philosophical inquiry. One of the indicators of his achievement as a writer is the way in which the two modes go along with each other, neither disrupting or contradicting the other, and both of them integrated seamlessly (usually) into the material that has come from his life and the research he did. (xiv)

Indeed, as the *Reader* illustrates, Manfred's writings have a broad and continuing appeal to both the rural and the broader, more "worldly" audience:

> Manfred immersed himself in the best of what European and American culture have to offer, and a good deal more besides. He was insatiably literate, inquisitive about physics, astronomy, linguistics, archaeology, anthropology, music, painting, architecture, botany, local gossip, the literary politics of New York, the give-and-take of political campaigning at the state and national level. . . . And that literacy and curiosity made him stick his nose and his fingers into the corners and crannies of American culture, and let him write of his beloved Siouxland in full consciousness of the whole America and the whole universe he revered with full Whitmaniac earnestness and energy. (xviii)

Thus, the reader of Frederick Manfred will not be disappointed. The possibilities of further study are endless. May the efforts made in this volume spur others to read, study, and analyze the legacy of Frederick Manfred and his contributions to Western, Midwestern, and American literature and culture.

Notes

[1] Manfred uses a number of terms to identify the "lizard" concept, including "Old Lizard," "Old Adam," Old Primate," and "Interior Commentator." See *Conversations with Frederick Manfred*, mod. John R. Milton (Salt Lake City: U of Utah P, 1974) 43, 45.

[2] Recently published in the essay collection *Duke's Mixture* (Sioux Falls: Center for Western Studies, 1994) 81-96.

[3] See Robert Wright's "The Myth of the Isolated Self," *Where the West Begins*, ed. Arthur R. Huseboe and William Geyer (Sioux Falls: Center for Western Studies, 1978) 110-118.

[4] Reprinted from *Western American Literature* 19.4 (February 1985) : 263-274.

[5] Reprinted from *Western American Literature* 18.1 (May 1983) : 21-31.

[6] The reader is advised to consult the following resources for a more thorough bibliography of primary and secondary writings on Frederick Manfred: *A Literary History of the American West* and *Updating the Literary West* (Texas Christian UP, 1987 and 1997, respectively) .

Part I

Finding a Voice: The Early Works

Introduction to
The Golden Bowl

by Arthur R. Huseboe

It is Frederick Manfred's most reprinted work, *The Golden Bowl*, or will be with this fiftieth anniversary edition; and its newest manifestation comes within weeks of the appearance of his novel number twenty-three, *Of Lizards and Angels*. Both novels, the earliest and the latest, are owing in large measure to Manfred's youthful life experiences in northwest Iowa and in South Dakota, and both contain some of his very earliest writing, and some of his most poetic. *The Golden Bowl* in particular consists of rich poetry. The elemental quality of the struggles of Maury Grant and the Thor family against the wild forces of nature calls for elemental language and rhythms. The dry wind lashes the land in Old Testament rhythms. The Big Wind, the Big Dust, pulls at the houses and barns, pushes at the people in them, and the people wait for the rains and for the sprouts to open and for the grain to grow tall and become golden and for the harvesters to gather-in the earth's bounty and for human life to continue and for men and women to believe in the work of their hands. Maury Grant and the Thor family of South Dakota, like Manfred and his Feikema family of northwest Iowa, become symbols of the struggle of the race to survive and to find joy in the battle and in the victory.

And so *The Golden Bowl* is first of all the story of a young man's growing realization of the part he must play in the human struggle to persevere and to prevail. It is a story, too, of love and separation, of love and restoration, and of the memory of a man recalling the golden age of the land—before the iron age of drought had overtaken it—and of his faith in that memory.

The Golden Bowl is also a geography lesson about the West, the northern prairie plains, South Dakota in particular. Lying near the center of the continent as it does, South Dakota is as far away from the sea as one can be in the United States and in North America, 1000 miles away in all four directions: from Hudson Bay, the east coast, the Gulf of Mexico, and the Pacific Ocean. South Dakota and the other northern plains states lie where great masses of air—rushing down from Canada, sliding across the Rockies, and pushing up from the Gulf—meet one another in terrible aerial conflicts that bring the deadly blizzards of winter, the tornadoes and torrential rains of spring and summer, or the prolonged drought that knows no season. When the east-flowing jet stream drops to the south and stays there for months and years, then the killing droughts take over the land and crops will not grow, and the people leave the farms and small towns and move to safer country. Some move to Sioux Falls, to the relative security of the city; more go to the West or Southwest, where there may be drought, but at least no raging tornadoes or winter storms.

The danger of a long-lasting and tragic drought is as great now in the northern prairie plains as it has ever been and perhaps greater. A second agricultural revolution has swept away most of the small family farms in the state, and with them have gone many of the wooded windbreaks that offered some hope at least of slowing erosion when dry winds blow fiercely over talcum-powder soil. As farms grow larger and larger, as the quarters and half sections are stripped bare of their clapboard houses and sagging barns, the land lies more and more open to the same big wind that battered Maury Grant and the Thors sixty years ago.

How timely *The Golden Bowl* is as a testimony to the fragility of life on the great American desert! As I drove west from Sioux Falls toward Mitchell one early May day four years ago, a gray cloud began to rise in the west ahead of me, and by the time I reached the James River, fast-moving dust-squalls from the north had begun to sweep thin drifts of black soil across Interstate 90. It had been a dry winter and spring throughout much of the state; and in North Dakota, I had heard, miles-wide dust clouds were a daily occurrence. We seemed on the verge of another Dust Bowl.

But this time the winds brought relief, the rains fell, and the specter of a decade of dust like the 1930s once again faded away. In the years since, ample moisture throughout most of the northern plains has kept our vast land productive, a green earth, a golden bowl of grain and cattle that helps to feed the world.

The Golden Bowl is also a story behind which lies a story. For the making of the novel wrought a sea-change in Manfred, turned him from a seeker to a finder, to one who, having found his voice, was now condemned for ever to use it. The great change began in 1934 when he hitchhiked across South Dakota to Yellowstone Park and home again.

Manfred says of the journey west, "That trip released my soul." It was at a party at Jim Shields' on a Saturday night in mid-June 1937, not long after Manfred had gotten a job with the Minneapolis *Journal*, that his creative spirit broke free. In a living room full of twenty people, late, after President Franklin Roosevelt's liberal program had been thoroughly analyzed and the conversation had run out of water, the talk turned to vacation trips. Said Shields: "You should hear Fred tell you about the trip he once took through the dust bowl in the Dakotas." Manfred demurred. "Fred really saw some pretty raw stuff." Manfred still demurred.

"Go on. Tell about the hobo and the snake. And oh yes, especially about that old maid." Encouragement from the group. And so Manfred began, reluctant at first, but warming up as the party in the living room grew silent. He began the story, added a little more detail, embellished some, enjoyed their laughter, answered many questions, and went home in a warm glow. "For once in my life," he wrote in 1979 in *The Wind Blows Free*, "I'd finally told a story well enough to hold everybody's attention." What a discovery and what a confession for one of America's foremost story tellers!

He now saw as wasted time the nights he had spent typing out stories in the manner of Ernest Hemingway and John Dos Passos and Thorstein Veblen and other writers current in the public eye. He had told a tale in his own voice, "the way I saw it in my head," and not through someone else's eyes. When he returned to his room he began to type and, as if he were harvesting against a coming storm, wrote through the night and into the following afternoon. More than fifty pages when he had finished. "The hell with Hemingway and Steinbeck and Dos Passos," he told himself. Over the next two months he wrote and rewrote, until the hobo began to emerge as the central character and a finished book took shape.

No matter that there would be major rewritings over the next seven years, or two years wasted in a sanatorium; the first draft of the first novel was finished. What Manfred needed next, now that he believed that he could tell a story, was an authoritative voice that would confirm his belief. That voice came from Meridel Le Sueur, a woman well known in the Twin Cities as a Marxist writer, critic, and teacher of writing. Manfred went to her for advice, and what she told him opened a door to the future that would never again close.

'In a passionate letter that August to his good friend John Huizenga, Manfred reported what had happened. He gave Le Sueur the manuscript to read and two weeks later met her at the Stockholm Cafe for her reaction:

> "May I go along with you to Europe next summer?" she asked him.
> "Whaaat?"
> "Yes, You can go, you know."
> I sat down. I tried to keep the table still.
> "Yes, Frederick." She pointed to the ms. "It's powerful. It should outrank and outsell John Steinbeck's *Of Mice and Men*. Of course, that's my idea. The prospective public is fickle and they may not do just that."
> My face was very red. Altogether in one guey lump I remembered my farm days, college days, basketball days, my days with you [John], my fumblings with writing before, my awkward handling of ideas and facts . . . . . no . . . . . no . . . . . she was just kidding.

But Meridel Le Sueur was not kidding. Her warm praise and mild criticism convinced Manfred that he would eventually be published. Years later he wrote to Le Sueur that she—with Helen Clapesattle of the University of Minnesota—had "turned open more doorknobs for me than all the rest. You told me long ago that I could write and that I had love in my heart." And Manfred needed that encouragement, for seven years and seven re-writings were to pass before the publication of *The Golden Bowl*. The rest of the compelling story, however, that Manfred told at Jim Shields' house that Saturday night had to wait until 1979 to be written out in full. You can read about "the hobo and the snake" and especially about "that old maid" in a book called *The Wind Blows Free*.

Along the way to the publication by Webb Publishers of *The Golden Bowl* in 1944, Manfred stumbled upon Sinclair Lewis. The young man had left the sanatorium in March 1942, carrying the manuscript with him and hurling a Parthian shot behind him as he fled: "My life is in the chance that I can become a really fine writer. And I mean that. I came in here not caring to live except that I had a faint hope that I could write in here . . . . I'm not living just to live. Hell, anybody can do that." Lewis was teaching writing at the

University of Minnesota in the fall of 1942, Manfred learned. He hoped that the famous author would read one of his novels and help him find a publisher, and so he prevailed on Joseph Warren Beach, chairman of the English department, to take Lewis's temperature on the subject. The answer was NO, in a letter politely dated November 22, 1942. Lewis had to read student papers, he wrote, and there was desperate work to be done on his new novel, and reading Manfred's ms. would be "quite impossible." Many months later, when Lewis learned what the title of the dust bowl novel was to be, he protested vigorously to Manfred's publisher against the appropriation of a title that Henry James had already used. But it was too late, and Manfred risked the wrath of his principal household god and held on to *The Golden Bowl* with its glittering edge of irony.

Lewis was not finished. When the book came out, he read it. He liked it, in spite of the title, and he sent the book and a recommendation to the American Academy of Arts and Letters. The award that followed, coming as it did on the heels of a regional writing award from the Rockefeller Foundation, was a wonderful confirmation of Manfred's faith in and labor on *The Golden Bowl*. Best of all in a way, the novel finally brought the two men together. The voice on the phone was high-pitched and nervous. "Mr. Feikema? This is Sinclair Lewis. I've read your *Golden Bowl* and I'd like to meet you." But that meeting, told about with relish by Manfred in *Prime Fathers*, is, as they say, another story.

And now, nearly half a century later, *The Golden Bowl* is returning in this new edition, published by the South Dakota Humanities Foundation in recognition of Manfred's lifetime of accomplishments.

When novelist Wallace Stegner heard that *The Golden Bowl* was going to enjoy a fiftieth anniversary edition in 1992, he wrote to me of his pleasure at the prospect: "It is one of the best works about the Dustbowl years," he wrote, "which for some curious reason never got much of a play in fiction except in *The Grapes of Wrath*. Maybe the urban and rural Depression crowded the drought off the pages of novels." Stegner went on to compare his own health and the younger man's, noting, regretfully, "The habit, the pleasures, and the capacity of work are all fading. Please give Fred my felicitations on his vigorous youth and my congratulations on the reissuing of his good book, but tell him I'm not Lord Grizzly, able to crawl a hundred miles after being skinned alive." The friendly call of one old mountain man to his younger companyero a few rods behind him on the trail.

Manfred's vigorous youth *is* remarkable. It would be so if only because he has survived a near-fatal dose of tuberculosis in 1940-1942. But it is still more remarkable because he has translated his survival into a half century of booming good health by placing his determined faith in quantities of fresh air and fresh vegetables. Home grown, the latter, and nourished up by his own broad hand. Most remarkable of all is the youth of his imagination, a well of memory so deep that characters continue to climb out, often unbidden, clamoring to have their tales told. Some of the youngest memories are now the newest works, and Manfred has been lately inviting in and conjuring up a new cast of characters, and so *The Wrath of Love* is in the making, novel number twenty-four.

This latest effort is the result of no sudden burst of energy but rather is further evidence of the disciplined writing that has characterized Manfred's creative life from the very beginning. A review of his career over fifty years reveals the remarkable consistency of his creativity as well as the equally remarkable inconsistency of his acceptance by readers and critics.

The Golden Bowl was generally considered an impressive first novel. Rose Feld, for example, in the *New York Herald Tribune Weekly Book Review*, wrote of the book as a "moving story" which effectively creates a realistic past. Manfred's critical reputation reached an early peak with the publication of *This is the Year* in 1947, an expansive novel of the soil that went into two printings. It was his first national best seller, was the near-unanimous winner of the Associated Press editors' award as best novel of the year, and brought praise from Sinclair Lewis and Van Wyck Brooks. A *Time* reviewer found it a "unique regional novel."

With the relative success of his first books, Manfred in 1947 undertook the vast trilogy *World's Wanderer*. Critical response to the three parts, *The Primitive*, *The Brother*, and *The Giant*, marks a turning point in Manfred's reputation. Although many reviewers pointed out the same qualities that had been praised in Manfred's earlier novels, critical reactions were markedly negative.

The success of *Lord Grizzly* in 1954, however, with its three printings in hard cover, subsequent paperback edition, and appearance on the *New York Times* best-seller list, helped to reestablish Manfred's reputation as a writer of merit. Highest praise was forthcoming from William Carlos Williams, who stated, "I have never in a lifetime of reading about our West met with anything like it," and from Walter Havighurst in the *New York Herald Tribune*, who found the book a "hair-raising novel" with "strong, clear characterizations," "the most physiological narrative ever written." These judgments were confirmed when Manfred narrowly missed the National Book Award for 1954. As Manfred himself tells the story, his mountain man novel *Lord Grizzly* and Faulkner's *A Fable* "were two of the five novels nominated in the fiction category. There were three judges and Robert Penn Warren was one of them. The judges were to vote five for first place, three for second, and one for third. As it turned out, Faulkner, who'd never won an NBA award, got it for his *A Fable*."

"Some months later, I learned what had happened. Warren voted five for *Grizzly*, three for *Fable*, and one for someone else. A second judge voted the same. So *Grizzly* had ten votes, *Fable* six votes. Malcolm Cowley, critic, was chairman of the three-man panel, and he didn't like *Grizzly*, and to make sure that it didn't get the prize, he voted five for *Fable*, and three and one for two of the other books in the final five nominated. Result: Eleven for Faulkner and ten for Manfred. Had Cowley even given one vote for *Grizzly* it would have been a tie, and then the two men who'd voted for *Grizzly* could have outvoted Cowley two to one."

In the years since the success of *Lord Grizzly*, Manfred's critical reputation has benefited the most from the publication of the other four novels in the Buckskin Man Tales series: *Riders of Judgment, Conquering Horse, Scarlet Plume,* and *King of Spades*. These five together received their highest praise in 1975 when Madison Jones (*New York Times*, February 16), in a review titled "Frederick Manfred—Parallels with Homer," spoke of his enormous energy, his careful research, and his narrative strength. "Not many novelists can match Manfred's powers as a story teller," said Jones. "The whole world is alive for him."

This review, coming at a time when more than a million copies of the Buckskin Man Tales were circulating in low-priced Signet/New American Library reprints, marked the highest point in Manfred's reputation right up to the present. While Jones gives *Riders of Judgment* faint praise and *King of Spades*, Manfred's favorite novel, somewhat less, particular praise is lavished on the three Indian novels. The essentially spiritual life of the plains Indian could not be more convincingly rendered, said Jones, than it is in *Scarlet Plume* and *Conquering Horse*. It is *Lord Grizzly*, however, that captures Jones's imagination and leads him to pronounce it a Western classic, an impressive creation worthy of comparison with the works of Homer.

It may be so. It may be, too, that sculptor Korczak Ziolkowski, he of *Crazy Horse* fame, will some long day hence be proven to have been right when he said, "*Lord Grizzly* will outlast my mountain."

But in the meantime, seventeen years after Jones in the *Times*, Manfred's reputation is reaching a new ascendant. A harvest of four new books in four seasons after nine years of scanty crops marks a return to the luxuriance of earlier stages in his writing career when a new book every one or two years kept his name warm among readers and reviewers. In 1989 appeared *The Selected Letters of Frederick Manfred, 1932-1954*, a massive collection of early letters that one reviewer has called a panoramic look at a modern son of the Middle Border gazing out, Janus-faced, on America east and west and proclaiming and championing his center in 'Siouxland' . . . (*South Dakota History*, Spring 1990)." The *Letters* were followed later in the year by *Flowers of Desire*, a World War II novel of betrayal, rape, and restoration. Neither sold well and neither was reviewed by the big-city or national publications. But the logjam was broken, and in 1990 the University of Oklahoma Press issued *No Fun On Sunday*, its first publication of original fiction. The reviewers have liked the new book, Manfred's only baseball novel, praising it for its rich detail, its deceptively simple plot, and even for the re-creation of rural Iowa life in the 1920's. And readers too are liking it, for it has gone into a second printing.

Now Oklahoma has issued Manfred's twenty-third novel, *Of Lizards and Angels*. When asked about it, he calls it his best, more powerful than *King of Spades*. It is the product of a new attitude toward his craft that Manfred has arrived at. Last spring he told the *Agassiz Review* that at age eighty he no longer worries about what his relatives and neighbors might say, and he no longer writes to please a wife or the *Minneapolis Star* or Edmund Wilson or an imagined audience, or even himself. "I decided," he said, "that I should just be the scribe and let the book write itself and not worry about what I think. And there's the big difference from where I first started and where I am now." "That's why I can say I feel like I'm just now learning to write, because I don't worry about all those little concerns I used to have."

Already Frederick Manfred has produced a body of writing that the world will not willingly let die. Already his books take up too much space to be ignored, and the readership he has already gained continues to increase as the Manfred canon enlarges. The early voices of Meridel Le Sueur and Sinclair Lewis, hailing a powerful new writer in the American midlands, have been echoed over half a century by major critics and fellow novelists. When Wallace Stegner writes, "Give Fred my felicitations on his vigorous youth," he is characterizing not only the young man of eighty but also the essential nature of his work, vigorous and youthful.

Afterword to
The Golden Bowl
by John R. Milton

In 1942 Frederick Manfred was released from the Glen Lake Tuberculosis Sanitorium in Minnesota, married Maryanna Shorba whom he had met in "the San," and had in his possession what was essentially the final draft of *The Golden Bowl*, to be his first published novel.

After a few minor changes, and the addition of the Black Hills section and the hobo camp scene, *The Golden Bowl* was published by the Webb Publishing Company in St. Paul, Minnesota, in 1944. A second printing came from Webb shortly thereafter, followed by a reprint from Grosset and Dunlap in 1946, a London edition (Dennis Dobson) in 1947, a Twenty-Fifth Anniversary edition from Dakota Press in 1969, and a reprint of that edition in 1976 by the University of New Mexico Press. The present edition is therefore the seventh.

Although the three most recent editions bear the name Frederick Manfred, it should be noted that the first editions were published under the name Feike Feikema. The Frisian family name was Feikema, and it had been the custom for many generations to name the oldest male child born to the oldest male "Feike." Manfred's grandfather was Feike Feikes Feikema V, and Manfred's father was Feike Feikes Feikema VI, although he went by the name of Frank in the United States because he had been born in the town of Franeker, Fryslan. Manfred should have been Feike Feikes Feikema VII, but his father wished to Americanize the name somewhat and also to honor his wife's father, Frederick Van Engen; and so Manfred was baptized Frederick Feikema. However, because of custom, Feike became his accepted nickname. When *The Golden Bowl* was published (his first novel), he decided to use the writing name of Feike Feikema, which was in a sense his true family name.

Manfred's first seven novels, from 1944 to 1951, were published under the name Feikema. Eventually he grew tired of having the name mispronounced, usually as Feékee Feekeéma instead of Fýka Fýkama. Study revealed that Feikema could be anglicized to Frederickman, or Fredman, or Manfred. After conducting two polls, one by telephone and one in person on Hennepin Avenue in Minneapolis, Manfred changed his name. Frederick Feikema became Frederick Feikema Manfred on April 25, 1952, by filing the name change in District Court, Hennepin County, Minnesota. Yet, as one can see, and as Manfred insisted all along, it was not really a change at all, but just an addition to the previous name. And, the added name was not really a new one but was a legitimate translation of the family name.

Lord Grizzly (1954) was the first novel to be published under the "new" name. Manfred decided that reprints of the earlier novels would use the present name, and *The Golden Bowl* was the first of these.

Frederick Manfred was born January 6, 1912, near Doon, Iowa. His Frisian father was six feet four inches tall, and his Saxon mother was six feet. All of Manfred's five brothers are over six feet three inches tall, but he is himself the tallest in the family at six feet nine inches. He attended Doon Christian School and Western Academy in Hull, Iowa, and then worked on the farm for two years. In 1930 Manfred left the Northwest Iowa farm country for the first time and enrolled at Calvin College, Grand Rapids, Michigan. He graduated with a B.A. degree and a Teacher's Life Certificate in 1934. (Just preceding him at Calvin College were Peter De Vries and David Cornel De Jong, who also became nationally known writers.) While a college student, Manfred held a number of jobs, played basketball (setting school scoring records), and participated in literary, dramatic, philosophical, and editorial activities. (Many of his college experiences are recorded in his fifth novel, *The Primitive*, 1949.)

Following graduation from college, Manfred hitchhiked around the United States, west and east. (Many people picked him up just to see if he would fit in the car.) In the *East Minneapolis Argus* of October 27, 1944, Manfred wrote: "As I lived in Iowa, near the border of South Dakota, I heard much about the drought there. In 1934, the worst year, I started out with $8 in my possession to see the country for myself. I was struck with the waste of the land and the way everything was burned. Here and there I would find people who were brave enough to stand against nature and wait until the rain came and their crops grew. Then the land would be their 'golden bowl.'" One result of Manfred's trip across South Dakota, then, was the novel *The Golden Bowl*.

By the time Manfred stopped wandering, in 1937, he had held some fifteen jobs, including semiprofessional basketball. (See his

AFTERWORD

sixth novel, *The Brother*, 1950, for a fictional account of the travels to the East.) According to newspaper clippings of the time, he was the tallest basketball player in the country. But he was also writing. In 1936 he won second place in a short story contest sponsored by Eerdman's Publishing Company in Grand Rapids. First place went to Peter De Vries and third place to David Cornel De Jong.

It was in 1937, while working as a reporter for the *Minneapolis Journal*, that Manfred wrote the first draft of *The Golden Bowl*, first called *Of These It Is Said*. In 1939 he rewrote it as a play for the local Federal Theater Project, but the project was discontinued by Congress before the play could be produced. In 1938-39 Manfred wrote his second novel, *This is the Year*. Both novels were rejected several times and Manfred was considering rewriting the second one in 1940 when he almost died of tuberculosis and subsequently spent 1940-42 in the Glen Lake Sanatorium, being discharged as "an arrested case of tuberculosis." From August 1942 to March 1943 he worked on a medical magazine published in Minneapolis, and then he decided to spend full time on writing novels.

By 1944 Manfred had rewritten *The Golden Bowl* six times, had two drafts completed of *This is the Year*, eventually published in 1947, and was well into *Boy Almighty*, a novel about his stay in the sanatorium. *Bowl* was published that year by Webb, and *Boy*, finished during the year, was published by Webb in 1945.

The Golden Bowl attracted its share of attention. John K. Sherman, writing in the *Minneapolis Tribune*, said: "It's rash to make predictions, but I'll hazard a guess that Feike Feikema in a decade will be, if not a household word, a name that brings honor to his state and added distinction to the craft of American fiction." Sherman was mostly right, although he could not know that the author's name would be different. Exactly a decade later, in 1954, *Lord Grizzly* was on the national best seller list, but under the name of Manfred. In other reviews, Wendell Johnson of the *Chicago Sun* called attention to the fact that most of the earth's population lived near the water's edge. People crowd the coasts, because their lives depend on water. Thus, the high plains, between the Midwest river valleys and the Rocky Mountains, is a special area where survival is difficult. Helen Matheson, in the *Wisconsin State Journal*, described *The Golden Bowl* as having dignity, sadness, and hope without being maudlin. She found weaknesses in the characters and in the plot, but she thought the writing was so skillful that it compensated for the other matters. She noted the strong rhythms, the figures of speech, and the style which approached blank verse. Andrea Parke wrote in the *New York Times:* "Mr. Feikema has not cluttered up his plot with trimmings, but has made of those black days of the dust storms a simple, powerful picture of human experience. His style has authority without forcing; poetic feeling without purple passages. With perceptions sifted through a discerning personality, his characters, dialogue and scenes emerge fired with life."

The Golden Bowl got good coverage around the country, and only a few reviewers complained that it needed filling out, or that it had unnecessary profanity, or that it was too similar to the work of John Steinbeck and Thomas Wolfe. The Steinbeck comparison was legitimate, both because of style and because of subject (at least in *The Grapes of Wrath*). The comparison with Wolfe was made not so much on the quality of the novel as on the physical size of the two men. Perhaps this latter comparison can be traced to James Gray's column in the *St. Paul Dispatch* for May 24, 1939: "That is more artist than anyone else has managed to be since Thomas Wolfe threw his incredible shadow across the American scene. I wish to go on record right now that I am a discoverer of the tallest novelist of our time."

In looking back, then, what does one say about *The Golden Bowl*? The fact that its surface subject matter was the depression in South Dakota during the 1930s does not diminish its importance in a later era. Dust bowl conditions have existed periodically in the past sixty years, particularly in the 1950s, in various parts of the West. South Dakota remains an agricultural state, which means that there is a built-in relationship between man and the land, even though it may appear to be somewhat different now in an age of machines and government subsidies.

Nevertheless, the importance of *The Golden Bowl* does not lie in the surface subject matter. It is a novel of the spirit, of the "long view," of man's attempt to achieve identity and to put down roots in order to maintain that identity. Maury's wanderings about the country are a kind of odyssey, or perhaps a quest, and it is what he finds that is important. He has three visionary experiences, of differing degrees, which finally add up to something meaningful for him. The first is his descent into the well to remove an obstruction which has halted the drilling. It is a deep well, and Maury is conscious of

AFTERWORD

being deep within the earth. Because there existed a real possibility of death in the well, the descent is much like one phase of the passion of Christ: "and He descended into Hell." Yet the symbolism here is not forced, and when Maury survives the experience and is, in a sense, reborn into the world from the womb of earth, he does not come out completely resurrected. The lesson is not complete.

And so he continues to wander, although the Thors urge him to settle down on their farm. His second significant experience comes in the dinosaur burial grounds of the Bad Lands. (In several of his books, Manfred looks back to the distant past, to the age of dinosaurs, for the beginnings of man. This is the search for origins, which is part of the search for identity. It is also an insistence that man has evolved and survived for so long that he is obligated to continue to do so. This idea is at least similar to Faulkner's continual emphasis upon endurance. Man must endure.) While in the Bad Lands, Maury senses that there is an origin common to all men, although he does not see it clearly. What begins to sink into his mind is the concept of rootedness.

Rootedness is positive, but Maury also sees, in his third experience, the negative view. It is found in the world of the hobo, the homeless man who is cold and lonely and who huddles together with other similar men who have only this temporary and unsatisfactory relationship, grounded not in the earth, or even in the spirit, but based only upon superficial necessity. Maury has been a spiritual hobo, and when he sees himself mirrored in the flesh of the lonely men gathered tentatively along the railroad tracks he completes his vision. What he learns may be stated in several ways, but the components of the vision are tradition, roots, brotherhood, and the long view.

The Golden Bowl, then, is a contemporary novel. Its experiences may seem a thing of the past if taken literally within the depression texture, but in the spiritual sense, which is finally the most real, the questions of identity and place and purpose reflect the major problems of our present time.

Frederick Manfred and the Anglo-Saxon Oral Tradition

by Nancy Owen Nelson

Frederick Manfred first realized his own ethnic link to Anglo-Saxon literature when he found, in a Calvin College dormitory, that he could easily read and understand a friend's assignment of Chaucerian English (*Conversations* 9). From this point on, Manfred was led to read and study the Anglo-Saxon and medieval poets and became aware of a growing kinship with their oral poetic tradition. As a result, in his early novels, he made a conscious effort to emulate the Anglo-Saxon poetic style, with its simple and clear diction, as well as the oral qualities of repetition, alliteration, parallelism, and incantation.

Early Manfred correspondence reveals his connection to the Anglo-Saxon poetic tradition. In the letters he makes frequent mention of books he is reading and of their impact on his artistic views. In particular, he often mentions Anglo-Saxon poetic techniques; two early letters clearly reflect this focus. As early as October 22, 1943, Manfred writes to prospective editor Frank Taylor about his Frisian origins and his consciousness of the "simple Anglo-Saxon style." (It should be noted that he had completed versions of both *The Golden Bowl* and *This is the Year* at this time.) :

> You might be interested to know that I've been reading Old English, or Anglo-Saxon literature. I'm a Frisian, and the Frisians, the scholars tell me, at one time spoke the original English, or at best, had an enormous influence on the early English. My old people at home still speak Frisian fluently and I understand them. I am learning in a concrete way what is meant by simple Anglo-Saxon style. If anybody wants to argue about it, I'll have a word to say now. I find it enormously fascinating and find too that I have been using an unnecessary amount of words of French and Latin derivation. Going through these early chapters 1 see many a word I can replace with a simple, clean-cut Saxon one And, I shall if it makes the book clearer and more poetic. (Letters, archives)

ANGLO-SAXON ORAL TRADITION 17

On April 28, 1948, in a letter to Max Geismar, Manfred discusses at great length his awareness of his indebtedness to the Anglo-Saxon poets. He is responding to Geismar's review of *The Chokecherry Tree*. In the letter, quoted in part below, Manfred discusses his growing appreciation of the Anglo-Saxon poetic tradition and his adaptation of its poetic quality in some parts of *The Chokecherry Tree* and *This is the Year:*

> ... I wish somebody would recognize my language. It is really poetry. It is loaded with semi-hidden alliteration, rime, with an undulating rhythm. I am very conscious of why my sentences do what they do. I study other poets and writers, and am aware of why they hit me. For example, in describing a musician working at white heat I wrote last week, "dripping pen in hand he *stabbed* the notes on the *staff*." Or, from *Tree*, "what is it that scuds us over the sudsing maelstrom." Or, from *Year*, "It sucked the succulent soils etc." "A noodle in his nose." "The ear-ringing singing was as sharp as a shriek. It was so near his teeth tittered together." ... My mind just runs that way, I love clean tone-ringing words. I usually detest abstract words, words of Latin or Roman origin, and when I do accept them I make sure that they are simple and sharp, and very similar [sic] in design to Anglo-Saxon Frisian. I happen to love *Beowulf*, and as a Frisian (from whom the Angles came) I have been trained in alliteration. (*Selected Letters* 263)

In conjunction, then, with the revelations in these early letters, Manfred's early novels reveal clearly his tie to the Anglo-Saxon poetic tradition; certain poetic passages in *The Golden Bowl* (1944), *This is the Year* (1947), and *The Chokecherry Tree* (1948), if examined closely for structure or if read aloud, have the characteristic techniques mentioned above. In addition, Manfred often uses the separate poetic voice of the singer of tales. As the poet of the Anglo-Saxon *Seafarer* comments on man's universal alienation, Manfred in the separate authorial voice communicates his belief in our link with nature, and specifically with the life forms which make up the evolutionary history of America. In these early three novels in particular, Manfred's authorial voice conveys his important theme of the "long view"—that though we live and die and turn to dust, yet we are a part of the cosmic whole, that our greatest achievement is to "come home to" that cosmic whole, or our roots.

This theme of the "return to sources," much written about by Manfred scholars, is evident throughout the canon. As early works of the young writer seeking his "voice," the three novels illustrate the characteristic position of the poet-commentator. In other, later novels, such as the five-novel Buckskin Man Tales series, *Green Earth*, and *Sons of Adam*, Manfred's comments about our role in the natural order are more subtly infused into the stories. Some feel that the technique of these early novels involves the writer's "push[ing] his vision in on the story" (De Boer 22). In the context of the correspondence we may view the early technique not merely as an inconsistency in authorial point of view, as critics such as Delbert Wylder have contended (21), but as the young artist's search for his voice through his own literary and cultural experience. Indeed, though the poet's and characters' voices are often intermingled, this intermingling happens for a particular reason when the character in question is beginning to share the poet's more universal vision. The character, then, joins the poet in understanding those themes which "transcend the region" to become "fictional explorations of the human condition" (Wylder 18).

In speaking on this broader plane, the poet in Manfred's novels is in touch with what he calls variously the "Old Adam," "The Old Lizard," or his "Interior Commentator"; it is linked intuitively to the rest of nature, not unlike "the kind of voice that once qualified a man to become a priest or a soothsayer, or the voice at Delphi" ("Space" 7). The poet, then, sings the message that we are all a part of cosmic nature; as Manfred states about the creative process in a recent speech at the University of South Dakota: "when any one of us takes on the task of studying nature, what we are actually doing is having nature study itself, since we are already a part of nature" ("Space" 19). In these three early novels, the poet's voice places characters and events on a universal plane.

The Golden Bowl, Manfred's first published novel, is a clear instance of his use of the separate poetic voice. Here the poet-commentator discusses the more universal significance of young Maury Grant's struggles with a family on a desolate farm in the Badlands of South Dakota.

The novel involves Maury's journey to find that "man's survival is tied to his environment; that the end of man's search for identity lies in the land and in rootedness; that he must not . . . doubt the land" (Bebeau 80). Maury's pilgrimage involves his internal battle between settling on the impoverished land with Kirsten Thor or traveling to find work further west. In the end, he returns to the land in its desolate and infertile condition and to the pregnant Kirsten. Appropriately, the novel begins and ends with passages significantly different in tone and structure from most of the rest of the narrative. The voice of the poet would be quite apparent, even if it were not separated from the regular text by the use of italics.

The novel begins with a rather straightforward description, much like the beginning of Steinbeck's *The Grapes of Wrath*, of the gradual desolation which the dust storms bring. Then three pages into the novel, Manfred provides an italicized passage which makes a definite shift in tone and structure; the poet's voice takes over, and the sentences become shorter, with parallel ordering and repetition more pronounced. For comparison, here is a standard brief passage of description:

> Still farther on, gray dust films everything, even the moving things. When the wind comes, the old structures shrug a little and the gray silt slides off in shivers. And sometimes, when a rain comes, the old buildings stand forlorn amidst the rustling of strange greens . (4)

. . . and three poetic passages:

> *And the wind came. Clear at first, it rolled and lifted, blustered hard and blustered soft.*
> . . .
> *And the dust came again. Dust that filled the sky, the fields, and the rivers. Dust that choked the lungs of the men and the cattle.*
> . . .
> *The stone-toothed wind hit the face of the sun and fretted and taunted the earth. Dust beat on the grain and killed it. Dust beat on the animals and choked them. Dust battered the barns and the houses.* (6-10)

The novel concludes with a passage of similar tone and structure, after Maury has decided to return to the Thors and make a commitment to the land. He has just heard Pa Thor, after a fierce dust storm, comment in his eternal optimist's way about the possibility of rain. With the old man's image of a Siouxland of fertility, Manfred closes the novel with the following passage describing a fertile and happy land. Again, the singer of tales projects the more hopeful, "long view" of the land; parallel and repetitive structure is evident:

> *In the hidden country of a pilgrim's heart, rains are falling. The sun shines there, and men go into the fields and work, and believe in the work of their hands. And sow grain, and broadcast the seed of grass for their cattle and horses. And plant corn and melon seed in the gray-black loam.*
> *And the land trembles with multitudes of germinant sprouts growing and leaping in the sun.*
> *And more rains come to interrupt the beating of the sun upon the earth.* (225-6)

Since *The Golden Bowl* does involve a young man's discovery of the truth of this cycle of life and death and of his individual part in that scheme, it is appropriate that some of the poet-commentator's voice be apparent in Maury's ruminations about his pilgrimage. One such passage, which Bebeau and Milton have called an important visionary experience (Bebeau 82, Milton ii), occurs when Maury travels west through the dinosaur burial grounds in the Badlands. Manfred records Maury's fascination with the "little castles and minarets. . . tottering candelabrums. . . a haunted city"—all forms which the Badlands create in Maury's imagination. Immediately following comes a significant passage in which the poet describes the evolutionary history of man, beast, and the land forms.

At this point, Manfred summarizes the natural history of the land to include the brontosaurus, the glacier age, erosion of the "bony spires," extinct animals such as the saber-toothed tiger, the drought, the cowboy era, and finally modern tourism. The passage has the alliterative and repetitive quality of the oral-poet. A sample follows:

> The land died still more. It became covered with short, sparse grass. Endless days of hot sun finally came. It cut the grass and

the roots of the grass and left the meat of the land open to the wind. And then, when the abrupt, ripping rains came, they slashed at the raw meat of the earth. Gullies soon ran east and south. Gullies deepened .... (148)

The passage also illustrates Manfred's belief in the cosmic unity of all things; appearing in the regular narrative, it symbolizes the joining of the poet's universal perspective with Maury's. This character is beginning to realize his need to return to the land which spawned all of these forms.

Like *The Golden Bowl, This is the Year* begins and ends with italicized passages, immediate clues to the poet-commentator's voice. These passages, all from the cock robin's point of view, are a three-page "Prelude" describing Siouxland's plenty, and a closing passage describing its desolation. Like the final passage of *The Golden Bowl*, the prelude provides an ironic contrast with the desolate land with which Pier Frixen will struggle in *This is the Year*, and it gives the reader an overall thematic view of this book which, Manfred states, "came right out of the earth itself" ("Narrative" 124).

To write *This is the Year*, Manfred studied the weather patterns in Iowa for the years 1918-1936 and focused on a five-year period (*Bibliography* 26). The novel concerns a second-generation Frisian, Pier Frixen, and his stubborn resistance to giving caring treatment to both his wife and his land, resulting in the death of both. In Manfred's universal scheme, then, nature has turned upon itself and has wrought destruction. Manfred makes a parallel between Pier's wife Nertha, whose name means the Anglo-Saxon "goddess of plenty, of cornucopia" (Manfred, *Conversations* 88), and the land, which he tries unsuccessfully to make flourish.

Thus the "Prelude" provides a passage in which the poet will tell of a land of beauty and fruition which will deteriorate through a process well-documented in the novel. The robin begins his journey in Memphis and arrives in Siouxland in late March; the passage creates a point of departure for the novel's development. Here the poet describes the robin's flight:

The robin flew in swoops: some long and tiring, some quick and inquiring. And always he fanned out his white tail feathers plainly in flight.

> ...
> *He hopped around, caroling, going from tree to tree, looking, seeking, singing, calling and calling, happy at last he had found his true country. (This is the Year* xi-xiii)

In a similar passage, the robin makes Siouxland his home:

> *Bright morning came and he cheerd forth a great long song, yodeling beauteous peals of love into the red skies, calling, calling, halloing aloud for his mate. He sang loud all day long, calling, calling....*
> ...
> *Spring was here, cock robin said, spring was here, and blue eggs were coming, and roblings, and all the summer long.* (xiii-xiv)

Because *This is the Year* is a novel "right out of the earth itself," the poetic passages most often concern the land and its stages of desolation, often resembling either dirges to the dying land or exaltations to its potential fertility. As in the dinosaur passage in *The Golden Bowl*, the voice of the singer of tales is fused with the characters' consciousness of their relationship with nature. Manfred's description of a dust storm through Pier's eyes contains much parallelism in modifying words, prepositional phrases, and short sentences. The first part of this particular description stresses Pier's feelings of helplessness in the grip of a dust storm:

> Then he saw it; an unbelievable thing.
> ... The whole earth went into an uproar, exploding skyward, throwing chunks of dirt and humus into the air. It rushed toward him. Titanic winds shoved. The mass of brown-black harrowing horror droned toward him....
> ... His misery, his feeling of abysmal insignificance, was turning inside out.
> He had been born, he had grown up. He had eaten, he had dunged. He had pushed his father off his shoulders. He had bred and raised a son, who, in turn, was getting ready to push him off his shoulders.
> ...

Ae, life was like grass. It grew in the spring, it greened in the summer, it grayed in the fall, it rotted in the winter; and, the next spring, it made room for the new grass.
. . .
The storm brulled; bombommed.
He waited. He was sure that he was being buried
alive. He waited an hour.
He waited two hours. He choked . . . . (*This is the Year* 470-72)

Appropriately, the most significant passage from the poet-commentator follows Pier's revelation. It is the "Earth Sermon," and it is delivered by the County Agent, "Old Dreamer Pederson," to Pier, in an attempt to open his eyes to his ill treatment of his land; the parallels of the land to Nertha are quite apparent. County Agent Pederson here functions as the voice of the poet-commentator. His knowledge of the land has given him an understanding superior to Pier's. Pederson's sermon is intoned after the manner of the Anglo-Saxon scop, particularly with its use of parallel sentence structure and verbal phrases:

"After a time, man crossed a mountain and came to a valley. There he found a dusky woman of exceeding beauty and worth. And he fell in love with her, became enamoured of her. And he took her, possessed her, and made her his own.

"And after a time he discovered that the woman he had taken to his breast was a sister, and a wife, and a mother to him.

"As his sister she played games with him, hunted and swam and fished with him.

"As his wife, she gave him fruits: corn, wheat, grapes, honey, milk.

"As his mother, she gave him shelter. . . ."

The poet tells of the death of the woman—land —at man's ruthless hand, and of his searching out of another "dusky woman":

"The old lady, like man, is only a tiny creature in the vast outspread of chaos. And the endlessly undulating stretches of outspread chaos care not a snap of the fingers, not a whit for either. Whether she or he thrives does not interest chaos. His dying, her dying, will not disturb it, affect it, will not contort chaos into cosmos, or wreck cosmos into chaos." (479-81)

Here Pederson clearly delineates Manfred's larger themes.

In a final passage at the end of the novel, the poetic voice again assesses Pier's story. In these reflections, the voice of the poet-commentator joins Pier's to make a concluding thematic comment. Pier begins to realize the importance of the land and the secrets of the ancients which she holds in her bosom. Shortened sentences and parallel structure accentuate Pier's reflections:

> He strode on. He was a wanderer, a captain without a ship or port.
> . . .
> The ancients were gone forever.
>
> He nodded his head. Gone forever. Ae. Just as he too would soon be gone, soon be out of the mind of man.
> . . .
> Wal, such was life. So it went. Grass grew, grass withered. (609-10)

In this passage, which links Pier to the ancient mound builders, Pier recognizes his failure and comes to realize the importance of Manfred's message about unity with and care of nature. Yet failing to realize soon enough, Pier has lost the battle to make this year "*the* year"—he has abused his heritage as a member of the cosmos. The "Postlude"—an italicized passage—provides the tale-teller's final statement on this issue. The robin flew over a fertile land in the "Prelude," but in the "Postlude" he clings at first to his wretched wintry home, from which others are driven by the cold. The poet tells us that, like Pier, the robin has realized that he must give up the legacy of his beloved home.

The familiar shift to parallel modifiers augments the poet's comments:

> . . . *at last, a fifth flock came flitting and chittering by, riding a cold drilling wind, and cock robin and his mate, chilled, lonesome, flew up, and joined the climbing and diving brothers and sisters, and were gone.*

ANGLO-SAXON ORAL TRADITION

The fork in the box elder was empty.

The ball of earth was spinning: another year had vanished from view forever. (615-16)

The Chokecherry Tree, the third of the novels with the separate poet's voice, brings in a new technique. Here the poet makes himself known primarily in prefaces to each chapter.

The novel was written from Manfred's experiences in drought-ridden Siouxland in the summer of 1936 (*Conversations* 57). The plot involves the return home of Elof Lofblom, a failure in college and seminary, and his struggles to rediscover his own Siouxland roots. Elof's own physical limitations and his unrealistic heroic ideals stymie his growth for awhile, until he reconciles himself with his own roots, takes an earth mother/wife Gert, and buys a filling station at Chokecherry Corner. Throughout the novel, Manfred connects Elof symbolically with the chokecherry tree, a mere bush in contrast to the towering cottonwood tree representing a "real hero."

The chapter prefaces have puzzled readers; when asked in a 1981 interview about the conception of these prefaces, Manfred suggests their intuitive, poetic nature, describing them as "poems" which appeared to him in completed form after the chapter texts were written (May 8, 1981). This suggests clearly Manfred's link to the intuitive quality of the poet/*scop*. In addition, the prefaces reveal Manfred's conscious appreciation of precise language and his use of "semi-hidden alliteration, rime, with an undulating rhythm" which he described to Max Geismar in the 1948 letter, cited above. Here we recall that Manfred leans toward words which, if not precisely Anglo-Saxon, are "simple and sharp" like the Anglo-Saxon diction. Through the poet's separate voice, the prefaces take a "long view" of little Elof's pilgrimages toward self-understanding and link Elof's life with the larger cosmos.

Some prefaces, marked by parallelism, alliteration, and repetition, comment on Elof's early progress toward self-identity; for example, the preface to Chapter One:

Here from the brow of this Siouxland bluff, a stone my seat, I watch your troubled swervelings to and fro. The valley you live in is green and it is moving—its cells are proliferating and its people are working. I watch all this, and watch you, and this is what my laboring fingers write on this page (Chokecherry Tree 1).

The preface to Chapter VIII, highly alliterative and repetitive, comments on Elof's, and indeed all mankind's, reasons for "going on." Elof has just proven to be sexually inept, and in the Chapter VIII preface, Manfred raises the universal question—why do we bother to struggle with life?

What is this momentum that drives us on? This mighty urge that scuds us over the sudsing maelstrom?[1] From where comes it? When were its first arisings? When and where will be its final subsidings?

What is there in us that "goes on," and hence makes us believe in "going on"?

It is there. In me. In you.

It's strong enough in me to impel me to plant and grow a garden, and marry and have a family, and plan and write books. . . . (Chokecherry Tree 87)

Here, through the intoning quality of the singer of tales, Manfred brings the meaning of existence back to simple things.

As we near the end of the novel, the prefaces attempt to tie together Elof's search for meaning. The preface to Chapter XVIII announces the finale of Elof's search, in which he discovers that his roots, his answer to his identity, are in the ordinary things of life—the welcoming home. The preface links Elof with his intuitive core, the "Old Adam":

We know that way down, way back, deep in your fleshes (is it your Old Adam?), something is stirring within you. No, not a spectacular truth, or a colossal discovery affecting mankind—no, nothing so draniatic. Only the discovery of a place where you may live mostly happy, fifty-one to forty-nine, for better than for worse, happily, safely, happily within the cupped hand, your home. Slowly, indistinctly, like a room being lit up by a dim light coming from an opening door far down the hall, your mind is waking to a knowledge . . . . (233)

These prefaces to the chapters of *The Chokecherry Tree* are the clearest examples in the early novels of the separate voice of the poet/singer. As with Maury and Pier, Elof comes close to intuiting Manfred's "long view"; this is illustrated in two particular passages in the regular narrative in which the poet's chanting quality, characterized here with parallel modifiers and short sentences, takes over. Both passages occur while Elof is in a graveyard and discovers his kinship to the earth. Reflecting in the Old Settler's Graveyard on the causes of death, he joins in the poet's universal perspective:

He stood up and slowly turned and saw the land as the sorrowing mothers had seen it.

Pitiful. The prairie wind blowing against the tendon-tight frames, against stringy limbs, showing the cleft of legs entering the thigh, revealing the low much-suckled breast, outlining the hipbone sharp. The prairie wind drying the crying face, the wrenched muscles around the eye socket ache-swollen, the long hate-hot glance burning the vast sweeps of the undulating loess.

The father reading from the Bible. Praying.

Psalms bleated into the blue ears of the zenith. (31)

In the second graveyard passage, Elof reflects on the pioneers buried there; again the parallel modifiers, sentences, and verb forms are evident:

Pioneers. Pioneers. Where was the sweat now? Where were the eyes and the muscles that had made a home in this Wild? Where was the trail they had trudged? Where were the settings they had crushed in the grass, eating and dunging and mating? Man. A handful of troubled soil. Arising there and standing here and weathering there.

Ma? Where are you. I, Elof, I'm here. (195-6)

Elof ultimately discovers the importance of his coming home to himself—his role as husband of Gert and as businessman in Chokecherry Corner. As in *The Golden Bowl* and *This is the Year*, the novel closes with the poet's voice. This final passage again links the ordinary experience of an ordinary character to the "long view" of his place in the cosmic scheme. Like the continuum illustrated by the spinning "ball of earth" at the end of *This is the Year*, the continuum of man's link to past, present, future, to all life forms, is suggested by the going on of generations:

> We leave you now, Elof, leave you to your life. Whether you become the leader of your little family, or a wife-run male, does not concern us further. You have survived. You are safe . . . .
>
> The earth spheres, and the bluff on which we sit is hurled forward into darkness and into the next day. And so, gone you are. And when this crisp page at last shreds and rots, too, gone will be the knowledge that you were ever gone.
>
> The generations arise, they come and they go, each leapfrogging over the one previous, hopping off into the future. (*Chokecherry Tree* 266)

This ending suggests fertility and fruition symbolic in Elof's name: "Elof, the leaf; Lofblom, the flowered leaf" (266).

The young Manfred read extensively in almost every literary direction; his early letters reveal his growing consciousness of his ethnic and literary origins. In the Anglo-Saxon poetic tradition, Manfred found a tool by which to comment on his characters and their place in the larger scheme. In 1948 the young Manfred wished that somebody would recognize the poetry in his language. This examination suggests but one of a multitude of research possibilities which the publication of the Manfred letters offers.

Notes

[1] Note Manfred's citing of this phrase in the Geismar letter.

Works Cited

Bebeau, Don. "A Search for Voice, a Sense of Place in *The Golden Bowl*. *South Dakota Review* 7 (Winter 1969-70) : 79-86.

De Boer, Peter P. "Frederick Feikema Manfred: Spiritual Naturalist." *Reformed Journal* 13 (April 1963) : 19-23.

Manfred, Frederick. *The Chokecherry Tree*. Albuquerque: U of New Mexico P, 1975.

---. *Conversations With Frederick Manfred.* Moderated by John R. Milton. Salt Lake City: U of Utah P, 1974:

---. *The Golden Bowl*. Albuquerque: U of New Mexico P, 1976.

---. Interview with Frederick Manfred, May 18, 1981.

---. Letters, archives of the University of Minnesota Library.

---. "Narrative Interview." *Frederick Manfred: A Bibliography and Publishing History*. Ed. Rodney J. Mulder and John H. Timmerman. Sioux Falls: Center for Western Studies, 1979. 119-139.

---. *The Selected Letters of Frederick Manfred: 1932-1954* Ed. Arthur R. Huseboe and Nancy Nelson. Lincoln: U of Nebraska P, 1989.

---. "Space, Yes; Time, No." Presidential Lecture, U of South Dakota, March 31, 1981.

---. *This is the Year*. Boston: Gregg Press, 1979.

Milton, John R. Introduction. *The Golden Bowl*. Albuquerque: U of New Mexico P, 1976. vii-xiii.

Wylder, Delbert. "Frederick Manfred: The Quest of the Independent Writer." *Books at Iowa* 31 (November 1979) : 16-31.

This is the Year: A Southern Perspective

by Forrest M. Byrd

This is the Year, Frederick Manfred's third novel (published under the name Feike Feikema), is a sprawling serious novel that drives the reader before it rather in the manner of a plains dust storm. The novel is large, both in physical dimension and in concept. It is perhaps the most densely allusive of Manfred's novels, rich in direct and contextual reference. Like most truly fine novels, it is of a time and place, while being somehow more than either.

Few novelists have created a sense of place so convincing that the people and environs take on a reality that is hardly explicable in terms of any single work. Consider William Faulkner's works for example. Dilsey's endurance, Quentin's suicide, and Tom Sutpen's innocence have undeniable significance within the context of their own stories, but the level of significance becomes greater within the context of that little postage stamp of real estate of which Faulkner made himself sole owner and proprietor. Thomas Hardy's novels have this same quality. We cannot really understand the opacity of Jude's obscurity until we have plumbed Clem Yeobright's lack of vision on the dark heath. We know somehow that this is so, even as we are unable to explain the phenomenon in the same way that Marlow finally is unable to tell the other men in the boat about the heart of darkness.

Manfred comes into his own with *This is the Year*. Siouxland stretches before us and Pier Frixen's big fifty becomes our peak in Darien. The laws of Siouxland that were partially delineated in *The Golden Bowl* become established in *This is the Year*. We are in a land of rational insanity where the inexplicable is mundane and verities refuse to be jostled aside by hopes or fears.

That Siouxland is larger than the narrative that contains it becomes more and more apparent with each succeeding novel, and a relationship between place and world view develops, much as has been noted concerning the South and southern literature. C. Vann Woodward in *The Burden of Southern History* notes that there is a thing called the "South" as opposed to a simple geographical designation, which is responsible at least in part for the existence of Southern literature as opposed to literature written in the

South. Woodward posits three historical phenomena as the *sine qua non* of Southern consciousness: a knowledge of defeat that no other region shares, an enduring poverty that has marked the people permanently, and a shared guilt rivaling that of Cain (Newby 29). Whether these are *sine qua non* of novels about the South is an unanswerable and probably a frivolous question. That the novels out of the South that have enjoyed an enduring critical reputation are shaped around these notions is a given. *This is the Year*, and, to a lesser extent, all the Siouxland novels, are, while certainly not "Southern," bound within a framework fascinatingly similar to Woodward's paradigm.

Teo, Pier Frixen's son, puts it well toward the end of the novel when he

> [leans] forward, wagging a calloused finger at him. "Dad, when are you ever gonna learn that the normal crops you talk about are exceptions? Dad, let me tell you something once. The normal around this part of the country is this blazing incinerator we're livin' in right now." (573)

A good crop, an uneventful year is the exception. Defeat, seasoned with privation, is the normal course of existence. That the land defeats men as a consequence of their ignorance and misuse is not germane. If it does not defeat them that way, it defeats them simply by being eternal in the face of their too obvious temporality. If the land does not defeat them, relationships do; if not relationships, then religious hierarchies; if not hierarchies then governments; if not governments, the old Adam within. Defeat is all the more bleak in that it is not a communal thing finally but an individual, isolated, rural event.

Poverty, in the Southern sense, never really reaches into Siouxland, but few Siouxlanders escape the clutches of a raging thrift that makes them apt candidates for a Flannery O'Conner story. It is a question best left to theologians whether thrift is akin to poverty when practiced to the extent that it is indistinguishable from a cardinal sin, but such thrift does mark the mind and world of all Manfred's characters. *This is the Year* is a "depression" novel and thus inextricably wed to poverty, physically and psychologically. The characters are bound to the land and are in a situation akin to a person trapped in a poker game that allows neither winning nor quitting.

The people of Siouxland do not, of course, own slaves. Whether they are slaves is another question that we need not ponder. On the land, however, they do share a communal guilt. For a world so biblically referential, it is interesting that the sin all characters share to one extent or another is patricide. *This is the Year* begins with the story of Pier's ascendancy over his father, Alde Romke. Pier physically puts the old man off the farm and runs it to his own song. Piers' father is not simply displaced though. Midway through the novel he, the old man, visits Pier during a time of wood cutting. The sawblade escapes its holder and literally bisects the old man. Manfred, with his usual narrative power, renders the scene so effectively that the shock of the old man's death permeates the entire novel. Teo, like his namesake, deserts Pier, rejecting both Pier and his world quite as patricidally as Pier has done to Alde Romke. Like a world full of Oedipus figures, the characters of Siouxland continually kill their fathers, but unlike Oedipus, they do it knowingly and usually for the "right" reasons. Lurking in the background of any Manfred text is the father who so terrified Luther in the thunderstorm. The darkest aspect of Teutonic protestantism broods like an unholy spirit over the waters of Manfred's created world, a spirit that sows guilt for those who try and fail, for those who try and succeed, for those who despair and those who do not. They seem to have brought their European guilt with them and grafted the guilt of native American genocide to the old stock.

Since Ebenezer Cooke, American literature has tried to produce an epic—that is, an extended narrative poem that celebrates the ideals and aspirations of a race or culture. *This is the Year* comes as close as any to meeting those requirements, and, to the extent that the time and place allows, is more successful than most. *This is the Year* is a poem. When it is most prosaic it virtually scans, and with its labyrinthine plot and giant characters, it harks back to an older form. The action takes place in a tiny corner or northwest Iowa and an equally small part of southeastern South Dakota during the years 1918-1936, years during which the rural Midwest endured a lacerating poverty that leaves them scarred even now. The hero, and it must be noted that Pier Frixen is a hero and not a protagonist, is a farmer. At another time and another place, he might have been a slayer of dragons or a sulker in tents,

A SOUTHERN PERSPECTIVE

but this is his time and his occupation. Fatherless by his own action, he is caught in a love-hate relationship with the land, with his wife, with his son, with his government, and with himself.

Within an overarching context of guilt, deprivation, and loss, three themes flow through the novel, combining, separating, and coming together again to surround the characters in a continuum that seems to begin before the novel existed and to continue long after the last page is turned. The land is the Woman of the novel, the woman to whom Pier is truly married, and Pier's use and abuse of her is the mirror of all the action. Patricide is central to the novel but is diminished by the action of Old Time which, like a vast impersonal cat, plays with fathers and sons alike. Change in the structure of the society brings about change in the land and change in the family, a family that has lasted for centuries in the form that Pier breaks.

Manfred surrounds the novel with a framing device, a robin flying up from the Gulf of Mexico. It flies up the Mississippi to the Missouri, to the Big Sioux River and finally to a certain house on Blood Run Creek. The robin will not be seen again for some six hundred pages, when it will reappear in a postlude, inevitably reminding one of Bede's remarks on the brevity of human life.

As the novel opens we meet Pier Frixen on his wedding day, bursting with confidence, totally convinced of his abilities and quite sure that he is one of the lords of the earth. He is as innocent as Sutpen and as guileless as Oedipus. The ruling conflict of the novel is immediately apparent when his parents attempt to reject his bride to be because she is not a full blood Frisian. Pier seeks them out, raging like a berserker. When his father sees him he

> [waves] a weak hand, "Ae I see you've come."
> "You damn well right I've come, you old fool."
> "Nou, nou, breinroer, bedimje."
> "Breinroer? Who wouldn't have a roar in his brain with a pair of old skates like you mussin up his life: And I'm not bedimming until you two birds explain a thing or two." (31)

Pier's brusque coercion of his parents sets up one of the basic conflicts of the novel. Pier is, after all, doing the "right" thing, and he is right on several levels. He is faithfully quoting the catechism of the American dream. In America we are not only allowed to marry without concern for family or community, we are encouraged to do so. The American myth, from *West Side Story* to *Dirty Dancing*, insists that parents will eventually realize that actions born in a state of hormonal overload will eventually be proved superior to either rationality or tradition. He is also right in that sooner or later parents are replaced by their children. He is equally correct in insisting the he must make his own mistakes and suffer his own consequences. As the narrative unfolds we find that being right is very like being free. It can be a hard thing. The cyclical pattern of human existence assures us that when we are at the advantageous end of rightness, we will, if we live long enough, experience the other end.

Pier is the lover of a virgin land, a land more familiar to Kolodney than to Henry Nash Smith perhaps. The sod has been broken for less than sixty years. He forgets (or never knows), however, that there is no new land, just as there is nothing new under the sun. The land is the same one his ancestors ravaged in Scandinavia and before that in the fertile crescent. Manfred persistently uses cycles (bird migrations, seasons, generations, feast days, life stages) to emphasize the permanence of guilt, poverty and defeat, and the actions which invoke them. The same callous independence and confidence that enables Pier to break free of his parents in order to possess the woman he desires, work together to slowly grind his wife into a creature whom he will come to loathe. He wants her for the children she can bear, and for the animal pleasure she can provide, but it never occurs to him that she may have needs and desires that are less than congruent with his.

It should be noted that Pier is a good man. He is not a drunk. He never beats his wife. He is actually gentle with his son in terms of the time and place. In fact, he lives, works, and breathes for his family. Everything he does is for them. He does, after all, live on a quarter section of farmland in the years prior to air-conditioned machinery and one-crop farming. The work is unending and relentless, and Manfred understands and portrays that work with chilling and even exhausting accuracy. The mistakes that Pier makes are not pursuant to a desire to do wrong but to do better. He plows the land in an up-and-down pattern, not to cause erosion, which he certainly does, but because that pattern of plowing is an outward and visible manifestation of an inward and spiritual emancipation from past that he hopes and prays is dead, and because that pattern is more aesthetically pleasing to him. Note how Manfred takes us into Pier's mind:

> He studied the lay of the land for a few minutes.
> He lighted his corncob pipe, looking to the right and to the left.
> And at last he made up his mind.
> He would plow the big fifty east to west, instead of north to south as Alde Romke had always done.
> To have all the furrows lead to the yard would make the field more a part of the farm. (129)

The new way of plowing speeds the process of erosion, and the decision eventually actually undermines his house in both senses, just as his decision to be his own person and cast off the needs of others undermines his farm. Pederson, the county agent or the "Old Dreamer" as Pier calls him, warns him of the danger of soil erosion, but this is, of course, the very quintessence of the American dream—the inalienable right to ignore reality and the fervent belief that consequences should not accompany that ignorance. Manfred's genius here is in delineating the fact that this American notion has not succeeded in displacing millennia of older law. The freedom to be ignorant is the creation of an extremely short-lived species that seems not to have taken into account the temporal difference in the two systems.

Just as Pier lays waste the land through a combination of ignorance and good intentions, he destroys his marriage by doing the best that he knows how. When he marries Nertha she is a blushing silver-haired nymphet. One of the Garlandesque conventions of the agrarian novel is that farm work is so burdensome that it squeezes both life and beauty from a woman. Manfred knows better. The very structure of the novel is replete with the knowledge that all relationships are reciprocal. But Pier has no reciprocal relationships. When his wife does not regularly bring forth young, he takes her to a doctor just as he would a prize heifer in similar straits. The doctor immediately recognizes that the problem is not organic. He asks Pier:

> "Tell me, when you go to bed, does she seem to get as much out of it as you?"
> Pier fired. He stared angrily at the other.

"What's that of yer business?"

The doctor nodded..."You've been cheating your wife since your wedding day."

Pier jumped up. "What fool junk are you telling me now?"

"It's the truth."

"Horse collar. Any man knows a woman's not built like a man." (328)

The interview concludes when Pier storms out of the office, taking Nertha with him, having learned nothing. It is tempting for a careless reader to dismiss Pier at this juncture as a simple ignoramus. To do so would not affect Pier or the novel, but it would brand the reader as an ignoramus. We need to plumb the genesis of Pier's seeming bent toward self destruction. Briefly, it is that he is as good a man as his world allows him to know how to be. And that is why he is so intransigent. He has just seen a doctor miles from his home. The doctor, a man he does not know, suggests on the strength of a few moment's acquaintance that his wife has the same sexual impulses as a man. From Pier's perspective, the doctor has just asserted that Nertha is perverse, that she is somehow akin to the women that men and schoolboys tell smutty jokes about. In the light of a half century of change, if not enlightenment, we may well feel condescending toward Pier, but to do so would miss the thrust of the scene. We have an ordinary man faced with a pronouncement from the closest thing our culture has to a priest that the part of the world for which he is responsible has gone weird. Further, that weirdness is the direct result of Pier's right actions. Manfred has established a classic situation, one in which a protagonist is responsible for effects, the causes of which are beyond both his control and his ken. If Pier is to remedy the situation that is making his life unbearable, he must consciously do that which he knows to be wrong. Were he not a fictional character, he could presumably change. But then so could Macbeth.

As counterpoint to Nertha, Manfred creates the character Kaia. She is half Frisian, half Gypsy. After Nertha dies, Pier sleeps with Kaia, and she subsequently tells him she is with child (550). There is never any doubt that Pier will marry her. He has, after all, incurred the obligation. Kaia is less than a good wife. She has, ironically, married him for his money, which in this case he has not got, and she has lied about being pregnant. Pier has the full complement of human flaws and often seems too much a victim of time and fate, but in this instance, when he learns the full measure of Kaia's perfidy, he settles the matter forthrightly in one of the most satisfying passages in the novel:

> Pier aimed a kick at her fleeing wigging bottom, missed. He saw the bird cages in the corner, picked them up, sleeping birds and all, and heaved them out on the yard after her. He ran to the bedroom, jammed her clothes in a drawer, heaved it outdoors. He became angrier as he ran. He cursed. He snorted unintelligible sounds. He ran into the parlor, ripped down all her pictures, heaved them out on the yard. He stood in the door. He saw her hiding behind the woodshed. He roared, "Get the hell off this place, you washed out gully. Get back to yer nitwit brother. Go eat some a his moonseed, you whore-bitch burning bush, an' see how you like it."
>
> Then he slammed the door shut, stalked across the kitchen, sat down in his armchair, lighted his pipe with trembling fingers, leaned back on two legs.
>
> He smoked.
>
> After a while, he said to himself, grunting, "Wal, buck-nun again." (582)

That is all there is. We never see Kaia again. Pier has the weaknesses that are inherent in goodness, but the kind of good man that he is, is also an absolutist. When the duplicity at hand is clear and discernible, the absolutist has no difficulty in dealing with it. The weakness inherent in absolutism, of course, is that duplicity is not always discernible, and is almost never clear. But that is part and parcel of the mastery of Manfred. Siouxland will only abide an absolutist. The life is hard and uncertain. A relativist would measure the worth of alternative courses of action until the time for taking action is gone. So what then does a man do in a universe that allows no course of action that is salubrious? As a Manfredian character in a Kesey novel once said, "He never gives a inch."

Pier interacts four times with the society that surrounds him. He refuses to have his livestock checked for tuberculosis until he is forced at gunpoint to do so. He organizes a "penny sale", at the foreclosure of his friend Red Joe's farm. He refuses government aid even after it is abundantly clear that he will go broke. Finally, he participates in the forced sale of his own home. The interactions are presciently selected as they clearly delineate the ambiguous nature of an absolutist morality relative to a pluralistic society while reinforcing the Woodwardian themes of poverty, defeat, and guilt.

The effulgent optimism that American children are infected with is shown in its effects both good and bad. The notion that a man's home is his castle is examined minutely. Authority within and without that castle is the examining probe. To the best of his knowledge, Pier is sure that his stock does not have tuberculosis. He firmly believes that it is at least partially a trick of the government to force farmers to sell their stock at a loss, and he is filled with the notion that what a man does with his own farm is his own business. As he says, "We farmers didn't vote to have our cows tested" (398).

Whether the reader thinks that Pier should have his cows tested is not the issue. We are interested rather in the moral make-up of the character. We know that he cannot suffer the loss of his cows to faceless government agents any more than he could to thieves. We also know that he will suffer the tortures of the damned if his cows infect innocent children with tuberculosis. If he submits to testing, he loses what his fathers risked all to gain when they came to America. If he does not, he will lose his farm and his personal freedom. Putting aside the ethics of the situation for the nonce, we can see that not a few white southerners could understand Pier's difficulty. When he organizes and executes the penny sale, a morally "good" act, he is acting out of the same ethical dictates as the tuberculosis testing episode. He believes that home and family are superior to the will of the government, above the mandates of economics, above even the requirements of statutory law. The danger of violating this particular stance is universally recognized. On the other hand, if individual farmers are allowed to toss aside the foundations of the law that renders a society orderly, certain other difficulties arise. A refusal to cooperate with societal dictates, however, is less laudable if it only functions when it is economically advantageous to the refuser.

If Pier were to become independent only when it is to his advantage, he could be in the same ethical position as the average political reformer. Pier hangs to his principles long after his position is untenable. Friends, family, and society desert him. Although

A SOUTHERN PERSPECTIVE

they are not burdened with any other knowledge, young southern males learn this world view from "Coach" for twelve and occasionally sixteen years.

In late 1935, the government finally realized that something must be done if farmers were to survive at all. When Pier is apprised of the corn and hog program, he, of course, declines to join. To the men who approach him he replies, "I run my farm my own way in my own time. I don't bother nobody and nobody's gonna bother me (467). He further explains his stance,

> "I believe we got to work all we kin to make sure we done our duty by nature and by God. It's wrong to cut down acreage, to hold back hog breedin'. It's wrong to throw away pork and beef. And grain. Wrong." (469)

No one understands the Calvinist tenet of "the priesthood of the believer" on a gut level better than a rural American farmer. Balance comes to the narrative through Pier's refusal to participate in the government programs. Ironically Pier is the one who is hewing to the principles that are presumably American. Balance is further restored when his own farm is finally foreclosed. He goes to his friends and asks if they are willing to do as much for him as he has done for them. In essence, they refer him to the government for help. With no discernable bitterness, he lets the farm go.

The farm gone, his first wife dead, the second a proven slut, and his son gone, Pier's reaction is ethically and psychologically consistent with the character that has been presented throughout the novel:

> A bitter thought possessed him. The fiery Frisians had given England its law and language, had given her many of its legends and myths, had given her its heroes Hengist and Horsa, but had never been given credit for it. And now he too here in America, having given his work and his dreams, would never be honored for it. Ae, injustice was still afoot in the world. The Alde Han was still at work. The old song and dance.
> Wal, such was life. So it went. Grass grew, grass withered. (610)

The novel closes with Pier's defiant resolution to go and see his estranged son:

"Wal," he said to himself, "wal, why not? I might as well. It won't hurt none to go see the boy. See what he's up to. An' then go on. Somewheres. Shucks, after all, I'm a young buck yet. My heart's still green." (614)

Since the Greeks, one of the patterns of tragedy has involved what, for lack of a better term, we can call "dramatic tension." That is, the protagonist is in a state of ignorance (*Oedipus, Winterset,* et al.). The disparity between the truth that the audience perceives and the ignorance held by the protagonist widens until a state of tension is created. Some action causes the protagonist to perceive the same truth that we perceive and the tension is released. Manfred allows no such resolution. We leave Pier as we found him. He is older, tougher, and if possible, more adamantly absolutist in his own terms than he was at the beginning. The reader's knowledge of truth is at least as specious as that of Pier, and it would require Pier to forgo his integrity which would leave him truly a mere protagonist and not a hero. Manfred's refusal to provide a placebo of release from dramatic tension is of more than passing importance. The American tragedy is not, after all, Greek, nor is it Elizabethan; nor, perhaps, is the human condition. Manfred's unknelled and uncoffined hero lives on his own terms in a universe that is antithetical to him and to his dream. The timeless environment will not allow his brevity. And the temporal society will not allow the timelessness of his absolutism. The tragedy of American tragedy is perhaps that after four thousand years, we have finally found a tragedy that is tragic. Defeat, want (either physical or spiritual), and guilt, along with a seemingly ungovernable patricidal bent have finally given us passage to more than India.

Works Cited

Feikema, Feike. *This is the Year.* Garden City, New York: Doubleday & Company, Inc., 1947.

Newby, L. A. *The South: A History.* New York: Holt, Rinehart and Winston. 1978.

Someday Hero

by Patricia Marie Murphy

Like his *Chokecherry Tree* character Elof Lofbloom, who overcomes temptations of the world, the devil, and the flesh, Frederick Manfred resisted the blandishments, the tempting apples of success, preferring instead the "raw red snapping apples from the orchard" (*Selected Letters* 234). In a letter to his friend and confidante John Huizenga, written in October 1946, one year before he completed his creative work with Elof, Manfred reveals his distaste for an admiring coterie's promised worldly pleasures and compliments, what Manfred called "blandishments of empty souls" (234). Although he considered these blandishments to be "sweet," he preferred country life: "If one hears compliments day after day, the impulse to believe them is enormous, is almost undefeatable. In my own case I wasn't too sure I could stand it, so I made quick haste to get out of town and out in a part of the country where I might be relatively inaccessible. I like a few friends. . .my walks, my family, my garden. . . .I like my work as a writer, love it, and I think that saves me from being self-conscious about it. And keeps me what I was, a bumbling farm boy" (234-35).

At this time Manfred was at work on his novel *The Chokecherry Tree*. He had written Van Wyck Brooks earlier that same year that he identified with his character Elof, another bumbling farm boy, "a college graduate who has no specific training and so can't get the job that fits his notion of what a hero should have" (*Selected Letters* 219). Like Elof, Manfred had a "Good mind but can't turn it to anything that will give me a living" (219). Manfred also reveals his intentions for his character: "Gradually, despite struggle, and protests, he sinks slowly away into the common mass of people" (219).

Yet it is in this very sinking that Elof paradoxically attains the status of *Hero*, which was one of Manfred's working titles for his novel" (*Selected Letters* 218). Relying heavily on Biblical inference, Manfred raises that bumbling farm boy from dirt-bound clodhopper to mythic status by creating an Adamic character who creates a place for himself in the wilderness and causes it to blossom like a New Eden. Elof Lofbloom is finally worthy of his name's meaning

(Flowered Leaf). Through a series of engendering choices, he makes himself into a hero in Siouxland.[1]

In *The Chokecherry Tree* Manfred defines *hero* as one who individuates, becomes a "soul apart with a separate pride" and then makes life "eternal" for his family line (18). His bumbling hero Elof is rather passive as he takes his initial tentative steps along the "steeping" (266) path to personal and communal salvation: "Some mornings he would wake and there the big surprise would be" (5). At St. Comus Seminary, he fails to actualize the dreams of "two old visionaries," his mother and old Domeny Hillich. He fails at the university. Seeking work, he roams the byroads of the barren Great Depression until he bums a ride home. That he has to fling himself from the rig of a grotesque maddened truck driver is reiteration of his powerless, out-of-control condition.

He is given shoes worn by another wanderer, now dead, a Depression bum. His father, the donor, expects Elof will follow in the bum's footsteps. But the shoes don't fit him. Indeed, none of the roles Elof temporarily assumes—student, *Peregrine Pickle* reader, caretaker, salesman—are a fit. Yet he learns compassion by standing in others' shoes. By novel's end, he has gained a Christ-like vision of humanity. He is tolerant and loving. Casting off burdensome and smothering projections, separating the wheat of who he is from the chaff of who he is not, he winnows out self awareness and a personal vision. He is at least able to define hero for himself.

Elof Lofbloom—a shoeless Jason—comes home to gain his father's power, the male authority passed down from generation to generation, authority represented by patriarchal prayer. At his father's table, Elof sits: "With his eyes closed, still in the grip of the thought that he had just heard his eldfathers, all the way back to Adam, chanting at the table" (19). The genealogy is rootedness, Elof's father's patriarchal line.[2] Although Elof seems to extract some meaning in life from literature (19), and although he later refers to *Peregrine Pickle* as his *Bible* (119), his family tradition provides community. University and self-education have severed Elof from familiar camaraderie with Siouxland country folk: "The taste of books had forever spoiled him. He had eaten of the tree of knowledge of good and evil, and it made him forever alone and misunderstood. Alone" (61). Like Adam who ate the bitter fruit, Elof has chosen knowledge and, thus, separation. He senses the strength in continuity, in rootedness in the past, in the chain of dead ancestors. But he has yet to claim his seat among the Lofbloom patriarchs. He still sits at his father's table, still sleeps under his father's roof. He has not planted his own branch of the family tree. He has not yet flowered.

When his mother reads to him from *The Book of Job* 18:10-16 on the day he leaves for college, Elof is warned about his possible future destiny: "The snare is laid for him in the ground . . .Terrors . . . shall drive him to his feet . . . His roots shall be dried up beneath, and above shall his branch be cut off" (20). Since no siblings are mentioned, Elof carries the responsibility of the last male Lofbloom. He may feel tied to his eldfathers in the family prayers, but he himself has not propagated or settled. And sexuality tied to reproduction is an important theme throughout this novel and through many of Manfred's works. In later years Manfred, who had been spurned by his first love (she chose another), revealed in an interview with Nancy Bunge: "If you look around in the other species, the top alpha males get first chance with all the females and then later on when they're through, the other ones get a chance, but by that time the seed has been planted. That's how these species keep up. But if you let them all breed, it just goes downhill" (27).

Elof also returns home to his mother's kitchen (7), to female acceptance, support, and nurturing. As Manfred views it, nurturing paradoxically proffers support while acting as a vise to control and to castrate him. Only by asserting male authority can Elof dispel the enticing female-mothering power. Shoeless, "driven to his feet" (20) —as Bildad accused Job, another isolate, of being driven—and symbolically castrated because of his stubby first toe and stubby penis, Elof is powerless without male-patriarchal authority. He is still mama's boy, still "Sister son" (34). He eats mom's lemon meringue pie and accepts her stifling injunctions to make himself into a minister: "For her he just had to become a hero" (5).

His mother's enjoining him to become hero haunts him from the time he is first "chosen." He, young Bud Hillich, and Gert are the only survivors of a tragedy which takes the lives of all their friends. Elof and the future domeny are left to bring to pass all the unfulfilled dreams of Chokecherry Corner's mothers. The adult Elof realizes that his childhood playmates were at least "saved from having to learn that one was striving for goals never meant for one" (31). Any personal ambitions Elof may have had are smothered as surely as the breathing of his contemporaries is smothered by the landslide. After the accident, Elof, his name "laid for him in the ground" or in the landslide, attempts to actualize his mother's vision, a vision that smothers his true self. To secure her nurturing approval, he tries to make himself into something that he cannot comfortably become by first studying for the ministry.[3]

To understand how Elof frees himself from his all-devouring need for his mother's approval, one must look to Manfred's allusions to Adam, chief eldfather. Adam, like Elof, had gained knowledge that resulted in expulsion from the blissful unconsciousness of the garden. He is admonished by the Lord God: "In the sweat of thy face shalt thou eat bread, till thou return unto the ground; for out of it wast thou taken; for dust thou art, and unto dust shalt thou return" (*Genesis* 4:19). The earth and what sprouts from the earth, the chokecherry tree and its bitter fruit, are central images in the novel.[4] In the prairie graveyard, Elof refers to man as "a handful of troubled soil," the symbolic handful of dirt thrown on the coffin, the final reduction of flesh to dust (198). Man is expendable dust. Yet, in the graveyard he also senses the hope of rebirth: "The musk of last year's dust and leaf came to him—it was the smell of molting time. And with it rose the new flesh smell of this year's growth. Elof savored it" (196). In the land lies the promise of new life.

Responsible stewardship over the land ensures salvation. Old Pa Henson entreats: "Pray that we may truly labor in this land thou gavest us as Thy children, as Thy chosen people, so that the land will never vomit us forth" (129). In the course of the novel, Elof is cast out of city society—from seminary, the state university, and, finally, Kingsfood. Even his original arrival home is like a vomiting—he is spewed out onto the highway. Early in the novel he is ". . . a young man who was going places and would someday become a hero" (47). But after "going places," with his adopted goal of "someday" becoming a "hero" now seeming more chimerical than realistic, he returns to the rural area, symbolic of the earth itself, to work out his true relationship to it as did outcast Adam. Land can smother one or "vomit one forth." It can also engender "this year's growth." The only way to be at peace with it, to overcome the "snare laid in the ground," is to learn to climb up the "steeping" (266) path, to do the work of Adam, "by the sweat of [his] brow." Elof, the wanderer, who has attempted to escape work and restraints of the land, has suffered being both kicked about and smothered.

Elof yearns for a place where he will "be shed of hated work . . .where he could become the hero and be loved for it. If only he hadn't lacked technical knowledge, if only his father had been kindly, if only the world had been rid of greedy graspers, then, oh then, he could have been happy in the heaven-land of what might have been" (142). He only dreams of a new land/heaven where he could be a hero-god. He is still psychologically dependent on his mother's care, still at his father's table, still cared for instead of caring for: ". . . he remained a slowbull, a mama's boy" (63). Gradually, however, loosening the noose of his mother's apron strings, he reclaims his "mind, light. . .a possession worth having" (183). Working hard in the fields brings out the "beast" or the "old Adam" in him. By compassionate service to others, he creates a "heaven-land," a kind of New Eden for himself. Perhaps the first glimpse of "heaven-land" is the ball game. Before he bats, he connects with the soil when he rubs dirt under his eyes and muses on his failures (111). Hitting the home run frees him: "He had struck chains from his self" (112). Instantly he is hero and savior: "Life was eternal for everyone" (113). And with his "stubby arm"—a reference to his still being ruled by females, and therefore symbolically castrated—he pitches a play that cinches his fame: "Heaven had come to earth again" (115). The community lionizes him and a lovely for whom he has lusted calls him "hero": "You hero you. . .Quite a hero" (117). In Siouxland he is now a minor god, an incarnation who has made the plains folk forget their own struggles. When he finally settles in Chokecherry Corner, he retains his reputation as minor hero: "Young Domeny Hillich, Kaes, Wilbur and Cor, the Nelson triplets, many, many others, regarded him a sort of hero for having once hit a mighty home run, for having stayed on his feet while licking a bad infection, for daring to come back to the village to live" (248). Man may only be a "handful of troubled soil," but he can become hero, can blossom, even if only for the fleeting moment of "this year's growth."

Blossoming does not completely quench the "cork dry" taste in Elof's mouth (247). The bitter bite of chokecherry is never totally improved. However, attempts to eliminate conflict between his *need for* and *fear of* women act as catalyst to catharsis. Elof gains self-knowledge. The women he meets overpower him physically or emotionally. Each one of these females is another landslide, figuratively speaking. Marthea Dix is a smothering image: "Elof himself was having a devil of a time surviving a tremendous crushing. Marthea had enveloped him like some huge amoeba gone cellulation crazy" (177). He falls under the mesmerizing landslide of Marge, the local lovely: "She was above him. Elof couldn't unthaw the freeze in his limbs" (118). His attempts at love-making with Effie fade into farce when his shoe sticks under the car seat. Frustrated, she "high heels" away (86). Again he is emotionally crushed. His foot, a penis symbol, is caught. He is castrated—this time the victim of a car seat and a disgruntled woman.

A major focus of the smothering/castration theme is Gert. The one weakness he sees in Gert is that she is a "bit bossy."[5] He suspects Gert has manipulated him with her batch of chokecherry jelly: "There was just a chance that she had used it to mollify him, had kept the jelly handy for just such a situation" (260). Some of his eldfathers had also apparently been pampered in this way. Although Gert had substituted a modern recipe, she also owned Elof's mother's original: "Her old recipe. The one she got from Grandma Alfredson" (257). The implication is that women in his family had handed down this recipe for mollifying purposes, a kind of cabalistic sisterhood with the chokecherry jelly recipe as sacred writ. Elof is angered by Gert's attempts. He resists the traditional Eve-like beguilement of Adam that enticed him to join her in apple eating. Elof may belong to his eldfathers. But Gert certainly belongs to her eldmothers. In addition, Elof is enraged when Gert makes an inference that because his penis (symbolized by his big toe) is short, she would rule the home.

A careful look at the text shows that the chokecherry jelly pacifies because it has a psychological shrinking effect on the penis, symbol of male dominance. Experience for Elof is like tasting one chokecherry after another: "For the first instant they were sweet; then suddenly stringent, tongue-shrinking" (62). Elof initiates his projects with zest. The experience, like feminine beauty, is "sweet." Sweetness falls into the bitter grief of abandonment and garden-leaving when ambition dwindles. The experience, and by association, life itself, is a threat. He feels castrated. His penis is even smaller in his mind's eye. Desire for the female, like chokecherry eating, has a shrinking effect. Chokecherries are also symbols of his exodus from promising Edens—the accounting course never completed, *Peregrine Pickle* never finished, the easy farm job that overpowers him because of his own carelessness: "The chokecherry and Elof Lofbloom. A scrub tree and a stunted youth. And both a bitter fruit" (102).

The "cork-dust" taste is associated with eating chokecherries, first introduced into the novel when Gert brings lunch to Elof in the field. She does not bring the chokecherries, but he is thirsty from eating them when she arrives. Elof is attracted to her physically and calls her a "comely worker" (62). Gert may be seen as a worker bee when immediately following this passage, an extended bumblebee metaphor is introduced. This metaphor appears later in the book in direct reference to Gert:

> A yellow-and-black bumblebee sussed around his straw hat. He stood stock-still, knowing that a trembling finger like a fluttering leaf or flower, might catch the glossy, staring eye of the haphazardly flying insect. He stood like a statue, hoping that if he made no move the stinging creature would buzz on. A cold shiver brushed over his skin as he watched it. He noted the blue-black shine of its head in the glinting sunlight. He envied it its fancies. It was both beauty and threat. He thought a moment about the two qualities: beauty, threat. Perhaps it was for the lack of them that he wasn't traveling over the far curve of the earth-ball like a conquering hero (62).

Under threat of a stinging, Elof is as paralyzed or overpowered as he is in the presence of women. The beauty and threat Elof is really referring to is his attraction to female beauty, his need for female attention, and the threat of castration/smothering that Manfred's text suggests often accompanies nurturing by females. Elof attributes his failures to a dearth of feminine support. Manfred later suggested that he may have been somewhat harsh in his attitude toward his earlier heroines.[6]

To free himself from castration fear, Elof reverts to physical force. At first he tolerates Gert: "He didn't feel uncomfortable wearing clodhoppers in the presence of Gert. It meant he was in control, not the woman" (138). But in the novel's final struggle, Elof fights with Gert, the bumblebee, for control:

And her stinger continued to dig, going in deeper, going down to where his old Adam lived. All his little hatreds, hatreds that conscience had carefully encapsulated with the fibroses of faith and hope and charity now burst open like trampled-on eggshells spilling yellow insides. What Ma and old Domeny Hillich had done to him both in high school and in Saint Comus Theological Seminary, what State had done to him, everything evil, lavaed out. (261)

This time he resists the landslide. This time he fights back. Wrestling with Gert (similar to dancing with Marthea Dix), he claims power and authority over what Manfred sees as female manipulation.

For a time all outcomes are bitter, festering toes that never quite heal. His problem is that he has been *puer aeternus*, avoiding adult responsibility for procreation and the duties that entails, including accepting Adam's charge of keeping mankind "going as a species" (178). Easy sex could make him forget failure. While spooning with Effie, Elof thinks: "This was life . . . real life. Something like this once a week made a man out of a man . . . Helped one forget one was a flop in life" (82). But uncommitted sex results in his shoe's getting stuck. And the wounded toe reinflames.

Fear of his lust for Gert drives him to join the wanderer Fats, a city slicker, one of the "killer bulls" and a representative of Kingsfood: "Gert represented a way of life he had been trying to escape" (142). Manfred portrays hedonistic sexual conquest as antithetical to Siouxland's idea of hero. "Cut your wolf loose," Fats urges Elof. The salesmen hired at the Redstone Motel "astounded" Elof with their lists of detailed seductions, "plans for another frontal attack upon Dakota virginity" (184). Elof, no admirer of the salesmen or their values, eventually quits Kingsfood without ever cutting his "wolf loose."

His flight from Gert is similar to the flight of Adam's son Cain, the marked and convicted: "A fugitive and a vagabond shalt thou be upon the earth" (Genesis 5:14). Elof is a wanderer who endures bearing a mark of his own—a stubby penis and inability to make any of his plans bear fruit. Cain forfeits birthright because he murders to get gain. Elof will not deceive potential Kingsfood customers to line his pockets: "It's so false, false . . . because in about ten minutes after a nice heart to heart talk as old bosom friends, you're going to give me a hundred dollars for twenty dollars worth of goods—the other eighty representing fast and friggy talk" (163). Forfeiting the opportunity to nab his brother's flocks, he gives meaning to the word *brother*. Domeny Bud Hillich recognizes Elof's role when the two arrive home together: "Elof, remember, I'm always Bud to you" (230). Although it is also the domeny's given name, *bud* is a Midwestern term for *brother*. Elof is dedicated to truth, thereby turning his back on the Satanic role of polished persuading of the gullible.

The decision not to manipulate or to be manipulated frees Elof to become a separate soul, and, thus, a *hero*, while Fats uses awareness of his personal charisma to screw his customers. Elof discerns kindly Fats as Janus-faced: ""Underneath the covering of Fats's and Van Dam's badinage flailed a bitter, knife-in-the-back struggle to the death. Fats was out to climb over Van Dam's corpse, and Van Dam was fighting to prevent it" (182). Fats lives by the creed, ". . . first law is to fill that belly. No matter what. If somebody gets in the way, you get rid of em" (160). He is dollar-driven and feigns generosity in order to fleece his customers and to get laid; yet he is a tenderly endearing character and extraordinarily honestly generous to Elof (178). His kindness contributes to the clearing of Elof's vision.

Elof values compassion over competitive gain: "Just the same, I ain't leaning on no poor people" (191). Later Elof discovers that, like Christ, he himself has been an "innocent lamb led to slaughter," a pawn on the Kingsfood chess board (183). Unlike Cain, Elof does not refuse to be his brother's keeper. He relinquishes his much needed manure-spreading job to another man down on his luck. And as he chooses a magnanimous path, the effects of his mark begin to disappear. He is no longer isolated, even after he separates from his first friend, Fats, the friend for whom the young bumbler had hoped: "If there were only a friend. Only. A friend could salve his bleeding fingers, would reassure him his hoping mind" (101). Elof settles down in Chokecherry Corner. Fats continues chasing gain and skirt across the prairie vistas.

Elof escapes the wandering Cain existence: "Elof boy, what was it that helped you escape the crafty males, the scarred Toms, the killer bulls?" (221). Like the servant who informs Job of his losses, and like Job himself who refuses the arguments of his "friends," Elof has "escaped " to start a new life. The "scarred Toms" may be seen as a reference to Cain's mark. Elof, a man without guile, escapes but is "hornless." His essence of manhood is not animal bullhood so much as an incarnation of deity, the martyred hero, the antithesis of the image of conquest. Having refused the role of Cain, riding home with Bud, he imagines Christ entering his body, as a sufferer with the weak and humble: "Christ Jesus. Yes. And the reason I took over the body of little Elof, the little Elof who had been a bit shortchanged on everything, the reason I took over him was to see if the strong were treating the humble and meek with human love" (226). Elof, now identifying with mythical hero, has atoned for Adam's transgression. Adam was told he must till the earth. His happy lark in the garden was over. Likewise Elof's "happy lark is over." He feels his old Adam breaking through when he works hard in spite of his festering toe, and by novel's close, he has synthesized compassion (Christ) and Adam (male survival). Establishing kinship, accepting responsibility for his brothers, Elof gains the male authority he needs to overcome castration by females.

Elof returns to the chokecherry land with a developed ability to persevere. As a "cross-roads glad-hander," he builds a new kind of Eden, a "51 to 49 world," where one can live with self-respect and respect for one's brothers. To forge his link in this Adamic chain has been no easy task. Struggle has left a bitter "cork-dust" thirst of dissatisfaction. Eating forbidden fruit also symbolizes knowledge acquisition. Time in formal study and informal on-the-road training prepares Elof for the testing that makes of him a "separate" soul and gives him "a mind, light . . . a possession worth having" (183). To become a "separate" soul, Elof—although probably not conscious of his moves to self-actualize in the beginning—takes certain definite steps, each an act of refusal. Manfred ties Elof's stunting to his dominance by females, as reflected in the sky described as a "black tarpaulin of heaven with a mizzling spray of milk white drops of light" (102). In the last paragraph of the book, the threat of castration is still there. The sky is still described as "milk-sprettled" (266).[7] The reference is to the female, the milk producer, the mother. Perhaps he will be "wife-run" after all, but the god looking down is no longer concerned. Elof has chosen the path of stay, struggle, and fight. He will survive: "The accident that jarred you out of your path and made you go up a steeping one (Would you make it? Would you fail?) did not break you . . . You are safe" (266). Elof has learned to accept the bitter along with the sweet.

His refusing to be manipulated, action that culminates in physical wrestling with Gert, is initiated by his insight into the city slicker's deception. In reaction to the interface between city slicker and country sod, Elof remarks: "You city slickers had better go back to school and get caught up or we country hicks'll skin you down to bone and toenails" (71). Respect for himself and his kind, a result of overcoming the world's temptations, is revealed in its maturity in his return to his father's house. The new Elof no longer hates his father. In his first homecoming, "Pa looked like an angered bullheaded duke—all horns and shoulders" (10). Pa at the final homecoming is not viewed as a threatening Oedipal father, but as fragile, vulnerable. When he notices a tiny pear-shaped tear coursing down the side of Pa's nose, Elof withdraws quietly, leaving Pa the remnants of his pride (232). No longer mama's boy or competitor with his father, he is ready to take his place in the great chain of Siouxland being.

Elof is the true hero who returns home where he builds a place for himself and family out of the wilderness of possibilities. He is not a "wandering stallion," not a Kingsfood salesman with seduction lists, but a beast with a stall, rootedness. The sex to which he finally commits himself is marriage to "mare-breasted" Gert. Children will most likely follow. The god on the bluff comments: "You have survived...the generations arise, they come and they go, each leapfrogging over the one previous, hopping off in to the future" (266). Elof, his hand "freckled" from climbing the "steep forenoon" (91), has made his walk successfully up the "steeping" path. He will engender offspring. This is life eternal, the "hopping off in to the future," an infinity of posterity, and he, an heroic link in the chain stretching all the way back to his eldfathers and Adam.

After his trials he is centered and productive. He takes root, and although here are towering oaks in the world, he is like the stubby Chokecherry tree, for whom his town is named. A survivor against odds, he settles and begins to leaf, one leaf on the Chokecherry tree. For although he has become a separate soul, in Manfred's philosophy, life is not eternal for Elof alone, but for the group:

"Mankind says: We do; we beget.
Mankind says: We go on..." (54)

Notes

[1]Manfred explained his coining of the word in a letter to Van Wyck Brooks in May 1946: "*Hero*, then *A Child*, then *W. W.*, then *Pilgrims*, then *A son of the Road*, then *Idyll of the Old Faithful*. Another thing I noticed: that most of these people come from a territory called Siouxland. (I drew a map of this area for *This Is The Year*. I am sure than over half of my work will tie back to my "boyhood heaven and hell." It is land adjoining the Sioux River running between Sioux Falls, S.D., and Sioux City, Iowa. Already I've peopled it with many towns, mostly fictions (though real) and people, and situations, and tragedies) " (*Selected Letters* 219).

[2]Manfred refers to the eldfathers in a letter in March 1947: "Then too, reading in *Beowulf* was a surprise; probably because I could hear echoes of the old Frisians, my âldfaers (eldfathers), and could in many cases hear Beowulf talk, hear the exact sound of the spitting and coughing verbs, just as my grandfather and great uncle use to bray them" (*Selected Letters* 242).

[3]Manfred's father wanted him to become a minister. In the strictly autobiographical *The Wind Blows Free*, Fred's father tells him: "Too bad you can't strart the Seminary this fall yourself. That's something your Ma wanted." To which Manfred replies: "Me a minister? Never Pa" (4-5). Indeed, Manfred's own mother seemed to be the antithesis of Elof's. In a letter to the Reverend Henry De Mots in December 1947, Manfred quoted his mother's deathbed advice: "Fred, my boy, I can see that your path is going to be different from what mine was. I'd like to see you in heaven with Jesus and me, but don't act the Christian if you don't feel it. If you don't feel it, don't live it. Live out your feelings." He went on to say: ". . . I am in the service of absolute truth. That is not a pinned down truth such as the term God has become for you, but a living and vital principle which helps me see more and more just exactly "what is" (*Selected Letters* 255-56).

[4]To John Huizenga he wrote in July 1947: "We are awaiting word on *The Chokecherry Tree* from the publishers, and since we are down to our last few dollars again, we are just a trace uneasy. . . .the book is as biting as a chokecherry. The bite isn't on the surface, but underneath, after you've bitten into it" (*Selected Letters* 247).

[5]Manfred was concerned with issues of male versus female dominance. In a letter to John Huizenga in October 1946, he compliments his wife: "I know of dozens of women, nay, all the women I've met I'm sure I would have murdered or divorced by this time, because they would either have tried to boss me outright. . ." (234). And In his interview with Nancy Bunge, he revealed his profile of what he called the alpha male: "They tend to be arrogant. They tend to be bossy. . . .The Chamber of Commerce guy gets tin cans and pushes them on through town and calls attention to his business downtown. They become the alpha male on Main Street. But that's an utterly great picture of how males think. To become the alpha male, to become the most recognized male" (Bunge 33). Another interesting view of Manfred's struggle with dominate or be dominated can be seen in his relationship with Miss Minerva Baxter in *The Wind Blows Free*.

[6]"But from *Scarlet Plume* on I did write books with females in the lead roles. I had no sisters. Didn't date until I was in my twenties; didn't sleep

with a woman until I was 25. I got married at 30, and then I soon not only had a wife, but two daughters and a mother-in-law, who all lived with me. And that made up for a lot. From then on women got a better shake from me in my writings" (Bunge 20).

[7]Manfred was intrigued with the male's connection to physical motherhood. He told Nancy Bunge: "...when Freya was born, Maryanna had quite a time with Freya, so the doctor would come and talk and visit with me; he noticed that I was always going like this (scratching) and he said, 'Can I look at that for a minute?' so I opened up my shirt and one milk cell had awakened. He pinched it and a beebee of milk came out like a boil and there was milk in there. And he said that happens every now and then. A husband gets so involved with his wife having a baby that it awakens something and he said that what your mind thinks can affect your physical body very much. You can almost do anything with it. I said, 'You can't change me to have babies.' 'No,' he said, 'that's right.' So I've been intrigued about the whole business of femininity for a long time. And, of course, I think, too, that every male has a female component lying there unused, but it can be awakened as time goes on" (Bunge 28).

Works Cited

Bunge, Nancy, "Something Magical and Important Is going On": Interviews with Frederick and Freya Manfred. *North Dakota Quarterly* 61 (Spring 1993) : 19-36.

The Holy Bible, King James Version.

Manfred, Frederick, *The Chokecherry Tree*. Albuquerque: U of New Mexico P, 1975.

---. *The Selected Letters of Frederick Manfred*, 1932-1954. Ed. Arthur R. Huseboe and Nancy Owen Nelson. Lincoln: U of Nebraska P, 1989.

---. *The Wind Blows Free*. Sioux Falls: The Center for Western Studies, 1979.

The Search for Wisdom: The *World's Wanderer* Trilogy

by Lawrence I. Berkove

At some point in his life, Frederick Manfred separated himself from conventional Christianity and began to develop some independent ideas about religion. The change has attracted some scholarly interest[1] and, in fact, receives extensive fictional treatment in the *World's Wanderer* trilogy. It is not the purpose of this paper to dispute the authenticity of the change nor to speculate about the specifics of Manfred's new religious position, but rather to establish the enduring impression on him of his early religious training even while he chronicled in the trilogy the rationale for the separation.

The general nature of this new position should not come as a surprise to anyone who is familiar with Manfred and, especially, with the trilogy. It would be astonishing indeed if anyone as deeply steeped in the Bible and Christian values as Manfred were to turn entirely against them—and there is no reason to believe that he did. Certainly in his fiction we find a selective retention of aspects of his religious upbringing. Precisely because they were selected for retention they become valuable aids to the inference of Manfred's personal attitude and also to the interpretation of his works. This can be demonstrated in the case of the *World's Wanderer* trilogy, which appears to have been shaped to a surprising extent by the model of the Old Testament book of Ecclesiastes. What Manfred found in Ecclesiastes was a pattern of life experiences, a consistent attitude toward them, and an escape from tragedy. Each of these points will be discussed.

There are two levels of events in the trilogy. The obvious level is that of narrative. From this point of view, the trilogy is an account of the life of Thurs Wrâldsoan, an awkwardly large Siouxland farmboy foundling who turns out to have great creative talents which are discovered and stimulated and brought to fruition by his adventures on his way to manhood. Underlying this is a subtle but formative level that is philosophical, or even religious: a rumination[2] not of a life, but of life itself. It is on this deeper level that similarities to Ecclesiastes can be discerned.

THE SEARCH FOR WISDOM

The pattern of events in Ecclesiastes is determined by the efforts of its putative author, named "the Preacher," to search methodically for wisdom in the pursuit of the most important mundane "goods" known to man: knowledge, righteousness, pleasure, and wealth. The accounts in Ecclesiastes of each quest are very brief, and they all end with essentially the same conclusion: "All is vanity and vexation of spirit." It is worth our while to glance over the trilogy and note the extent to which the "world-wandering" adventures of Thurs also constitute a pursuit and scrutiny of these same "goods" and result in the same conclusion.

Although Ecclesiastes claims its author to be "the Preacher," his words preach skepticism as much as faith. As a consequence, Ecclesiastes is a disquieting book, one which is more famous for the Preacher's probing and painful honesty than for his orthodoxy and comfort. It is an interesting fact that Thurs is sent to Zion College in the first place not only to acquire knowledge but also for the specific purpose of becoming a preacher. Much of the drama of *The Primitive* develops as a result of his struggle with himself over his intended vocation, and consequences of his decision not to become a preacher reverberate throughout *The Brother* and *The Giant*, the second and third volumes of the trilogy. Thurs's life is a manifestation of his probing and painful honesty, and on more than one occasion not only does he come to the same conclusions as the Preacher, but the very words of the Preacher are recalled by Thurs or by those in his company, and parallels are thus explicitly established between Ecclesiastes and the trilogy.

The first and major phase of Thurs's search for wisdom turns out only to be a search for the lesser quality of knowledge. It begins but does not end with his enrollment in Zion College, a seminary of Calvinism in the stronghold of the Christian Church community of southwestern Michigan. The desire for college was truly Thurs's; he had natural intellectual curiosity. But the choice of Zion College—for mixed reasons—had been that of his guardian, Mrs. Brothers. "I'd like to have you set your mind on becoming either a preacher or teacher in the name of the Lord. . . . What a wonderful preacher you'll make. Roaring hell and brimstone fire at us sinners in that big organ voice of yours. From on high".[3]

At Zion College, Thurs soaks up his studies and begins to bud. He takes the courses in religion that are expected of him but is not convinced by them and remains only a nominal Christian. His interests run more strongly in the secular direction, especially philosophy, literature, and music. Uncontrollably in love with Hero Bernlef, a lovely girl whose petiteness against his massiveness makes them a grotesque couple, Thurs hopes to win her by excelling in academics. She does come to respect him, but not to love him. It is the first failure for him of knowledge.

"Be not righteous over much; neither make thyself over wise," says Ecclesiastes (7:16), "why shouldest thou destroy thyself?" Not only the limitations of knowledge are exposed at Zion College, but also those of righteousness. At least in the sense of the narrow and rigid orthodoxy professed by the members of the Christian Church Thurs has most to do with, what passes for righteousness is never made attractive in the trilogy. Mrs. Brothers is a hard, bitter, vengeful woman whose "piety" causes the death of Thurs's mother, ruins the life of Thurs's father, and seeks to break the free spirits, Thurs and Adam Skop. Her foreman, Alexander Paul, is humorless, mean, and hard. Domeny Donker, Mrs. Brother's preacher model for Thurs, is a zealot who dwells professionally on God's wrath. Ultimately, the faculty of Zion College turn out to be little better than witch hunters. Failing to prove anything conclusively heretical against the philosophy teacher, Prof. Hobbe, they turn on Broer Menfrid, the music teacher and secret father of Thurs, cause him to be dismissed for un-Christian attitudes, and, in effect, recommend his expulsion from the Church.

Perhaps because of, rather than in spite of, their extreme "righteousness," many of the Church members also appear hypocritical. This is especially obvious in the students Thurs meets at Zion. None of them are the apprentice saints one might like to expect at a strict denominational college, and human nature in the forms of selfish, mercenary, and sexual considerations regularly subordinates theology. The seminarians, for example, appear as a group to be petty, conniving, and malicious. Christopher Beoring is not ashamed to charge full fare to his passengers even though his substandard car risked their lives continuously during the trip from Siouxland to Zion. And the wealth of the Snortebull boys' father buys them special privileges at Zion. Thurs, among the most honest of the students, fights unsuccessfully with himself to avoid masturbation, but Happy Hoppen never bothers himself with repression and keeps himself relaxed with an adulterous relationship with his landlady. "Isn't she a good Christian?" Thurs asks. "Sure. But at the

THE SEARCH FOR WISDOM 57

same time she's a female. And I'm an available young male" (*Primitive* 318). Early in *The Primitive*, the naive farmer Willem Sourcole confidently recommends "godliness, fear of d'Lord" (50) as the antidote to the shortcomings of Washington, but at the book's end, when Thurs learns of what the godliest of the godly, the faculty of Zion College, have done to Broer Menfrid, he resolves to resign from the Church and observes bitterly, "Everything is sin with them. Everything. And the result is they chase love away. Warmhearted, spontaneous love—gone! Neither of brotherhood nor of sex. They have everything but the heart" (444). Thurs had found iniquity in this place of judgment and righteousness (Ecclesiastes 3:16).

Thurs is only a young man when he graduates college, and although his skepticism has been fed by the failures for him of academic knowledge and Christian righteousness as sufficient goods and goals, he cannot yet generalize these failures to the larger areas of knowledge and righteousness. He thinks that if he were to go East he would find a better sort of life, one that would give him some pleasure:

> Reading about the East in the Times and various magazines, about its art and drama and politics and music, hearing about it over the radio in programs originating there, he had often longed to see it. . . . The East. Besides, he could probably hide there among its tens and tens of teeming millions. There was probably greater tolerance in cosmopolitan New York for odd ones than anywhere else in the world (*Primitive* 457).

Thurs at first flourishes in the East. He becomes involved with the rich, with sophisticated artists, and is relieved, at long last, of the burden of his virginity. New York is tolerant, liberal, and morally almost the opposite of Zion. But at the end of *The Brother*, he is abruptly overcome by a spasm of deep revulsion for the city. As he walks through New York a sudden revelation makes clear that he had been deceived by illusions.[4] A "word of Truth" comes to him, the longest quotation from the Bible in the entire trilogy. It is Ecclesiastes 2: 1-13, the denunciation of what the King James Bible glosses as the "vanity of things pleasurable." It dawns upon Thurs that all he has done and learned in New York has been folly and he remembers "that wisdom excelleth folly, as far as light excelleth darkness" (414). This experience makes Thurs decide to leave New York immediately, to flee it and to escape from it as he would from a city about to be destroyed.

The East, of course, was not a simple experience for Thurs, and the charge of "vanity and vexation of spirit" applied not only to his pleasurable experiences and to the extension of his knowledge there, but also to a new aspect of his education: wealth. Thurs quickly learns how seldom a working man has cause to rejoice over the labor of his hands: at the Hammer Rubber Works, fellow employee Gabrielski loses an arm in one part of the factory, while in another, young girls strip rubber sheaths from penislike forms and fold them into contraceptive boxes. But labor is not only unpleasant for the workers; it also is "vanity and a vexation of spirit" for the owners. For all of his labor in establishing his company and making it a giant among corporations, Black Jack Hammer must leave it, as Ecclesiastes 2:21 gloomily anticipates, to those who did not work for it, to those, in fact, who never even worked at all. Hammer at the peak of his career is married to a woman he cannot tolerate, and whose daughter—by another marriage—is affected, spoiled by wealth, and sexually frustrated. Hammer is obligated to bankers, shareholders, and unions, and is afraid of government controls. And he feels his body giving out. Our last glimpse of him is as an invalid in a wheelchair, crippled by arthritis, attended by a nurse, and so thin his face is almost a death's-head. His pursuit of wealth is ultimately only another "vanity and a great evil."

The vanity of knowledge was not exposed once and for all at Zion College. Thurs continues to be tempted by it throughout the trilogy. He encounters three great systems of thought and value in his lifetime. The first is Christianity, oriented to the past. Although Thurs breaks away from the Christian Church upon graduation from Zion College, Christianity nevertheless leaves a permanent imprint upon him. Thurs retains a memory of the Bible, and particularly of *Ecclesiastes*, a memory which continues to influence him at critical times and to affect his opinions of the other two systems.

Thurs continues to search for wisdom when he reaches the East, and thinks for a while that he may have found it in Marxism, the second and present-oriented system. It is natural for him, involved as he is in the labor union, to meet dedicated Marxists and to become interested in the theories of an ally against the oppres-

THE SEARCH FOR WISDOM 59

sive Hammer Works. Having seen through one system, however, Thurs is already prepared to be skeptical of Marxism. Thurs eventually comes to see that it is divided into two camps: the one, led by Malcolm Makepeace, which gently idealizes its theories; and the other, led by Fritz Blutschwert, which applies it brutally and cynically as an instrument of power. As Blutschwert gains the upper hand, Thurs becomes increasingly disenchanted with Marxism. The last straw for Thurs is the nonaggression pact that Hitler and Stalin sign. It is a sellout of Marxian principles, and Thurs realizes that Marxism, for all its appeal to the downtrodden, is "a theology every bit as thorough and dogmatic as was old-time Christianity" (*Brother* 417). He sees that it blinkers its adherents both to the world outside and to its own contradictions and hypocrisies. It is another "vanity and vexation of spirit," and he rejects it.

The third system is science, oriented toward the future. Its god is named Scire, from the root word of science, meaning "to know." Its priest in the trilogy is Bruce Farrewell, a lapsed Quaker who is now a nuclear physicist. Both Thurs and Farrewell are aware that Scire is a man-made god, a myth, as Marx has become and as they both believe Christ is. But Farrewell nevertheless believes that the knowledge of science is the best truth man has, whereas Thurs, unable to understand science as Farrewell does, remains skeptical of it. He notes critically, for example, that Farrewell maneuvers his car "more as a scientist than as adroit driver" (*Giant* 55), trusting a theory of acceleration rather than the feel of the car on the road. As a consequence, although the two men become friendly, they pursue different courses of life. Farrewell worships the knowledge of science and participates in the development of the atom bomb; Thurs remains skeptical of science as an ultimate value, and seeks to find fulfillment in life by following not an abstraction but something simpler and personally satisfying, his talent for music.

He is encouraged in this career choice by his dying father, the former Zion College music teacher Broer Mcnfrid, who clinches an appeal with a quotation from Ecclesiastes: "Wherefore I perceive that there is nothing better than that a man should rejoice in his works; for that is his portion: for who shall bring him to see what shall be after him?" (*Giant* 244). There is nothing better for Thurs than music. He loves it, composes it, and rejoices in his work. Following yet another precept of Ecclesiastes: "Live joyfully with the wife whom thou lovest all the days of the life of thy vanity . . ."

(Ecclesiastes 9:9), Thurs marries and is happy. At the peak of his success and happiness, however, at the moment when his wife is about to give birth, Thurs asks Farrewell to drive them to the hospital. Still convinced of his theory, Farrewell turns a curve too fast and in the resulting accident Thurs is fatally injured.

The sudden and unexpected death of Thurs is a difficult but critical part of the trilogy. It clearly does not lend itself to autobiographical interpretation. It also does not lend itself to the position that the trilogy ends with a tragedy, for the trilogy does not end at this point. Little is said in Ecclesiastes about the personality of the Preacher; it is because he is not at the center of the book. Although the trilogy would be inconceivable without Thurs, yet it is an arguable paradox that he also may not be at its center. The Preacher is a means to an end: a statement about existence. Thurs has the same function. When he dies, the trilogy proceeds first to link Thurs's life with those of all men and then to arrive at a conclusion ambiguously balanced among Darwin, Whitman, and Genesis, among ontogeny and ontology: "Beginnings: origins: always beginnings" (*Giant* 400).

If it can be granted that the trilogy parallels Ecclesiastes in its consistently skeptical view of the tendencies and capacities of human nature, then one more parallel will complete the comparison. Again like Ecclesiastes, the trilogy escapes tragedy by balancing a prevailingly skeptical view of human enterprises against a mystical affirmation of a mysterious order to existence of which human existence is only a small part, and which human wisdom is insufficient to compass. The point of the trilogy's conclusion saves it from tragedy and from melodrama too: the death of the main character of the story cannot mean the end of everything; "one generation passeth away, and another generation cometh: but the earth abideth forever" (Ecclesiastes 1:4).

Thurs's death is a corroboration of the observations that "the race is not to the swift, nor the battle to the strong . . . but time and chance happen to them all" and that "man also knoweth not his time" (Ecclesiastes 9:11-12). Although the Preacher was skeptical of what man can know, he was not skeptical of God. Nor is Manfred skeptical of a God who is ultimate Truth, a Purpose behind the incomprehensible scheme of life. He is skeptical of what men call God, reductionist myths of infinite Truth, adapted to man's measure. Manfred learned from Ecclesiastes to see the folly of the pretensions to absolutism of institutions and thought systems which are only wishful projections of human vanities. But he also learned not to deny the sense of an infinite mystery, incorporating the past as well as the present and the future, that is the source of all existence and all value. In the final analysis what Thurs shows and Manfred intimates is that the search for wisdom exceeds mortal limits; for an infinite truth there must be an infinite search.

Notes

[1] Peter Oppewall, "Manfred and Calvin College," *Where the West Begins*, ed. Arthur R. Huseboe and William Geyer (Sioux Falls: Center for Western Studies, 1978) 86-98. See also Robert C. Wright's discussion in *Frederick Manfred* (Boston: Twayne, 1979), especially 101-106, 141-44, 154-58.

[2] My use of "rumination" does not necessarily imply agreement with Manfred's theory about "rumes" as a genre; I allude to his idea here primarily becuase it does emphasize the importance of writing out of deep reflection. See *The Giant*, 418.

[3] *The Primitive* (Garden City: Doubleday, 1949) 19. The other two volumes of the trilogy are *The Brother* and *The Giant*, published respectively in 1950 and 1951 by Doubleday.

[4] The incident, too long to be quoted, appears on p. 413.

Part II

Finding a Name: Buckskins and Other Matters

"Wolf That I Am . . . ":
Animal Symbology in
The Buckskin Man Tales

by Mick McAllister

No reader of the Buckskin Man Tales can fail to notice the neat symmetry of action and symbol in *Lord Grizzly* and *Scarlet Plume*. In the first, a white man has his baptism into the American wilderness and emerges radically changed by his experience; in the second, a white woman, Judith Raveling, suffers similar baptism and transformation. Among the symmetries of the two works are a set of parallel incidents that have considerably more than a merely stylistic function: the pursuits of the fleeing protagonists—Hugh by the "hant bear" that follows him down the White River, Judith by the Yankton in a wolfskin who shadows her across the Minnesota prairies. Frederick Manfred's choice of a key animal symbol for each novel is an important part of the thematic fabric of the series as a whole. Bear and wolf: the nature of the beast explains an aspect of each book.

Most readers are familiar with the traditional symbolic meaning of bear and wolf, whether European or Indian or both, and those symbolic meanings are pertinent to the themes of *Lord Grizzly*, *Scarlet Plume*, and the novels that precede or follow them. Manfred cues us to consider such meanings in *Lord Grizzly* when he has Major Henry discuss with his trappers the religious significance of the bear in Plains Indian culture:

> They think the grizzly some sort of god. One tribe I have in mind, when they need food in the winter, go hunt out the bear and bring him the best food they have left, and bow to him, and ask him to forgive them for what they are about to do, saying they know he is their friend, saying they know he wants to live up to his name as the giver of life, saying they know he wants to die for them. (*LG* 78)

American bear folklore fills the book, especially in the early part, before the attack on Hugh. Throughout, we are given bear lore—in the stories told by the mountain men and Indians, in the behavior of the bears themselves.

The nature of the bear is central to the meaning of *Lord Grizzly*, especially certain aspects of its social behavior. The bear is a solitary creature, a classic loner; only the female is likely to be accompanied, and then only by cubs. The male has no parental function beyond impregnating the female; none of the raising, training, feeding, teaching, punishing the cub is done by the male. He, like Hugh, can't father. Like Hugh, he has no male bonds, either—no community of bulls, like the bison, like the wolves who will form artificial packs of unmated males for no reason but socialization and the practical necessity of pack hunting. Throughout *Lord Grizzly* we are reminded of "Old Ephe's" hermit nature, and throughout the book Hugh's great spiritual conflict revolves around his growing recognition that he can no more be a bear than he can be an Esau.

Esau is the Indian, the red one, the hunter. Hugh in his she-rip nemesis' fur hide is a Jacob in disguise—the wolf-reliant, antisocial, self-nucleid white man, needing nobody, he claims, better off alone than on the riverboat the Rees ambush than in the party of trappers slaughtered on the North Platte, than with the other hunters who might have saved him from the mother grizzly who give him his savage initiation into the meaning of independence.

Hugh could be a bear, if that were truly what he wanted; he could adopt the hermitage solitude of the medicine beast if he wished, but clearly something in his nature rejects that choice. He wants—demands—loyalty from his fellows, loyalty no bear would ask of another. He longs for community just as the wolf needs his pack; he weeps with joy and sentiment when he finds even the poor companionship of a dying old Ree woman abandoned on the plains.

The Plains Indians honored and emulated any number of the animals in their rich natural environment. The bison is a source of tribal wisdom, teaching communal dance, bringing peace with the sacred pipe, bringing holy maize, teaching the mature lessons of conservative, sedentary age. The bear is the medicine beast, solitary philosopher, treasurehouse mind of sacred things, earthbound spiritualist, brother of eagle. His solitude is the hermit's, the holy man's, the privacy of permanent introspection, the loneliness of the endless vision quest, life of the elder priest and hierophant. Hugh is an old man, but no philosopher, no hermit. His flight is not positive, not into the spirit but negative, away from demanding responsibilities. He is not the priest seeking private, holy mountaintops but a boy who won't grow up, Huck lit out for the territories, a child demanding fealties he will not reciprocate. Having abandoned his natural sons, he demands love and loyalty of his adoptive sons.

"Old Ephe's" blessing, bestowed at a critical moment of the Crawl, is no confirmation of Hugh's acceptance into the fellowship of nature. Hugh has chosen the wrong totem, or the wrong course of life for his chosen totem: something is out of sync. It is the nature of man to be social, to bond, to mate, to father his children as the wolf fathers pups. For all his resistance to these imperatives, something in Hugh is drawn to them, some muley hankering after colts, some unsatisfied, unquenched need for pack fellows. He has the potential, after his forced intimacy with the landscape—the Crawl, his second and third loner treks—to grow into a grey ghost of the spirit, Lord Grizzly, patriarch of a new white male covenant with the wilderness. Instead, he chooses, when he chooses to forgive, the other path; he chooses to acknowledge the need for his hant companyeros, ghost companions of the social beast. He accepts his wolfishness.

In *Lord Grizzly* the bear is at once the spirit of the wilderness and emblem of a certain potential accommodation of white man and American land. In *Scarlet Plume*, the grizzly is replaced by the wolf as central symbolic creature of the Buckskin Man Tales. From the horrifying image of the crucified wolf that signals the beginning of violence, to the wolfskin that Scarlet Plume adopts as a disguise while he follow Judith, to the "Werewolf women" who attack the Indian prisoners, the wolf is the totem of this book, present in fact, image, or metaphor on nearly every page.

In the massacre sequence, at the beginning, the wolf and the Indian are equated. The Indians will kill the white man as the wolf kills rabbits (*SP* 22); they range around the settlers "like a pack of wolves" (27): their battle cries are "wolfish barks" (67); one attacks like "a lean wolf" (48). They are perceived at the worst moment of the massacre as "worse than wolves even" (49). The wolf-crucifier Crydenwise insists that Indians and wolves are alike in one important respect—they can't be civilized (38). The white settlers of Skywater voice the common view of the wolf: it is a cowardly, ravening monster-symbol, as it has been for European man for centuries, of the savage wild. For the Indian, the wolf is also important, even threatening, but in a different manner.

Indian dead are raised on scaffold "to save them from the wolves" (77): and anyone left alone in the wilderness can expect the wolves to find and eat them (83, 85, 114). A bad wife is like "a crazed she-wolf" (108). But the Indians voice more than the one-sided view held by the white man. The Yanktons have learned from the wolf how to hunt, using the wolf's trick to lure antelope into traps, driving the buffalo pack-style. Their dogs are part wolf. Their negative feelings about wolves are never expressed in terms of an irrational, blind horror, but always their image of the wolf is neither sentimental nor irrational, merely informed and realistic, merely reflections of a healthy respect for the wild. Never do we see any wolf commit any act of aggression against a human—against anything, in fact—despite all the talk of savage hunters and the long section when Judith (and we, on first reading) believes that she is being stalked by a wolf.

It is in a wolfskin that Scarlet Plume pursues Judith—not to attack her, not even to capture her and return her to the village, but to protect her. He takes the skin she slept in at Sioux Falls and follows her like a grey wolf, only visible in the periphery of her vision. Once they are together, she readopts this skin she became so enamoured of during the idyll at Sioux Falls, and at times she wears nothing else. It is the wolfskin, not the deerskin—wolf's prey—recently acquired at Lost Timbers, that Scarlet Plume hides her under when Mad Bear and Bone Gnawer come nosing about, the wolfskin that serves as blanket and bed for their lovemaking. It is still with them as they make their way to Camp Release. They use it to cover the Codman children when they find them wandering—naked, starved, disoriented—near Skywater. Back among whites, the skin is replaced with "a smelly red and black horse blanket" (295).

Since the wolf is a key to the novel, it would be well to consider the real wolves, so seldom visible in the book. The first one we see sets the tone for the rest: it sits on a low mound near Judith's house, sunning itself and lolling its tongue as if it were laughing (4). While we cannot help, in retrospect, but see ominous foreshadowings in the picture, the fact remains that the beast itself is a very image of innocence. During the buffalo hunt, many pages later, the picture is repeated. Two scout wolves trailing the buffalo observe the Yankton's surround and, "laughing with long red tongues"

(134), they slip away. Only once more does a free and living wolf appear—part of a triptych of sexual images.

The central event of the triptych is the "Virgin Feast," which Judith calls a dramatic pageant as moving and sumptuous as a St. Paul play. On one edge of the feast are three sleazy boys, spoilers who try to besmirch the celebrant's honor. On the other side, noticed only by Judith, is the flirtation between a camp dog and a male wolf. The bitch frolics a bit; the male approaches her. Judith reacts in character, first thinking the wolf intends to attack the dog, then disgusted when he "pumps her out of sight into the bushes." Like the rooster who offended her early in the novel, the wolf reminds her of animal lust, the demon she fears most, being a proper nineteenth-century American lady. Like the yielding hen she despised, the dog is a willing lover, even initiator of the loveplay, and disgusting for it. Judith has far to go emotionally, even this late in the novel, before she can throw herself at Scarlet Plume near Lost Timber.

There is, of course, one other real wolf in the novel, the one no reader will ever forget—Crydenwise's victim. It should not be forgotten, in the context of all the horrors that fill the following fifty pages of the novel, that the first victim we observed directly is just as savagely tortured, as sadistically murdered, as any white sufferer to come. Even the mind most irrevocably locked into the view that human suffering is of greater significance than animal cannot help but respond with sympathetic horror at the picture of the crucified wolf. At this point, Henry Christians has been killed—neatly, with one swift arrow. Judith is out hunting for her daughter and nephews, who were last seen playing with an Indian child and who, she fears, are being tortured even at that moment. Her nightmare reveries are broken by a scream. When she investigates, expecting to find her mutilated child, she comes upon Crydenwise skinning a timber wolf alive. Manfred spares us no detail of the sight: the raw look of the beast as it shivers and jerks, crucified on a wooden "X" frame, "glistening body muscles" clutching spasmodically while the animal screams.

Crydenwise is "teaching" the wolf not to steal calves. Crydenwise had brought a pregnant cow with him from Ohio, and a wolf—somehow he seems sure it was this one—killed the cow and ate the calves, twin bulls. While Crydenwise finishes his grim business, Judith reports to him the death of Henry Christians. At the moment she finishes speaking, while Crydenwise stares aghast at her, the wolf dies "on its crude cross." If there is a lesson to be learned from the scene, it is not about stealing calves, it is about the bestiality of Crydenwise and the white man's inability to comprehend and accept the laws of the American wilderness.

There is, first, Crydenwise's foolish assumption that wolves should not hunt, should respect his private property, and then the even more foolish rationalization that the torture he is inflicting on this particular wolf is something other than sheer, vengeful sadism. Twice he uses the phrase "teach him" to describe what he is doing to the wolf. Not even able to admit his own savagery to himself, he must invoke some Biblical concept of justice, some peculiar notion of "rehabilitation," so incongruous as to seem insane, to explain his cruelty. It is Crydenwise—he, and the trader Silvers—who is the primary spokesman for the traditional frontier view of both Indian and wolf. For these two men, the two "wild devils," neither a respecter of John Locke's moral perspectives, are equally undomesticable, completely incompatible with civilization:

> "'Ever try to domesticate a wolf?" Crydenwise said. "Try it some time and see what you get. I know. A wolf'll snap at anything that comes near him even after he gets used to livin' with you. Same thing goes fer a red devil." (38)

It is a point of view that Barry Lopaz spent a chapter of his *Of Wolves and Men* analyzing. Lopez covers the issues so well, I will refer the reader to that chapter, "The Beast of Waste and Desolation," and merely summarize his main points here. Tracing our hatred of wolves back to medieval bestiaries, he describes the connection in the European mind between the wolf and the very concept of wilderness. It is wilderness, Lopez argues—as Frederick Jackson Turner III would argue a few years later from a slightly different perspective in his *Beyond Geography*—that we truly fear and hate: the chaos of the wild. The wolf—wild outlaw cousin of our civilized, tamed, and servile "best friend"—and the "wild man," the indigenous folk of the uncivilized American land, became interchangeable ideas in the mind of the New Englander, then the Westerner, as agents and symbols of the Christian Devil.

Seeing in each Satanic allegiances, we condemned their behaviors in the light of our prejudgements. The wolf learned quickly to avoid a man with a gun. For the white man, this was not a sign of wisdom, but of cowardice. Trappers would report on the one hand the savagery of the wolf, tales of attacks on defenseless deer—and men foolish enough to expose themselves to such attacks—and on the other they would tell of incidents when wolves stood by barking ineffectually while their very pups were stolen from under their noses. The Indian too was perceived as a brutal coward—eager to injure the defenseless, equally eager to avoid anyone capable of fighting back.

No two creatures have been more thoroughly invested with the idea of wildness in all its most frightening aspects than the wolf and the Indian. How many Indians the white man killed, slaying his own nightmares, no one is sure, though the tally equals, over a span of four centuries, the devastation of the Nazi holocaust. How many wolves? In the thirty-five years between 1883 and 1918, nearly 81,000 were slaughtered in Montana alone. Like the Indian, the wolf is all but exterminated in the United States, and now the coyote is being slaughtered in its place, new scapegoat for an atavistic fear.

The connection between wolf and Indian was established in white literature as far back as Cotton Mather. The Indian, ironically, also felt a connection between himself and the wolf, but for utterly different reasons. For the plains tribes, especially, the wolf was the ideal creature to emulate—good hunter and fighter, superb tracker, family man, tribal creature, quick to learn and adapt. Indian folklore is full of stories that emphasize these positive qualities of the wolf, often in contrast to the accommodation the dog sold his freedom for.

When the white is "wolfish," he imitates not the natural beast but the nightmare invention of his own mind—this is the significance of the wolfish metaphors all through the description of the attack by New Ulm's "werewolf women" on the Sioux captives headed for Mankato. In *Scarlet Plume* the wolf itself is a neutral creature, neither hateful nor admirable, merely a normal, dangerous part of the whole landscape, no more evil than fire or lightning—a bit more to be feared, but feared because its good is not the good of the people, any more than the people's good is that of deer and buffalo. There is in the Indian view none of the anthropomorphic silliness that sees the wolf's hunting as a morality play with the deer as poor, defenseless Good and the wolf as fiendish

Evil. Scarlet Plume himself describes and demonstrates the Indian view of the hunter after he has shocked Judith by playing on a deer's female instincts to lure her to her death.

Imitating the sound of a frightened fawn, he has brought the sympathetic doe near enough for a sure shot. Judith is scandalized, moved by some sense of what she calls fair play. Scarlet Plume is unabashed. They needed the food; she, desperately in her starved condition. To emphasize the naturalness of this hunt and death, Manfred includes a scene parallel to the skinning of the wolf; Scarlet Plume strings the corpse of the deer up to a tree and lays back the hide with neat precision, making the flesh appear not in tortured spasms but "as if with the motion of birthing." He butchers the meat efficiently, without wasted motion, without leaving any usable parts aside. Finally he prays over the body, asking its forgiveness, vowing to practice such economy in all his future hunting.

When Judith protests that he preyed on a mother's love, he argues that the deer understands the meaning of the hunt, that he and the deer are cousins and must help each other. When Judith pushes his argument to the logical extreme—what if the deer could eat him?—he replies that if it were so, he would accept it. He carries her own logic still a step further, remarking that the white man will eventually consume the Indian even as the Indian consumes the deer, and in the final pages of the book he demonstrates the sincerity of his resignation by refusing to resist his own inevitable death at the hands of the whites, placing dignity and identity above personal safety.

It is no accident that in the book about the white woman's attempt to come to terms with the meaning of wilderness, the wolf replaces the bear as symbol of that wilderness. For Hugh, solitary and self contained, the bear is a natural symbol. Like the bear, the white man is essentially an individual, self-reliant, committed to personal freedom, valuing self above community. The woman, the Indian, and the wolf share one characteristic antithetical to that white male ideal—a strong sense of the value of the community. The wolf is a pack hunter, a creature of communal consciousness, placing the needs of the group above any personal concerns. Like a plains Indian community, a wolf pack is organized loosely around a leader couple—a male and female of great charisma—then less loosely around the pups, the children, whose welfare is the first concern of parents, uncles, cousins. When Scarlet Plume follows Judith wearing the stolen wolfskin, he is costumed in his personal and racial totem. After he joins her, during their idyll at Lost Timber, Judith adopts the wolfskin, symbol of her partial acceptance of the natural relationship that should exist between man and wife. Still later, the wolfskin bestows a kind of baptism into the generating family when the two adults use it to cover and protect the Codman boys. Judith's failure to understand the essential need for a community implied by the symbol leaves her baffled by Scarlet Plume's unwillingness to run away with her, dark Adam with his pale, pregnant Eve and two towhead boys.

The hoary pop historian's claim that civilization comes with the woman, not the man, is a generalization that carries a great weight of truth in the history of American expansion, and even greater truth in the literary history of that expanding western movement as it appears in the Buckskin Man Tales. It is with the arrival of white women that communities of white culture begin to appear in the tales; it is the women, not the men, who are the tamers of Deadwood in *King of Spades*. Judith, like "the white women," that creature somewhere between archetype and stereotype, is a communal person, a mother, teacher, city person, with the same civilized values as Hugh's "she-rip" Pennsylvania wife.

Hugh's accommodation with the wilderness experience must take the form of a personal recognition and growth, and the ability to accept his individual relationship with the land and its values. For Judith, the accommodation must include family, community. She will have children; she vanishes pregnant at the end of the novel with Scarlet Plume's half-breed child. She defines herself by relationships ("Without love I am nothing") rather than by identity. She is not so different from her Yankton captors, or from Scarlet Plume, who goes to his death not merely because it is "fated," but because he cannot go back to his tribe, because he is cut off from most of his defining relationships and—cut off—must wither and die. He has sinned against the community spirit by first rescuing and then becoming the lover of the white woman, and it is a sin that makes him, tragically, unfit for Yankton life. A communal man, the final tragedy of his life is that he must die with only his personal identity intact.

This interplay of personal and group identity Manfred accentuates with a number of devices as the book draws to a close. Scarlet

Plume is absorbed into a nameless crowd of men who were victims of what a monument in Mankato, Minnesota, once proclaimed the greatest mass execution in American history. He may have died merely because a pardon intended for him was given another man, named "Red Feather," his identity lost in a bureaucratic bungle. Going to his death, he swallows his own red honor feather when told he cannot wear it under the blindfold. At the moment of his death, he is merely one of thirty-eight bodies hanging on scaffolds; he may be the one who fell from a broken noose, maybe not. He is finally nothing more or less than his fellows—at once a sad dissolution of personal identity and an appropriate fate for a man whose self was less important to him than his social being.

If we see the Buckskin Man Tales as a working out of the conflict not only of man and nature, white and Indian, male and female, but also that between individualism and socialization, then the parallels between *Lord Grizzly* and *Scarlet Plume*, paired centerpiece and fulcrum of the series, are even more striking.

There is first the contrast of Hugh and Scarlet Plume: Hugh makes a virtue bordering on mania of his self-reliant individualism, and learns that he is a social creature, dependent upon his fellow men, hungry for the company of male and female both, craving fatherhood, forced to accept the necessity of his social obligations. Scarlet Plume is the ideal man, pure wolf— father and son, ready to accept his social place and destroyed because of the tragic conflict between his personal feelings of love for his mate and the communal imperative of his social being. Unable to deny his wolfish nature, to adopt permanently the nuclear solitude of the puma, he walks into his death.

There is the contrast of Hugh and Judith: Hugh is old, past the ideal age for parenting, ready to become, could he accept the implications and necessities of the change, an Odin-like patriarch for a new order, a new fellowship of hunters and hunted, but he is ultimately unequal to the demands of the apotheosis offered him. Judith, too, has the opportunity to begin a new order upon the land. Young, healthy, initiated painfully but wholly into Indian life, she could be mother to the golden race, synthesis of red and white, not half-breed children but true hybrid. Her failure is less sure than Hugh's. When she flies Camp Release, pregnant with the child who could be Erden Aldridge fourteen years later, she is flawed only by her inability to understand that essential element of Indian life, community. She cannot accept the absolutism of Scarlet Plume's commitment to his communal nature; his refusal to adopt a nuclear existence with her she regards as whimsical, then willful rather than as his recognition and acceptance of the inviolable given of his nature.

Not man into wolf, as the women of New Ulm become when they fall like ravening beasts on the defenseless Sioux warriors being hauled off to trial and execution and destroy, in their frenzy, the gentle Indian woman who saved their holy book for them, thinking she had the only copy. Not man becoming wolf, but man accepting his wolfishness, in all its varied implications, is a theme of the Buckskin Man Tales, and there is no better image of our failure to do so than the sudden moment at the beginning of *Riders of Judgment* when Cain Hammett, bearer of the last drops of good blood, tainted spiritual grandson of Judith and Scarlet Plume, last remnant of the half-wild spirit Hugh Glass nearly adopted, symbolic child of Erden and Earl Ransom, absent-mindedly kills a wolf, the last wolf in all the books, for target practice.

Works Cited

Manfred, Frederick. *Lord Grizzly.* New York: Signet, 1964.
---. *Scarlet Plume.* New York: Pocket Books, 1966.

From the Usable Past, Models for Postmodern Readers: Student Responses and Theoretical Approaches to *Lord Grizzly*

by Larry R. Juchartz

In the epilogue of her book *West of Everything*, Jane Tompkins outlines how and why the Western story appeals to us through its nearly universal culmination in righteous vengeance taken by the hero. By resorting to violence, Tompkins writes, the hero "prov[es] his moral superiority" to his antagonists[1] and the vengeful act, when performed at last, "feels biologically necessary" to the audience anxiously awaiting its happening. Her explanation of this necessity for violence in Westerns—and our acceptance of it—is thorough and compelling, so it's surprising that she closes the epilogue not on this note, but rather with an appeal for *peace*. Reflecting on the academic custom of slaying one's adversaries (i.e., intellectually destroying the work of one's colleagues) in the quest for scholarly reputation, Tompkins writes:

> [I]nstead of offering you a moral, I call your attention to a moment: the moment of righteous ecstasy. . . when you know you have the moral advantage of your adversary, the moment of murderousness. It's a moment when there's still time to stop, there's still time to reflect. . . to say, "I don't care who's right or who's wrong. There has to be some better way for people to live." (233)

This same kind of reflective process is undergone by Hugh Glass in Frederick Manfred's novel *Lord Grizzly*, and as old Hugh wrestles with the vengeance demon that keeps him alive, after a ferocious attack by an enraged grizzly bear, eventually to forgive the men who've left him for dead near Thunder Butte, students reading his story take from it a wealth of learning. The subjects of their more superficial responses range from awe at the novel's depth and structure (John R. Milton's *"Lord Grizzly:* Rhythm,

Form and Meaning in the Western Novel" offers a particularly rich structural analysis) to an enhanced appreciation for the "authentic" mountain-man speech which Manfred gives his characters, difficult as that speech may be at first for students to read. But over the semesters when I've taught *Lord Grizzly*, it has become clear that most student responses will fall overwhelmingly into three main categories: the novel as a source of strong reader identification, the novel as a stimulus for a desire to escape, and the novel as a guide for survival.

What the students respond to in general is fairly simple: They latch onto *Lord Grizzly* because, just as Tompkins advocates a time-out from academic infighting, they too want some peace from the steady diet of violence and noise that they've endured. And Hugh Glass, speaking from a time of violence and action-over-words, has taught them how to attain the "better way of living" they seek. Such an education from this improbable model might seem ironic, but now I'll let students add their voices to those of literary theorists to explain why that's not so.

Using the Past to Identify with Race and Gender

In a 1958 interview, Fred Manfred explained that, before writing *Lord Grizzly*, he'd felt a marked "thinness" in the heroes of his earlier novels, observing that they lacked "all the dimensions" (*Duke's Mixture* 49). Realizing that this weakness stemmed from a lack of "enough history or country or culture"—what Richard Etulain articulates as "a useful or usable past" (148) —behind the characters, Manfred set out to research their ancestry and happened upon the barely-sketched tale of Hugh Glass in the *South Dakota Guide Book*. "It struck me," Manfred told his interviewers,

> that here was the first real contact of the white man with the raw West. And since then there has been a series of generations; they don't necessarily follow one another. . . in a family, but in sequence. [T]hey are sitting behind these, and even further back behind the first furtrappers are the Indians who really lived here first. (50)

Combining this realization with the knowledge that the United States missed the long, rich history, both literary and cultural, enjoyed by England, Manfred decided that he would have to create a usable American past himself. "My work lacked the resonance of olden time," he notes in "The Making of Lord Grizzly" (*Duke's Mixture* 141), "[and] I wanted echoes of an earlier American era in my novels. By writing about Hugh Glass and others, I'd be my own progenitor. . . . [The book] would be a history, in fiction, of our country."

The historical value of the novel isn't lost on students who read it. They frequently write about, and discuss, their surprise and eventual sense of betrayal when they realize that even such things as interactions between humans and animals in the wild have been misrepresented to them by television and films. ("I found it hard to believe that Hugh was awakened so often by wolves and bears standing right over him," writes one student, Ted, "but after hearing my classmates explain that these animals are not known to devour people still living, I realized how much research Manfred put behind the facts in the book.") More significant are the interactions between whites and Native Americans, which have certainly suffered from an even higher degree of misrepresentation by the same media. "The fact that the mountain men traded with the Rees [Arikara] and other Native tribes, both peaceful and violent, allows us to see both sides of the story and be more objective about the Indians' struggles," writes another student, Kelly, who goes on to say that the novel "taught me about a lifestyle that is long dead, yet should never be forgotten."

Echoing Kelly's mention of "seeing both sides" of white-Native interaction, and applying postmodern terminology in his response, Chris writes that "as the structure of our literary canon becomes ever more diverse, it is important to look at the historical and cultural value of *Lord Grizzly*. This entire book screams of racial tension." This observation is shared by Manfred himself, who notes that Hugh's marriage to Bending Reed, a Dakota (Sioux) woman, stems largely from his attraction to her *hoyoka*, or contrary spirit, but that "there is also his and the white race's addiction in wanting to touch strange skin, either to love it or destroy it, or both" (*Duke's Mixture* 76). And while the race issues in *Lord Grizzly* are confined to those concerning white mountain men and their neighbors in the Arikara, Pawnee, and Mandan nations, this doesn't preclude students of other color from finding their own ways into the narrative. "As an African American," writes Anthony,

> I struggled with my responses to the Indians. Since many of them were Hugh's enemies, I disliked them, but since he referred to all of them as "red niggers" so often, I sometimes became his enemy, too. Luckily, Hugh's good qualities are stronger than his racist ones, and I could identify with his struggle against hardship and come back to his side again.

Alex, a Colombian emigrant, likewise takes offense at Hugh's "red nigger" slur, using it and *Lord Grizzly* as the basis for a lengthy term paper about racial aspersions in much of the literature he read during the semester. No one blames Manfred for Hugh's derogatory labeling, however; the fault lies with the unfortunate fact that race pervades so much of the American "usable past" itself.

But Hugh, being very much the same sort of *heyoka* figure as his wife, is a man of contradictions, and the same lips that speak of Indians in such troubling terms can also speak a gentle prayer over the body of an old Arikara woman left by her tribe to die along the trail (*Lord Grizzly* 159-60). Moreover, nearly every instance of his speaking the words "red nigger" or "red devil" in the novel is accompanied by a clear irony: Hugh has, in true mountain man form (see Smith 81-9), embraced so many Indian ways that he's as "savage" and "uncivilized" as the fiercest braves he goes up against, earning the name "White Grizzly," a title of respect, from them as a result. Additionally, his marriage to the Dakota woman Bending Reed is the sole point of entry into the narrative for women readers who find themselves undergoing what Judith Fetterly, in her book *The Resisting Reader*, has called "the experience of immasculation" (xxii) that arises when a male-centered text forces them into the role of banished "Other" (ix). Without Reed, women readers would have only Mabel, Hugh's fairly cartoonish "rakehellion sherip" of a wife left behind in Pennsylvania, to represent them—yet even Mabel, voiceless and caricatured to such an extreme that women students can't identify with her as a realistic female figure, at least gives them something to remark upon as they validate Fetterly's point that

> women obviously cannot rewrite literary works so that they become ours by virtue of reflecting our reality, [but] we can

accurately name the reality they *do* reflect and so change literary criticism from a closed conversation to an active dialogue. (xxiii)

One student, Kristen, illustrates these words especially well as she talks back to Manfred in a confidently active voice to name the fact that "Hugh has some pretty glaring shortcomings during his married life in the east, among the biggest of which are passivity, alcoholism, cowardice, and a complete lack of any sense of responsibility for his family. But these apparently don't carry as much weight or blame as the faults of Mabel, the castrating bitch wife."

Mabel's one-dimensional portrayal, fortunately, is overshadowed by the strong presence of Bending Reed. As defined by Robert Wright in his book *Frederick Manfred*, Reed is an agent of positive change for Hugh, and without her the mountain man would never have been instilled with the capacity to learn forgiveness—the central theme of the novel—at all. Because Reed is filled with the spirit Heyoka, Wright notes, her contrariness is "able to turn hatred to love and vengeance to compassion. She is Hugh's better self" (63). She is also the intellectual "better" of a whole village of Arikara—especially the men in it—who purchase her from the Pawnee during the four years that Hugh is away from her early in the novel. After the *heyoka* possesses her, she does everything completely opposite to what she's been told, and when her Arikara husband instructs her to come into the tepee for lovemaking, she walks, backward, in the opposite direction. The louder the man shouts for her to turn around, the faster she moves away, until she has run all the way out of the village without anyone recognizing her escape (*Lord Grizzly* 30-2). This combination of intellect and strong independent spirit, along with her physical beauty and skilled craftswomanship, is what makes Hugh love and admire Reed as a complete person—and this completeness of her character helps women readers to forgive Manfred's caricaturizing of Mabel. "Bending Reed represents a woman who is neither all good nor all bad," Jennifer writes, "who is in other words a *believable* human being. By focusing on her character and the positive messages that she brings to readers in the 90s, women will be able to validate this otherwise exclusively mountain-*man* tale well into the twenty-first century."

Jane Tompkins, after giving a lengthy account in *West of Everything* of her personal history as a woman admirer of, and respondent to, Western literature and films, concedes that a major problem with the genre lies in its "forc[ing] women to look at women from the [view]point of men, seeing women as sex objects, forcing women to identify against themselves in order to participate in the story" (17). Here Tompkins echoes Fetterly, who points out that such a forced reading produces in women a "powerlessness which results from the endless division of self against self, the consequence of [having] to identify as male while being reminded that to be male—to be universal, to be American—is to be *not female*" (xiii). But if much of the story offers only a solitary male figure, as *Lord Grizzly* does through most of its second section, then "identifying against the self" takes on an added dimension. Such an expanded form of anti-identification shows in what a student, Donna, writes in her journal entry:

> Like Hugh, I have been on a frightening journey in the wilderness and been unaware of my bearings. I was lost in the mountains three years ago, and I remember being scared to death, convinced I would die before anyone found me. But more than that I remember my huge relief when I saw a familiar landmark—a huge rock called Horsetooth. That rock was my Thunder Butte. My journey wasn't nearly as long and painful as Hugh's, but still I felt close to him as I read of his trials and remembered my own.
>
> There are many other things I have in common with Hugh, to differing degrees. I've sat around campfires, I've ridden horses, and I have been loved and abandoned.

The first paragraph of Donna's response reflects a (genderless) commonality with her subject, but the second shows an almost painful lack of any more points of entry into the narrative. Reading against herself, Donna is forced to wear a label of generic person, not woman, lost in the mountains—and then she quickly runs out of any more parallels. One of her classmates, Marcie, can't even participate as a person; her only way into the story is by identifying with a *horse*, then forcing herself to free-associate from there. Marcie writes: "I found myself saying out loud, 'Oh, you poor thing' when the buffalo bull gored Maggie in the belly and ripped out her insides. And then I realized how she symbolized all of the women who struggled and suffered as they played a role in shaping the West."

This may seem a bit of a stretch, especially since Marcie chooses not to elaborate on the connection she made, but much of the reader-identification in *Lord Grizzly* takes place at an intuitive level. Like Hugh, student readers are "us[ing] the past to build the future" (Austin 130) —which for them is the present—and in the process of this complex reconstruction, they "reconcile conflicting elements of nature, savagery, and. . .Old World cultural inheritance" to form "new revelation[s] from within." Moreover, as some of their responses here will indicate, they are simultaneously performing two types of what Robert Stepto calls "re-authoring" by trying to discern the novel's meaning while at the same time deconstructing it, working through both the "artistic" and "esthetic" poles of the text (see Iser 274) in which credit for the former goes to Manfred as textual creator while the challenge to discover the latter goes to them. For instance, students often find that as Hugh tries to define himself, each definition he chooses is canceled out by an opposing anti-definition—he is at once a cowardly deserter and a fiercely loyal companion, a drunken fool and a wise mentor, a white soldier and an Indian brave, to list only a few of the oppositional labels—with the end result being not an orderly list of separate, meaningful words, but a random juxtaposition of meaningfree symbols that ultimately create a blank slate on which Hugh can write his discovered name as he becomes enlightened. That he lacks the insight to write the name clearly at the end of the story only invites students to write it for him. "Turned tame, this child has," he says after forgiving the subjects of his previous hatred, "[p]assed through such a passel of things he don't rightly recollect wrong from right no more" (*Lord Grizzly* 281). But this confusion goes unshared by Hugh's reader authors who have, as Stepto defines, both discovered the pedagogical merit of the narrative and "conquered" its quandaries (832).

Addressing this postmodern approach to reading and reauthoring text, linguist George Steiner argues that "[t]he audience/reader is not merely a loyal echo to the artist's genius, but a joint creator in a conglomerate of free-wheeling, imminent energy. Away with masters" (162). Yet it's difficult to dismiss Manfred's genius in *Lord Grizzly*. Like his character when interacting with Bending Reed, the author has a clear sense of play, and the myriad inversions, ironies, and counterstatements in the novel seem so carefully chosen and well-placed that we'd be remiss in renouncing the artistry involved. While Manfred attributes a great deal of his most inspired writing to a mystical force he has alternately called the "lizard," the "Interior Commentator," or simply "the deeps,"[2] he is also quite proud of the *conscious* efforts behind his writing as well, such as are reflected in the postscript to a letter he wrote to his agent, Alan Collins, in December 1954:

> Facts: the wonderful title is mine; the arrangement of the plot is my original idea; the working out of how come [Hugh] forgave is my original idea; the research for background is enormous and very accurate; the speech is accurate down to a cough—no one can improve on it; and the material on the Indians. . . is the best yet to appear in any book, [James Fenimore] Cooper's included. Whoever buys it is buying a masterpiece: flawless, solid, enduring. (*Letters* 396)

Whether conscious or not, one of the more playful aspects of *Lord Grizzly*, and one which gives another point of narrative access to women readers especially, is Manfred's inversion of Western-genretypical male/ female positions in the relationship between Hugh and Bending Reed. As Tompkins points out in her chapter "Women and the Language of Men," the traditional Western hero has little use for language, for words, since these are "false or at best ineffectual, [and] only actions are real" (51). Moreover, she notes, language is "always associated with women, religion, and culture," functioning primarily as "a critique of force and. . .a symbol of the peace, harmony, and civilization that force is invoked in order to preserve" (55). In the typical Western, words belong to women, actions belong to men, and the male hero's stoic silence functions as "proof of his manhood and trueheartedness. In Westerns, silence, sexual potency, and integrity go together" (54).

But in *Lord Grizzly*, Manfred has turned this definition upside down. During Hugh's crawl back to Fort Kiowa after the grizzly attack, the mountain man hides within earshot of a passing band of hostile Arikara, and their speech as they pass makes him "hunger with tears in his eyes for the friendly sound of a human voice" (149). When the group passes and Hugh discovers the old woman it has left to die at trailside, he speaks almost nonstop while giving her food and drink, hearing only silence from her in return. No matter this, however; so persuasive is the sound of his own voice that when the woman dies (159), Hugh weeps and asks, "What? An' we just friends?"

Likewise, earlier in the novel when Hugh returns to Reed's tepee after four years away, much of the scene consists of his babbling happily as she remains silent. While his language is at times ultracompact and dense, especially when he knows that the *idea* behind the words is faulty—"I'm back. It's too bad I was gone so long, yes. But that I couldn't help. I'm back. That's it"—it is more often rambling and full of joyful colorisms that seem to be spoken merely for the pleasure of their sound: "By the beard of bull barley, Reed . . . cut out the peedoodles" (28). Reed has told her story first, but as Hugh narrates his own long account for the time away from her, she interjects only to ask brief questions pointing out logical flaws or narrative discrepancies, and as his tale is still in progress, it's Reed who pushes Hugh back against the buffalo skin, silencing him as she "bec[omes] his wife again" (37). Here it is the woman as hera, not the man as hero, who foregoes words to speak instead what Cixous would label a "language of the body" which concomitantly empowers Reed with sexual potency when she "inscribes" her husband with that forceful text. And later in the novel when Hugh returns from his long crawl for survival and Reed once again initiates sex, she finds that the lack of effective words to define his conflicting emotions over abandonment has rendered him impotent—*his* body, unlike her own, cannot speak. Not until he engages in full dialectic with one of the deserters, Jim Bridger—and then forgives him—can Hugh once again "long with a great longing" for Reed (231). Citing Peter Schwenger's book *Phallic Critiques*, Tompkins writes that through speech comes vulnerability, the "feminizing" of emotions which can only "retain a male integrity" when they're kept locked up, unshared and unexpressed (56) — and if this theory holds, then both Bending Reed and Hugh Glass, as written by Manfred and read/rewritten by students, are nothing short of strong rebellions against genretype. Hugh's entire experience—past, present, and future—is overwhelmingly defined through clearly expressed language, in both interior and exterior speech, and only when interacting with other men does he resort to the clipped, pithy syntax of the typical Western hero. What's more, when he speaks with men, Hugh uses words mostly to instruct or to learn practical information, while his speech with women or alone is used to reflect, define, and understand the vast range of largely-ineffable emotions and conflicts inside him. He is an androgyne wrapped in consummate macho-hero leathers, and in that sense, could be a reflection of Manfred himself. In a chapter titled "What Makes a True Soul Mate" (*Duke's Mixture* 74), the author recalls that, as a young man, he

> began to look for [a] perfect friend in a girl. I hoped to find that perfect complement mate, in which the man in me would love the woman in her, while the woman in me would love the man in her. And vice-versa. By doubling our eyes we would quadruple our insights into The Darks and magnify our ecstasies into The Lights.

This "inner woman" quality has been infused into Hugh, and the inner man into Bending Reed, his "perfect complement mate." Together, the two characters serve as guides for students who follow Hugh's journey through the long bitter darkness of hatred, out to the warm glowing light of compassion—a journey in which reader identification is intensified even more.

The Land and a Longing to Escape

Throughout *Lord Grizzly*, Hugh Glass expresses worry that his beloved wilderness will be encroached upon by the "civilized" East—that, as Henry Nash Smith puts it in *Virgin Land*, "the pioneers with their axes and plows will convert the forests to farmlands" (132) which in turn will grow into settlements, then communities. Perhaps as a result of his encounter with the dying Indian woman, Hugh takes time to "brood on the lonesome country" (*Lord Grizzly* 161), and his vision of the future is a bleak one. In that future, he sees

> ... she-rips and their cubs coming in and destroying a hunter's paradise. The white queen bees would come in with their tame worker bees and build honeycomb towns and cities.... Ae, the enslavement of both land and man was coming here too. [He]

they were men, and free men at that. . . . (161-2)

Of course, the West appeals to Easterners for the same reasons that it appeals to Hugh, symbolizing for them the same freedom and opportunity for a new life that it grants him—but he overlooks this comparison. Student readers, however, do not, especially if they're geographically centered in the same East that Hugh dreads and ridicules. As Tompkins explains, the West offers "escape from the conditions of life in modern industrial society: from a mechanized existence, economic dead ends, social entanglements, unhappy personal relations, political injustice" (4) —all of which are now magnified a hundredfold since the time when Hugh escaped them, so it's little wonder that many young readers want to join him in both his time and his place. "The desire to change places also signals a powerful need for self-transformation," Tompkins writes, explaining that while some Western heroes seek to conquer the land, others want "to merge with it completely— they are trying to get away from other people *and* themselves" (7, italics added).

These sentiments come through clearly in Kristina's response to the novel, in which she writes with stark honesty the following personal creed:

> I can completely relate with Hugh's escape from eastern life because I don't want any part of society. I don't want any part of the person I've become in it. There is nothing worse than slaving away for someone else, 40 hours a week, just to save enough money to buy a second VCR. I have nothing against hard work, but it should be something you believe in and enjoy doing. So many people around me are obsessed with making money, completely addicted to it, buying material "fixes" that they don't need and aren't even sure they want. It's very easy to get wrapped up in society and its money and to think this is life. I know; it happened to me.
>
> But I also know that true gratification waits in jobs that have been around for centuries: farming, teaching, owning a small store. I want to move to Montana, grow my own gardens of vegetables and herbs, craft my own clothes and blankets, carve little trinkets out of wood. I want to know myself and not be diagnosed with an ulcer at the age of thirty-five.

I am making a vow: the tradition of mountain people like Hugh Glass will be carried on by me.[3]

We might be tempted to write that final pledge off to the romantic daydreams of a freshperson, but as she makes it, Kristina is a twenty-five-year-old single mother who has already lived the life she seeks to escape. Interestingly, though, her writing does not mention her young child, a marked contrast to the pattern that Lillian Schlissel has observed in her book *Women's Diaries of the Westward Journey:*

> [I]f the westward migration became an expression of testing and reaching for men, then it surely must have been an "anti-mythic" journey for women. . . . When women wrote of the decision to leave their homes, it was almost always with anguish. . . .
>
> [Women] found nothing grand, nothing wonderful, nothing to suggest what [their] husband[s] so clearly saw. . . . [W]omen did not find the new country a land of resplendent possibilities. They heard their children crying, and longed for their old homes. (14, 53)

Of course, there's a vast time difference between Kristina's journal entry and those of the women whose diaries Schlissel studied, and gender roles have undergone radical revision during that period. But Kristina's apparent desire to escape *alone* can also be explained by Tompkins, who writes that the Western hero "has no friends, just temporary allies, no family, only some shadow people back home or dead. The excitement of hunting or being hunted, of living close to the land, is enough. . .the cycle of fear and relief from fear keep the isolation from appearing" (217). While family may have been a primary concern for pioneer women in the nineteenth century, in the postmodern age it can become secondary to personal freedom without affecting one's "hero" status at all—as Hugh's desertion of wife and sons clearly reinforces for readers. The model does not appear to be problematic for them.

And whereas the hero's place—the wilderness—has often been described through what Henry Nash Smith calls "a haze of rhetoric" (131), filled with abstract romantic symbolism or idealized images, Hugh and his readers see it clearly for what it is: land vast enough to move in, air clean enough to breathe, and forests thick enough to offer good hiding. One of Kristina's classmates, Lorne, puts his own desire to escape into a military context:

> *Lord Grizzly* brings memories of my tour in the Marine Corps. As a grunt in a recon unit, I spent many days and nights training in some of the worst conditions nature could offer. But like the Corps itself, the land has a way of breaking you down and building you back up again so you can survive in its environment.
>
> Hugh Glass is very similar to the platoon sergeants I served under in my unit. Seasoned combat veterans, they had made it through when the shit hit the fan in Vietnam. They were our teachers, our mentors; far from perfect, but knowing what it takes to survive in the bush. What's interesting is that the sergeants, like Hugh, all had an alibi for choosing to live out in the field. They were running away from the civilized "civilian" world in which they could not fit. I think that every Marine, myself included, was running away from something. We hid in the woods, playing war games, and we learned that nature charges a high rent for her land. But now that I'm back, I'm thinking like Hugh. I don't miss the Corps at all—but I sure would like to renew my lease on a place in those woods again.

Lorne's desire to leave the city comes because he has lived in "the bush" and felt its power, an experience shared by many with military backgrounds. Former Vietnam infantryman Tim O'Brien, in his excellent novel *The Things They Carried*, describes a scene in which a relative newcomer to the land[1] gestures out at the lush jungle beyond the firebase and says, "'Sometimes I want to eat this place.... I want to swallow the whole country—the dirt, the death. ... When I'm out there at night, I feel close to my own body, I can feel my blood moving, my skin and my fingernails.... You can't feel like that anywhere else'" (235). A very similar human/landscape interconnection is described by Manfred in *Lord Grizzly* as well: "The contrast of green cedar against red soil raised involuntary sighs.... Faces brightened; voices lifted; blood pulsed sweet and clean. They were true men of the wilderness" (225). Taking on both biological and spiritual presence, the land filters its way into the veins of those living in it until they and it are one, and for some students, the land's appeal lies exactly in that mix of biology and spirituality. Troy shows this in his highly-detailed account of a camping trip he experienced in Yellowstone Park:

> I lay there under the dark night sky and listened to the sounds of the wilderness around me. I could hear animals snuffling around in the distance, and from closer by I thought I heard a small rodent scream as it got snatched up by a feathered night hunter. I wasn't afraid, though, because I knew this was where I belonged. Wild and free like those animals, with no one keeping track of me except the Great Spirit above.

Others simply just want to go to open land without articulating their reasons, and in their responses to *Lord Grizzly* lies a strong subtext of the "need for self-transformation" Tompkins mentions. "Manfred writes that the West has 'no laws around but your own,'" Michael writes, "and I want away to a place like that. I want away from the rules my parents use to control me. I want away

> from restrictions on everything I do. I want away!" Likewise, Betsy states simply that she would like to escape from the life I am living and become someone like Hugh Glass, fighting for my life as I hike across the wilderness, using only my will and my wits to survive. *Lord Grizzly* gives a clear assessment of how the east is seen from a Western perspective: "Deceit. Selfishness. And the white girls looking and acting too much like pictures." We need to do something about this.

While Betsy seems to be responding mainly from gender, rebelling against the quiet, well-mannered personality she displays in class, she goes on to say that "in Hugh's eyes, we [in the East] are cold, distant, and treacherous. This lets us change our way of thinking—maybe we are not as civilized as we think." Her reflection is shared by many of her peers who likewise find their description from Hugh's point of view troubling, and who use it as a basis for introspection about themselves and their postmodern culture. They do not like the image that forms.

Surviving in the Wilderness of the City

The student responses cited thus far reveal a strong willingness by their authors to open themselves to the text lying open to them, and are intended to illustrate how reader-response criticism (see, for instance, Tompkins' anthology; also Eco, *Role;* Fish, *Artifacts*) finds particularly rich application in Manfred's work as those students use his novel to make, as Stanley Fish describes, "a succession of decisions about [the] author's intention . . . decisions that are precisely the shape, because they are the content, of the reader's activities" ("Interpreting" 765). The student writings that follow now, however, may show even more clearly how Manfred's readers have used their own world to construct the one inhabited by Hugh Glass, allowing Hugh's past experience in turn to reconstruct their present one, to reshape and redirect it toward a more positive future—demonstrating as this process unfolds how reader response can present literature as a construct of individual experience that transcends the traditional meanings constrained by textual form when its readers search out, as Catherine Belsey writes, "not the unity of the work, but the multiplicity and diversity of its possible meanings. . .and above all its contradictions" (57).

Before examining those responses, though, it might be helpful to first offer a brief paradigm for the interpretations students have made. For this, I'll turn to a recent ethnography[5] which recounts that, following the purchase in 1856 of 840 acres which would become New York's Central Park, landscape architect Frederick Law Olmstead wrote: "We have nowhere on the western frontier a population. . .in which it is possible to live so isolatedly from humanizing influences and with such constant practice of heart-hardening and taste smothering habits as [those] found in our great Eastern cities" (39). By installing nature in the middle of the metropolis, Houston Baker writes, Olmstead hoped to "extend the civilizing effects" of what the architect called "scenery" to the city's swelling population. However, Olmstead had to admit that this "civilizing effect" would only take place during daylight hours. "The park . . .will be useless for any good purpose after dusk," the designer wrote, "for experience has shown that. . . the public cannot be secured safe transit through large open spaces of ground after nightfall" (qtd. in 41).

Similarly, Native American author Vine Deloria, in *We Talk, You Listen,* writes that "[t]he white man has tried to make Nature adjust to his whims by creating the artificial world of the city. . . [b]ut he has failed. . . . Everywhere there is indiscriminate violence[, and] with the rising crime rate, people will only be able to go about in urban areas in gangs, tribes if you will. . . . The only answer will be to adopt Indian ways to survive" (196-7). That warning came in 1970. Today, as most students see it, their "artificial world" has become a menacing and wildly overgrown Central Park with the clock stuck at midnight, and to survive in it, they look to Hugh Glass and his Indian ways for direction. As Brian puts it: "The West from *Lord Grizzly* isn't in the West anymore. It's right in the middle of the glass and steel and concrete city, and the same primal instinct Hugh Glass needed to survive in nature is the one we need to survive in our urban wilderness." Even the landscape of this wilderness, he explains, looks the same in the silhouette of night. "Our tall trees are metal streetlights; our mountains, towering buildings; both loom over us, but neither will protect us from the wild animals that are ourselves."

Continuing the analogy, Brian writes:

> Hugh Glass appeals to me because he knew how to survive. He knew nature, where to find its food, its water, its shelter. He tapped into his primal instinct and used it to stay alive. How is he different from someone living in the streets where nothing is given? Where you have to find it all yourself, to know where to get food, where to sleep, how to stay warm, eat, steal, fight, survive? Since our new wilderness is the city, Hugh is that street person, and an admirable one.

But then Brian's thesis takes a marked turn away from survival and back toward our earlier category of personal freedom. If the West has come East, he asks, then where is the new division between "land" and "city"? Where does one look for escape? The answer, he implies, can be found in the difference between homed and homeless:

> This comes from a boy with a good home where everything is handed to me. My meals, my bed, my faith, my knowledge, everything already written, everything already packaged in neat little bundles. Keep that. Put me out there on the street where I can say forget rules, forget order, give me something

real, something that screams *FREEDOM*, give me people who have dealt with real problems, show me the human spirit at its most degraded, therefore its most noble when it overcomes degradation. Let me live day to day with no set schedule. . .let me learn from experience, like Hugh did, what is in this world around me. How can any of us survive so far removed from nature? I can't figure out why we all haven't gone to the streets.

In seeing his home as the crowded East and the broadly-defined "street" as "nature," Brian engages in a phenomenon known to geographers as "perceptional geography," through which "a subjective [and] linguistically filtered perception of space, and not an empirical, measurable, or statistical description of it, controls human spacial relations" (Ellis 120). His home presents no risk, no variety, therefore no freedom to discover; it presses in on him with its safe, stale emptiness. Outside on the streets, however, is an energy field—raw, boundless, and ungoverned—empty of order but full of challenge and danger. By that personal construct, the street is (subjectively) his free West, no matter that both it and the home it borders make up a microcosm of the antithesis of both "free" and "West" which (objectively) contains them.

Many of Brian's classmates, however, take a much starker view of the city streets around them. Kerry, for instance, writes that

[t]he most valuable of Hugh Glass's traits is his ability to be aware of his surroundings. In cities where we're afraid to speak for fear of being attacked, where we can't walk without risk of being killed, the ability to see danger, listen to the warning sounds, and then find a way to *live* with both is the key to survival.

Hugh skillfully uses his sight and hearing to help him locate food and water during his crawl, [and] if the youth of the 90s could learn to look and listen to situations, to *analyze* problems before right away trying to solve them, our solutions could be more effective. The method that too many of us use today—a quick thought and then a shot from a gun—is no kind of solution at all.

Like Kerry, Tom also focuses on urban violence in his response to the novel, drawing a unique comparison in the process. The mountain men of the 1800s, he writes, are the early models for today's criminal street gangs, and to support the argument Tom emphasizes how

> The mountain man was a tough, sometimes reckless individual who rejected the rules of society and lived by his own code. He relied on experience and instinct to survive in his cruel, harsh environment. He rejected his family, or was rejected by them. He was loyal to others who ran with him, contemptuous of those who didn't. Surrounded by enemies, his thoughts were often focused on destruction and killing.

Although he then goes on to develop the gang parallels, the enthymeme is enough. What might not be clear, though, is that Tom isn't condemning Hugh Glass, nor does he condone street gangs. Instead, he draws the comparison between them in order to conclude that "[y]oung people today can look to Hugh Glass and see a gang member who broke free of the gang's mentality by thinking independently. Using his mind as a weapon, he thought through his anger and was freed from his manacles of hatred and rage."

For still other students, the term "survival" appears to take on a broader meaning, which nonetheless remains centered within a more abstract, less immediate life/death dichotomy. Having just returned from their journey with Hugh as they write their responses to him, their voices fret about surviving as humanity in an age of technology, echoing the lament of Earl Shorris in *The Death of the Great Spirit:* "On a crowded earth one surrenders to the machine or perishes. . . . Humans, the tool makers, are being made over by their tools[, and] it is one's uniqueness that is devoured by the machine" (250). The same sad reflection is present in what Mark writes in his journal:

> Today's world is made of cellular phones, microchips, cars that go four times the speed limit. There are no more mountain men, there are only machines, so most of us lack the time and ambition to get to know anything about nature. The average college student, I think, would describe a "mountain man" as the TV defines him—as someone who drinks Busch beer. Luckily, reading of Hugh Glass's crawl for life is a crash course in survival—but not necessarily for surviving outdoors. The

lesson can be just basic hanging on, no matter how crazy our mechanized lives are. Hugh teaches us to never give up.

Mark's classmate Lori then takes the subjects of technology, violence, and forgiveness and mixes them together into one telling paragraph:

> Children today sit passively in front of television shows and video games that teach them nothing. There's no creativity, so there's nothing to learn except for how to kill your opponent on "Mortal Kombat." I wish they would read something like *Lord Grizzly* instead. With all the violence going on between teenagers today, this book can teach them a lot about forgiving. With vengeance comes only hate and death, but Hugh overcame his hatred and forgave instead. With forgiveness comes love and life. I wish Nintendo could make a video game about *that* for a change.

That Hugh's survival is almost entirely due to his violent quest to kill others isn't lost on his audience, however, nor is the fact that his rage is heavily based on his deserters' having dug him only a shallow grave from which "a half dozen strokes and the varmints [would have] had him dug out of the sand, tearing and gorging before he even turned cold" (*Lord Grizzly* 102) —that, in essence, he is angry over the treatment of the corpse he did not become. But it's this kind of unrealized, and even subtly humorous, irony around his character that helps students to clearly follow his development toward enlightenment and, in a sense, divinity. Were Hugh not such a simple man of simple means, of complex knowledge but uncomplicated ways of knowing, the progression would rely mostly on intuition to be detected. Instead, Manfred presents Hugh as a genre-atypical "talking hero," a man whose survival may rely even more on his language—both thought and spoken—than on his instinct and familiarity with nature, so readers can track his move toward forgiveness one revised word at a time.

As Manfred recounts in an interview, the forgiveness theme of *Lord Grizzly* posed the most problematic aspect of prewriting for him. "I didn't know how to end the story," he says (*Duke's Mixture* 50). "I could see intellectually why [Hugh] would forgive the [deserters], but I could not feel it emotionally." But this dilemma ended for the author when the false arrest of a relative in California gave him, as Nancy Owen Nelson puts it, "the emotional opportunity to explore the forgiveness process" firsthand (4). The relative's huge capacity to overlook the wrong he'd been done by the state is infused directly into Hugh's eventual compassion for the *compañyeros* who left him alone in the wilderness, and it is also passed along to students like Robin, who notes that Hugh "could only forgive others after accepting the parts of himself that others would never forgive," and Aaron, who observes that "Hugh's heightened state of existence does not come through religion, which preaches 'an eye for an eye,' but through spirituality—by *transcending* the confines of religion to find what's actually right and true."

In a South Dakota public television broadcast, Fred Manfred says that "when young people come into our classes, not all of them have a notion of what they want to become yet. Some of them take the [literature] class to find themselves, in a way. . . . 'What's your real name? What's your real purpose in this world?'. . . . Many modern kids may go up to the mountain, but they can't find the vision—what are they going to *become*?"

Based on their responses to *Lord Grizzly* here, it might not be too much of a speculation to say that at least some of them will become postmodern "mountain people" in the way of Hugh Glass—living in the moment, not for it, learning to enjoy the land, not destroy it, and overcoming both adversity and anger to create the "better way of living" that Jane Tompkins, and they themselves, desire.

That's a pretty fine legacy for a forty-year-old Western novel.

Notes

[1] In the body of Western literature that Tompkins has examined, the central figure is almost exclusively male. Her choice of the masculine pronoun here reflects this.

[2] See, for instance, "Old Voices in My Writings" in *Duke's Mixture* for a discussion between Manfred and his daughter Freya of "the lizard" as a force behind writing, and "Space, Yes: Time, No" in the same volume for a description of the "Interior Commentator." Manfred's term "the deeps" is

used in a 1984 television interview with John R. Milton and Nancy Owen Nelson on *Great Plains Literature*, South Dakota Public Television.

[3] After completing the semester in which she wrote the journal entry cited here, Kristina left the university and moved to Colorado, where she took a job in Boulder and began saving money to move to Nederland, a small community high up in the Flatirons. At the time that she sent word of this important step toward fulfilment of her pledge, her child was in the temporary care of relatives.

[4] The words are spoken by a young woman named Mary Anne who comes to Vietnam to visit her fiancé, an infantryman. By attributing this dialogue to a female character, O'Brien magnifies the power and attraction the land holds for those in it. See "Sweetheart of the Song Tra Bong," 100-125.

[5] *Black Studies, Rap, and the Academy.* Chicago: U of Chicago P, 1993.

Works Cited

Austin, James C. "Legend, Myth, and Symbol in Frederick Manfred's *Lord Grizzly.*" *Critique: Studies in Modern Fiction* (Winter 63-4) : 122-130.

Belsey, Catherine. "Constructing the Subject: Deconstructing the Text." *Feminist Criticism and Social Change.* Ed. Judith Newton and Deborah Rosenfelt. New York: Methuen, 1985. 45-64.

Cixous, Hélène. "The Laugh of the Medusa." *Literary Criticism and Theory.* Ed. Robert Con Davis and Laurie Finke. White Plains: Longman, 1989. 732-748

Deloria, Vine, Jr. *We Talk, You Listen.* New York: Macmillan, 1970.

Eco, Umberto. *The Role of the Reader: Explorations in the Semiotics of Texts.* Bloomington: Indiana UP, 1979.

Ellis, Reuben J. "The American Frontier and the Contemporary Real Estate Advertising Magazine." *Journal of Popular Culture* (Winter 1993) : 119-133.

Etulain, Richard W. "Western Fiction and History: A Reconsideration." *Critical Essays on Wallace Stegner.* Ed. Anthony Arthur. Boston: Hall, 1982. 146-163.

Fetterly, Judith. *The Resisting Reader: A Feminist Approach to American Fiction.* Bloomington: Indiana UP, 1978.

Fish, Stanley. "Interpreting the *Variorum.*" *Literary Criticism and Theory.* Ed. Robert Con Davis and Laurie Finke. White Plains, NY: Longman, 1989. 757-774

---. *Self-Consuming Artifacts: The Experience of Seventeenth-Century Literature.* Berkeley: U of California P, 1972.

Great Plains Literature. Prod. Richard Muller. With Frederick Manfred, John R. Milton, and Nancy Owen Nelson. South Dakota Public Television, Jan. 1984.

Iser, Wolfgang. *The Implied Reader.* Baltimore: Johns Hopkins UP, 1974.

Manfred, Frederick. *Duke's Mixture.* Sioux Falls: The Center for Western Studies, 1994.

---. *Lord Grizzly.* Lincoln: U of Nebraska P, 1954.
---. *The Selected Letters of Frederick Manfred*, 1932-1954. Ed. Arthur R. Huseboe and Nancy Owen Nelson. Lincoln: U of Nebraska P, 1989.
Milton, John R. "*Lord Grizzly:* Rhythm, Form and Meaning in the Western Novel." *Western American Literature* (Spring 1966) : 6-14.
Nelson, Nancy Owen. "At Last, the 'Truth': The Manfred Letters, *Lord Grizzly,* and the 'Usable Past.'" Paper at Western Literature Association. Moscow, ID, 1989.
O'Brien, Tim. *The Things They Carried.* New York: Penguin, 1990.
Schlissel, Lillian. *Women's Diaries of the Westward Journey.* New York: Schocken, 1982.
Shorris, Earl. *The Death of the Great Spirit.* New York: Simon & Schuster, 1971.
Smith, Henry Nash. *Virgin Land: The American West as Symbol and Myth.* Cambridge: Harvard UP, 1950.
Steiner, George. *Extraterritorial: Papers on Literature and the Language Revolution.* New York: Atheneum, 1976.
Stepto, Robert Burns. "Distrust of the Reader in Afro-American Narratives." *Literary Criticism and Theory.* Ed. Robert Con Davis and Laurie Finke. White Plains, NY: Longman, 1989. 828-842.
Tompkins, Jane, ed. *Reader-Response Criticism: From Formalism to Post-Structuralism.* Baltimore: Johns Hopkins UP, 1980.
---. *West of Everything: The Inner Life of Westerns.* New York: Oxford UP, 1992.
Wright, Robert C. *Frederick Manfred.* Boston: Twayne, 1979.

I am indebted to my friends and colleagues Elizabeth Capwell and Nancy Owen Nelson for their thorough critical readings, insightful questions, and thoughtful suggestions as this work developed, and especially to Christy Rishoi for texts and contexts that would otherwise have gone unexplored.

And to the students who opened their hearts and minds to me along with their journals, whose questions, suggestions, and insights taught me more about Lord Grizzly *and the western genre than I could ever hope to teach them, I dedicate the work itself and hope it makes a fitting tribute to the countless mutual discoveries we enjoyed during a semester that ended much too soon.*

Gender, Power, and Knowing in *Conquering Horse*

by Richard Bailey

In an interview dated May 8, 1981, Fredrick Manfred makes the following comments about how he writes:

> The reason I use certain incidents is not because I think it means something so much as it's dramatic and I feel drawn towards it, and I feel my excuse for using it is if I feel drawn to use it. I may not understand it. There may be a whole lot more meaning in it than I know, but if I'm drawn terribly to use something I put it in on the grounds, first of all, I'm human like everybody else, and number two there may be a bigger reason than me that wants it in there so I should follow it.

What do we call this? Following intuition? Trusting the composing process? I understand the author refers to it as "getting his lizard working," paying attention to something deep, something below the level of conscious understanding, and waiting for meanings to present themselves. Maybe they will, maybe they won't. The writer does not fret about the whys; he concentrates on the hows. "A bigger reason than me wants it there." This is always a startling admission from a writer, suggesting less than complete control of the writing, of the meanings he makes, of the meanings available to us as human beings.

I begin with this consideration—this kind of *surrender* Manfred speaks of—because I think the experience of being drawn, led, moved, guided, conducted, conveyed (I'm getting my thesaurus working) is primary in Manfred's *Conquering Horse*. The focus of this paper is gender, power, and knowing in that novel. I will try to show that male characters, especially the protagonist, a young brave initially called No Name, becomes truly masculine, or deeply male, as they—he—takes on female characteristics, and that this process results in a kind of oxymoronic state: aimless directedness, vulnerable powerfulness, which enables them to be drawn into a deeper unity within themselves, with the earth, other living things, and other humans.

In brief, *Conquering Horse* tells the story of a young brave who wishes to receive a vision. The vision will enable him to be a full participant in his community. Great things are expected of him; lacking his vision, however, he remains a nobody. Hence his name, No Name. In two extended episodes, No Name does what needs to be done. With his rival, Circling Horse, he travels to Butte of the Thunders, where he receives his vision; then with his lover, Leaf, he sets out to conquer the great white stallion, hoping to bring it back to his village, where it can sire a new generation of horses and insure the continuity and prestige of his tribe. This is No Name's story, told by a third person narrator, limited omniscient, limited almost exclusively to No Name's point of view. What readers see and know, we see and know pretty much through No Name's eyes and sensibility.

At the outset, we see that No Name is preoccupied by two things through which he gains entry to manhood: sex and vision. Over the first he has some control; over the latter, none. He is planning things, as the first paragraph of the novel shows:

> No Name waited until it was dark. Then he threw a white robe over his shoulders and stooped out through the door and quietly made his way toward his sweetheart's lodge. (3)

He is mad about Leaf, but he cannot have her, as he is not yet a real man. He proposes that they run away together, to his uncle's village in the next county. That failing, he comes to her in the night, creeps into her tepee and attempts to untie her. (Her parents, no fools, lash her to the earth, to protect her virginity.) That failing, he follows Leaf and her mother to the place where they bathe in the river. He spies on them, and when her mother naps, he surprises Leaf. She tries to hold him off, telling him, without her virginity she won't be worth an old horse. Also, she appeals to No Name's stake in remaining pure: "My father says that a man should suffer and see a vision first before he lies with a woman. Otherwise he will not become a great man" (70). But No Name's need is great. While he has no control over when his vision will occur, he has control over the immediate situation. He plans, conspires, whines, and wheedles, until finally, Leaf submits.

Her troubles begin. His only worsen. Leaf disappears, presumed dead. No Name sinks into a funk. This No Name, at the out-

GENDER, POWER, AND KNOWING 99

set of the novel, is all frustrated will. He wills his way into Leaf's embrace, defiling both her and himself. Really, it is no kind of manhood he experiences. He would like to make his vision happen, but cannot. There are greater powers than he. He is subordinate to them. No Name thus begins a process of purification, which will enable him to receive his vision.

How different the dynamics are when Leaf and No Name meet again, more than half way into the novel. He has had his vision, which comes to him in the form of a white mare, telling him that he must conquer the white stallion and that his father must die. No Name has set out to find the white stallion, only to become lost in the wilderness, alone. Yet he is learning to be drawn, to be led by things he does not completely understand, such as finches, eagles, sacred stones, and, of course, his "helper," or fetish.. Awakening one morning, he feels a pull. "It drew hard on his flesh soul. It was as though someone had grabbed up a handful of flesh on his chest and were pulling him forward" (185). He is led in its direction, where he discovers an abandoned Pawnee camp. He walks "in a half trance," Manfred writes, detached yet completely alert to his surroundings, which are richly detailed. As No Name moves through the scene, Manfred accentuates No Name's mental state through stylistic choices like these, "His feet moved under him. They took the path to the stream" (187), signaling a profoundly altered will. In a stream, buried up to her neck, he discovers Leaf. Pregnant, she has been abandoned by the Pawnee. No Name frees her, cleans her, and revives her: "He kneeled beside her and stroked her arms from the shoulders to the wrist. He rocked her from side to side, gently, firmly" (190). It is as if Leaf has been reborn, and No Name is a midwife.

Something has happened within No Name. He has become a nurturer, although on the very next page, hunting, we see his "dark predator eyes roving to all sides" (191). More than simply becoming a nurturer, he has taken on greater dimension than he has at the beginning of the novel. He has ceased attempting to control and plan. He has acquiesced to other powers. There may be a bigger reason than he for what he is supposed to do. He just does it.

How do we account for this change in No Name? What does it mean that Leaf has been reborn? that she, rather than a man, she, pregnant with No Name's child, accompanies him on his important mission? that No Name's vision is mediated by a mare? How do we account for the fact that the magnificent white stallion, rather than be vanquished, dies before No Name can return with it? What good is a dead stallion? What kind of manhood can a man boast of when the symbol of his manhood, the vehicle of it, no longer exists?

Like Leaf, No Name, in the process of receiving his vision, has experienced death and rebirth. I would argue he has experienced a death of false manhood in himself, the planning, calculating, exploitative manhood that enables him to use Leaf to prove himself a man. The death of this false manhood occurs through two experiences: his actual near-death experience when he is traveling to Butte of the Thunders with Circling Hawk; and, then again, in the sun dance ceremony when he returns after his vision.

In a critical scene, crossing a river, No Name is pulled into a whirlpool and nearly drowns. Circling Hawk saves him. Returning to consciousness on the river bank, No Name says, "A part of me has died." What part? Circling Hawk is No Name's rival. Both men would like to be the tribe's next leader. Both men desire the same woman. Circling Hawk believes (correctly) that No Name has "wived" Leaf. Worse, both believe she is dead. The circumstances of their journey are ideal for what I am calling the false manhood to surface—competition, hatred, the desire for revenge. Manfred constructs scene after scene in which predators appear—eagles, wolves, hawks—and the characters attempt to interpret them. One evening No Name awakens to the sound of "thick breathing," and he reasons that it is Circling Hawk. No Name reasons thus: "[He] accepted the mission to come with me, because it was wakan and worthy to do, but he also hated me with all his soul and therefore has decided to kill me" (109). He looks up to find actual wolves in their campsite. No Name has difficulty thinking of Circling Hawk as anything other than a rival. When he wakes Circling Hawk, he learns that Circling Hawk also has dreamt of wolves. During his fast, however, weakened and vulnerable, something happens to No Name. He is able to see Circling Hawk in a new light:

> He was glad to see his ugly friend still in attendance. He remembered how Circling Hawk had held him in his arms and warmed him after he had nearly drowned in the Great Smoky Water. He realized at last that Circling Hawk was truly an older brother to him. He wept about it. He swore to reward him for it.

He opened his arms as if to embrace what had once been his hated rival. (122-23).

The parallels between this scene and Leaf's rescue are apparent. We see No Name learning from his rival to be a nurturer, a life-giver. It is No Name's weakened condition that enables him to see his rival in this new light. This sympathy seems to be essential to actually receiving the vision. It is not until he is rid of his feelings of rivalry that No Name arrives "in a world where there was nothing but the spirit of all things. He saw it was the real world, the one behind the world of shadows he usually lived in" (129).

Returned from his vision, No Name must next present a scarlet blanket to Wakantanka. That is, he must give his own blood in a sun dance. In this ceremony, yet another death occurs. The focus of the dance is a pole, a phallic symbol inserted in a "fat-filled hole," through which the people conjure "the Obscene God." "Kill the Obscene God," they cry. "He has power over us. Help us before all the virgins are taken" (141). Moon Dreamer, the holy man, shoots it with his bow and arrow. But it is not enough that they condemn promiscuity and exploitative sexuality in the abstract. No Name is then brought to the pole, to be tormented as a mock enemy, by the gods' decree. He is to be purged of whatever rapaciousness still lives in him. Skewered above each nipple, he is attached to the pole by leather thongs tied to the skewers. As he begins his dance, Moon Dreamer tells him, "Let the child in you die and the man in your come forth" (144). What kind of man? No Name leans back, pulling away from his tethers. "Flesh rose off his ribcase in two places like the small sharp breasts of a young girl" (144). The child in him, associated with sexually hungry man, must die. What takes its place is portrayed to the reader in female images. Ultimately, he literally pulls two patches of skin off his body, bleeding profusely, creating the scarlet blanket. The female imagery is reiterated at the moment he succeeds: "The bleeding slits on his chest lay open and swollen as if they had just given birth to puppies" (150).

Taken together, these androgynous images are outward physical signs of changes occurring within: death of the child, death of the false man; emergence of another sensibility, less calculating, more intuitive, more feminine. Recall that at the moment No Name feels himself drawn toward Leaf—at the time, toward he knows not what—the sensation is "as though someone had grabbed up a handful of flesh on his chest" (185). He is led to Leaf by what has been ripped from his body. He is led toward a new unity with her made possible by a more integrated soul.

This mature, real manliness is portrayed in androgynous form in other characters in the novel. McCallister speaks of "the unselfconscious androgyny of Redbird in *Conquering Horse*" (10). Then, too, Sounds the Ground, the Pawnee chief No Name surprises in his lodge, shows restraint and respect for No Name, welcomes him, eats with him, communes with him. Doing so, Sounds the Ground is reviled by his wife: "You are a soft-hearted woman to welcome this snake of a Sioux into your lodge. That is what comes of smelling pretty flowers when alone, like some silly goose of a girl" (211). Yet Sounds the Ground, himself opposed by a Pawnee rival (appropriately named Rough Arm), is secure in his power, because, the novel would seem to suggest, it is grounded in a more fully human character.

This androgyny, I think, compels us to re-evaluate Manfred's work. That re-evaluation is given urgency and focus by feminist theory in recent years, which has made a case for other ways of thinking about literature and alternative ways of knowing. One of the challenges in feminist thought has been to question the epistemology of Western culture. *How* we think determines *what* we think. *Women's Ways of Knowing* points out that, historically in universities, and by extension in Western culture, a male way of knowing has been privileged, and that, in a broad range of institutional life, we have perpetuated this male way of knowing, emphasizing head over heart, rationality over intuitiveness, the logical over the affective, left brain over right brain, conscious over unconscious, an agonistic posture over a sympathetic one, argumentation over narrative, third person over first person. Jane Tompkins attests to a struggle within herself, in her attempt to use a female voice that has been submerged under the weight of her own training as a literary critic. She writes of two voices in conflict within her: "the voice of a person who wants to write about her feelings (I have wanted to do this for a long time but have felt too embarrassed)" and the voice of a critic, who "believes that such feelings, and the attitudes that inform them, are soft-minded, self-indulgent, and unprofessional" (24). It is precisely because of feminism that novels such as *Conquering Horse* should be read:

GENDER, POWER, AND KNOWING 103

because it takes the reader into a world from which, if she is a well-schooled American, she has most likely been cut off.

The epistemological issue—how we know what we know—is central to western fiction's struggle for legitimacy as a literature. In 1966 Max Westbrook notices a critical difference between the realism of Western fiction and that of Eastern—which is to say, canonical, literary, highbrow, and mainstream—varieties of fiction. That critical difference, he argues, hinges on consciousness and will. In conservative and liberal realism, "The place of consciousness," he writes, "in the mode of apprehension remains requisite. . . . [The] act of discovery must be or become a conscious act in order to be genuine for the individual" (14-15). Not so in the case of the Western realist. Says Westbrook:

> The real lies in dark caverns of the unconscious and cannot be penetrated by the rational (or conscious) mind. We think with the conscious mind, but thereby apprehend only the effects of the unconscious, rather than its true nature. . . And yet the Western rejection of will is not a rejection of any function of will; it is rather an insistence that will keeps its proper place and not be used to betray the primary unconscious" (15-16).

Conquering Horse, and the experience of No Name, dramatizes the individual's effort to become attentive to what comes from the dark caverns. The effort is not a "conscious act" (Westbrook 15) on No Name's part; in the course of the novel, he becomes increasingly receptive, allowing himself, as Manfred has said of his composing process, to be drawn. "Will keeps its proper place." And most importantly, the capacity to be drawn, the action of the novel suggests, is enhanced by emerging female attributes in No Name.

This claim is powerfully born out in the final episodes of the novel. In many ways, No Name's pursuit of the white stallion is a descent into the primal, the most elemental part of himself. In pursuit of what he repeatedly refers to as "his god," he is transformed into a predatory creature, into the stallion's likeness. Repeatedly we see Dancing Sun as predator: "His growl was like that of a monster wolf, deep, primordial" (242). In the depth of its fury, Manfred describes Dancing Sun as "a raging predatory lizard" (250). And then, at the moment No Name is about to actually capture the stallion, the powerful image is reiterated, this time in a description of No Name:

> His pulse beat painfully in his wound. His head came up. He sniffed in anticipation. His fierce black eyes glittered. Red passion glowed in his brain. A cold-blooded green-eyed predator writhed in the old darkness of his belly. He licked his lips, once, already wildly happy that he had seized the white one. (276)

To conquer the horse, No Name has surrendered completely to the predator in himself, attentive to signs, to the voice of his helper, and, significantly, to the aid of his female companion. Leaf is constantly there, enabling him. She guides him, helping him first to find the stallion, then actually saving his life, when No Name is being attacked by the stallion, driving it off with a firebrand.

But *Conquering Horse* is not about man finding the predator within himself. In a stunning move, Manfred kills off Dancing Sun at the end of Part III of the novel, which is a terrible setback for No Name. Just as he thinks he has triumphed, just as he thinks he finally knows what he is supposed to do, what everything means, all of No Name's certainties are dashed. He awakens at the beginning of Part IV, mourning the loss of Dancing Sun: "I have lost the white horse that was promised me. My heart is on the ground" (289). Once again he is in a position where he must be led. He has nothing to go on. He has no plan, no strategy. "Where is your wife?" a voice asks. No Name cannot reason it out. Dancing Sun is dead. And what of the second part of his vision, which says that his father must die? "Where is your wife?" the voice asks again, and again, and again. Six times, before No Name is led to her, where she has given birth to their son, and where, nearby, Dancing Sun's favorite mare has also given birth to twins, male and female. The colt is white, with a reddish mane, the same horse it was prophesied he would find.

This is the moment No Name has been prepared for. *Conquering Horse* is about man finding the nurturer in himself. No Name vows to take care of the sacred colt as if it were his son. Embracing it, he feels its heart beating against his chest. He breathes life into it:

He cupped his hands around its soft protruding lips and breathed into its mouth, deep, long; breathed until the colt's chest began to lift and fall on its own a little. His breath and the breath of the colt became one. (299).

He lifts the colt to its dying mother's belly, helping it to drink life-giving milk. He passes the night with it, nestling with it as if it were his newborn. Then, in an extraordinary turn, once the mare dies, he cuts a belt from the mare's hide, including the nipples, and wears it around his mid-section in an effort to become its surrogate mother.

No Name's act is a culmination unthinkable at the outset of the novel. Unthinkable by both him and the reader. The stallion, his divine counterpart, is dead, and No Name is birthing a new stallion, a new maleness. This is a radically new notion of the hero. Manfred involves his character in an archetypal adventure: a journey into manhood, involving an initiation into adult sexuality, separation from the community, descent into the unknown, or unconscious, death of the father, birth of a son, an encounter with the godhead, and a return to the community with special knowledge. But No Name's return is a departure from the mythical hero's journey, especially in this emphasis on the anima he discovers in himself.

Further, No Name's return with the son of Dancing Sun is not altogether triumphant. It is also burdened with a terrible foreboding, a terrible knowledge, that his father must die. The death seems inevitable, necessary in the harrowing tragic sense as Oedipus moves ineluctably in the direction of his terrible knowing. But what a critical difference there is between Oedipus and No Name: Oedipus' tragic knowledge is that he himself is responsible for everything, that he has chosen his destiny. Oedipus' knowledge is an affirmation of his will. No Name's knowledge, as he grapples with his father's prophesied death, pertains to a will larger than his own. He must acquiesce to his father's death, and in doing so, acquiesces to a larger power. That acquiescence can be seen in No Name on the night before his father dies, before his father is conveyed to heaven by a blinding thunderbolt. No Name, who is now Conquering Horse, prepares for the day with his uncle, Moon Dreamer:

"But, my uncle, when must I kill my father?"

Moon Dreamer looked gently down at Conquering Horse. Carefully he reached a finger under his buffalo mask and wiped

away a sliding tear of yellow matter. "My son, tomorrow, at dusk, it will be given to you."
"My father is greater than I. Yet I hear you, my uncle."
"My son, do you feel the power of the white mare?"
"It is entering me."
"My son, do you feel the power of the white mare?"
"Ai, it is warming my belly."
"My son, do you feel the power of the white mare?"
"Aii! It is making me a mighty man."
Yet a fourth time Moon Dreamer asked it. "My son, do you feel the power of the white mare?"
"Hi-ye! Yes, I am a great man! I am happy! Thank you, thank you." (340)

What will happen, Moon Dreamer says, "will be given" to Conquering Horse. He will be drawn to act in a certain way, consistent with larger powers. Importantly, Conquering Horse's surrender to these powers is expressed, not in terms of the white stallion, but the white mare, four times, which is growing inside him, warming his belly. His empowerment, his connection with the divine, is gestating inside him, making him a mighty man. In a state of profound spiritual arousal, he senses the interconnectedness of life:

> He could still feel the power of the white mare throbbing in him. He now saw all life as one huge flow, with himself in a streaming part of it. And being a part of it he felt the whole of it. The huge flow included the lives of the wingeds and the fourleggeds and the twoleggeds, and also his life and the life of his father. One part of the flow was exactly like any other part of it. It was all one and the same. Therefore he no longer needed to think about how his father's life would end. (340).

This is Conquering Horse at the height of his powers, a fully realized male, in complete sympathy with other living things. It is an extraordinary moment in Western fiction, and an equally important image of man—and I mean man—in Western culture.

There is plenty of work to be done on Manfred's fiction, especially as it relates to his treatment of gender. In a novel like *The Manly Hearted Woman*, it is clear to the reader that Manfred's view of gender is complex and richly androgynous, that something like a new vision of the sexes is being offered. That vision is available to us even in what seem like overtly "manly" stories, such as *Conquering Horse*. It is a vision that may creep into Manfred's work without his being fully aware of it, because his lizard is at work, because he is terribly drawn to such a way of thinking about gender, without fully understanding why. It is our task as readers and explicators to engage the why, leaving the how in his very capable hands.

Works Cited

Belenky, Mary Field. et al. *Women's Ways of Knowing*. New York: Basic Books, 1986.

Interview with Frederick Manfred, May 8, 1981.

Manfred, Frederick. *Conquering Horse*. Lincoln: U of Nebraska P, 1983.

McAllister, Mick. "The Sundered Egg: The Sexual Issue in *The Manly Hearted Woman*." (Presented at the Western Literature Association Conference, St. Louis, October 1980.)

Tompkins, Jane. "Me and My Shadow." *The Intimate Critique*. Ed. Diane P. Freedman et al. Durham: Duke UP, 1993. 23-40.

Westbrook, Max. "Conservative, Liberal, and Western: Three Modes of American Realism." *South Dakota Review* 4 (Summer 1966) : 3-19.

The Land, History, and the Self in Fiction by Margaret Laurence and Frederick Manfred

by Barbara Howard Meldrum

The Great Plains know no national boundary—Canada and the United States share this distinctive region. Yet the culture that has developed reflects differences that may stem from variations in settlement patterns and in political, social, and historical development. Literary critics as well as cultural historians have theorized about national-regional traits, but in the works of some novelists we can experience the kind of cultural analysis that comes from an artist's empathetic portrayal of human experience in a particular region. Comparing these fictional probings by representative Canadian and American novelists can shed some light on the differences and similarities of prairie life on the two sides of an unnatural political border that nonetheless separates two distinctive cultures.

I have chosen Margaret Laurence and Frederick Manfred as representative novelists because they are near-contemporaries and because each has created a body of work that explores their respective prairie worlds in interrelated novels. Like William Faulkner, each has created a fictional world—Laurence's Manawaka and Manfred's Siouxland.[1] Each writes from the perspective of Anglo-colonization, but each seeks to portray sympathetically the native inhabitants of the region. Both have sought connections between the past and the present: Laurence states that she tried in her fiction "to assimilate the past, partly in order to be freed from it, partly in order to try to understand myself and perhaps those of my generation through seeing where we had come from" ("Sources" 81). Manfred tells how he turned to historical fiction because he felt "the characters in my books up to that point were somewhat two-dimensional. . . . There was a background missing in all of them" (*Conversations* 68). Discovery and consequent freeing of self seem to be the goal for each. For Laurence, that self seems more personal and individual; the past which she explores is primarily the personal, remembered past, and flashbacks are structurally integral to her fiction. For Manfred, the self is primarily the authentic American self which D. H. Lawrence urged us to realize; the past he explores is not only the remembered past of his own lifetime, but the historical past dating from the last of the pre-white days on the plains in the early 1800s. Structurally, his progression is usually linear chronology; the interconnections come not from flashbacks, but through images forming a mythic geography and through echoes from a sacred time.

Laurence's Manawaka world is a prairie town that is both a place and a particular culture. She says that her "way of seeing . . . remains in some enduring way that of a smalltown prairie person" ("Sources" 84). This prairie was settled by pioneers. "The pillars of the Nation," young Vanessa called them when she started to write her first novel—romantic pioneers, until she learned that her grandfather was considered to be one: "If pioneers were like that, . . . my pen would be better employed elsewhere" (*BH* 56).[2] No, Grandfather Connor was not obviously heroic to young Vanessa; he was, in fact, autocratic, patriarchal, dominating, seemingly devoid of human feeling. Vanessa hates him and lives for the day when she can escape his influence and his presence; not until years later does she recognize that "he proclaimed himself in my veins" (*BH* 179). Grandfather Connor had walked as a boy from Ontario to Manitoba, had started as a blacksmith, then built up a hardware business, and proudly affirmed his dynasty by building the first brick house in Manawaka, a house Vanessa calls "Jericho's Brick Battlements"—truly a fortress, a garrison which is both monument and refuge, a mode of conquest in that vast and alien land. Both he and Hagar (*SA*) pay a high emotional price for their pride which makes their survival and conquest possible. Writing of "that whole generation of pioneers," Laurence acknowledges "how difficult they were to live with, how authoritarian, how unbending, how afraid to show love, many of them, and how willing to show anger. And yet—they had inhabited a wilderness and made it fruitful" ("Sources" 82). Henry Kreisel states that "Prairie puritanism is one result of the conquest of the land, part of the price exacted for the conquest. Like the theme of the conquest of the land, the theme of the imprisoned spirit dominates serious prairie writing, and is connected with it" (Kreisel 265). Both Grandfather Connor and Hagar are crippled emotionally, hiding behind a bear-mask (Connor) or becoming a stone angel (Hagar). Hagar, Mrs. Reilly, Mrs. Fennick (of *The Fire-Dwellers*), Prim (of *The Diviners*) —all are fat women imprisoned by their own flesh. Hagar vividly portrays the imprisoned self; she clings desperately to her house which is her identity, both a prison and a refuge, resisting the move to Silverthreads Nursing Home; she discovers as she nears death that she was "never free, for I carried my chains within me, and they spread out from me and shackled all I touched"; she is both snow angel and stone angel, who could not share the pleasures of the flesh with her husband and could not cry at her son's death: "Pride was my wilderness, and the demon that led me there was fear. I was alone" (*SA* 261, 70, 216).

Whether pioneer or a contemporary figure such as Rachel (*A Jest of God*), Laurence's characters need and seek freedom of spirit and emotion, which have been isolated and repressed through cultural influences directly related to the prairie setting. How do these characters achieve that freedom which represents a wholeness of self? One avenue they try is escape. All of Laurence's Manawaka female protagonists leave town and go to Vancouver, British Columbia. Why Vancouver? Because it is a city, not a small prairie town; perhaps because it is on the coast by the sea, nearly as far west as one can go; most of all, because it is a new place where one might make a new beginning, leaving the past behind.[3] But of course, these characters carry something of their Manawaka past with them, both the good and the bad. A journey west, Morag learns, is ultimately a journey back into time and the past where she constantly changes her own past, "recalling it, revising it," for the lesson that she learns is not that "You Can't Go Home Again," but that "you have to go home again, in some way or other" (*D* 5, 60, 302).[4] Like the "River of Now and Then" which seems to flow both ways at once, Morag learns to "Look ahead into the past, and back into the future, until the silence" (*D* 453).

There is no escape, Laurence's successful heroines discover. A new beginning can be cautiously hopeful, as Rachel knows when she departs for Vancouver (*JG* 245-46). A "venture and launching" sometimes becomes necessary—even the illusion that a new beginning brings freedom from the past (*SA* 120, 137). Eventually, however, one is thrust back upon oneself. Freedom involves finding and making one's own place, living in the present moment with full awareness of the past, and being both alone and united with others. All of Laurence's fiction moves toward such a recognition, but the

THE LAND, HISTORY, AND THE SELF 111

revelations are sharpest in *The Diviners*. Morag Gunn is a writer working on a novel which is probably an autobiographical rendering of the memories she reviews as the action switches between past and present. Her friend Royland is a water diviner from whom she has felt she "was about to learn something of great significance . . . something which would explain everything. But things remained mysterious, his work, her own, the generations, the river (*D* 4). Appropriately, her moment of greatest revelation comes in his presence while they are boating on the river. They chat about swimming, Morag admitting that she avoids swimming because the weeds seem like some prehistoric river-monster attacking her: she fears the primordial even though she has chosen this rural setting as an escape from cities, "making this her place, her island." Then she asks herself whether islands are "real" and concludes that they "exist only in the head," for no escape is complete; survival depends on our interconnectedness with others, personally and economically. Then Royland draws her attention to a rare sight—a Great Blue Heron, now nearly extinct, which spreads its vast wings and gracefully takes off in flight, "like a pterodactyl, like an angel, like something out of the world's dawn. The soaring and measured certainty of its flight. Ancient-seeming, unaware of the planet's rocketing changes. The sweeping serene wings of the thing, unknowing that it was speeding not only towards individual death but probably towards the death of its kind." Royland and Morag share this moment in silence and awe; she begins to see that "here and now was not, after all, an island. Her quest for islands had ended some time ago, and her need to make pilgrimages had led her back here" (*D* 356-57).

Her pilgrimages have also been revelatory, involving both place and history. One pilgrimage was personal and cultural: her attraction to her British-born English teacher at university, whom she marries, joining herself literally to that which she felt lacking in her Manawaka past. But her life with Brooke is urban and sterile; she leaves him for Jules Tonnerre, who represents the other polarity of Manawaka life: the Metis, half-breed Indians, remnants of those who were native to the land but are now cultural outcasts in white Manawaka. Their child she names for Jule's sister Piquette, who died a victim of her futile efforts to join the dominant white culture. Although Jules and Morag never marry and spend most of their lives apart from each other, they share a love and respect on a level deep enough so that they can at least honor each other's existential aloneness. Their daughter may not succeed in uniting the diverse strains represented by her parents, but she seems to be heading in the right direction when, at the end of the novel, she returns to her mother's Manawaka and beyond, to the Galloping Mountains and her Metis uncle from whom she will learn the ways of her ancestors.

Morag's ancestors were Scottish Highlanders who came to Canada during the Clearances. Inspired by the legends her stepfather told her, she intends to make a pilgrimage to Sutherland and even gets as far as Scotland, then backs away, recognizing that "the myths are my reality" rather than the real place or the facts of what actually happened (all we have are versions—*D* 350). She also discovers that her ancestors are not in Scotland, but in Canada—her own people of her own land (*D* 390-91). This knowledge frees her from an ancestral past too remote in space and time to be helpful to her and makes possible a more direct integration with her Canadian homeland.

Her final pilgrimage has brought her to McConnell's Landing, located east of Manawaka, a rural setting where she makes a place her own, putting down roots and growing as person and artist. Here she invokes another ancestor, one of this place: Mrs. Catharine Traill, a pioneer woman who succeeded in coping with the demands of being wife, mother, innovative homemaker and gardener in that once wild land, naming the plants and establishing order out of chaos. At first her spirit is an intimidating role model for Morag; but finally, sometime after her vision of the blue heron, she reaches a point of reconciliation: "in my way I've worked damn hard, and I haven't done all I would've liked to do, but I haven't folded up like a paper fan, either. . . . this place is some kind of a garden, nonetheless, even though it may be only a wildflower garden. It's needed, and not only by me" (*D* 406). Morag has made her own garden, her own Eden, east of Manawaka, a garden of the mind which bears the fruits of her labors in works of fiction.[5] The blue heron suggests the primordial, prehistoric life of paradoxically fragile strength and beauty which moves in a sacred time that is threatened by death-dealing profane changes of modern life; yet it serenely pursues its way and thereby inspires Morag to accept the here and now. Royland the diviner exercises what he recognizes as a mysterious gift until the day he discovers he has lost that gift and is an "*ex-shaman*" (*D* 451). His acceptance of his fate is another example for Morag. Moreover, he acknowledges that there are "inheritors" who will carry on the divining, which is both gift and the result of learning. The final image is the river itself, which seems to go both ways at once, the river of now and then, life and death, shallows and deeps. We end with a tenuous, living balance, both passive and active, both giving and taking, accepting and striving, an inner freedom which makes it possible to survive and to grow.[6]

Frederick Manfred's temporal scope is historically broader than Laurence's, but like Laurence his theme pertains to the realization of selfhood. Russell Roth was right when he said that "the unifying theme of the Buckskin Man Tales" is "the search for the true self in a context of an evolving and generic *American* self." Writing in 1969, he saw in Manfred's work a "progression from green earth to dust bowl." (Roth 89, 98). Today we have other novels to fit into the overall pattern, especially *Green Earth* (1977) and *Milk of Wolves* (1976), both of which suggest that death and what D. H. Lawrence referred to as "post-mortem effects" may possibly lead to rebirth. The apocalyptic vision of the Buckskin Man Tales may not lead directly to a millenium; but some sort of renewal, a new life, may indeed be possible.

The fabric of Manfred's fiction is deceptively simple. Lacking are the complex time-patterns of Laurence's novels which interweave past and present until united in the present moment at the end of her novels. Each Manfred novel progresses through linear narrative; the complexity comes through motifs, locations, and symbols that are repeated with variations throughout his fiction as a whole. Reading each novel, we are caught up in the narrative; but we keep stumbling across familiar landmarks until gradually the pieces begin to fit together like a jigsaw puzzle as gigantic as Siouxland itself. These puzzle pieces are places such as Thunder Butte and Pipestone; animals such as the wolf, grizzly, and horse (especially stallions): birds, such as the meadowlark and eagle; Biblical tales, especially the story of Abraham and Isaac, Jacob and Esau; Greek myths—of Oedipus and Odysseus; and motifs—twins, incest, barrenness and fertility.

Manfred begins his historical account with pre-white Indian times in *Conquering Horse*. If ever there was a time of Paradise, this would seem to be it: not a state of perfection, but truly a state of integration where men and women live fully in the present moment, yet also experience a sacred time beyond time as all life flows as one. The protagonist is No Name because he has not yet had a vision and so has not earned a name befitting his adult identity. He must find himself. Significantly, he earns the name Conquering Horse through a process that not only brings him self-esteem and fulfilled love, but brings gifts to his people. A. H. Maslow would recognize Conquering Horse as a self-actualized person who in fulfilling his own inner potential also benefits others through meaningful work.

Conquering Horse is not only an individual hero but a culture hero, re-enacting the beginning of a new world for his people by bringing them the gift of a seed horse that will make his people mighty. This act recapitulates the white man's gift of the horse to the plains Indians: one instance of positive interaction between the two races which revitalized Indian culture. Symbolically then, the action of this tale suggests what was possible in a positive way through interaction between whiteman and redman. That such was not to be historically fulfilled is borne out in the next two novels which reveal the demise of the Indian before an encroaching civilization so structured that an either-or struggle for survival becomes inevitable.

In addition to the individual and tribal or social levels, the story also operates on a third, archetypal plane. The archetype pertains to the relationship between fathers and sons and between brothers; manifestations of that archetype take various mythic forms. One version Manfred works with in a number of novels is the Biblical story of Abraham and Isaac, Jacob and Esau.[7] We can recognize the outlines of the Biblical story in the sibling rivalry between No Name and Pretty Rock, in No Name's wrestling with an eagle to gain his vision, and most importantly in the father's refusal to sacrifice his son for personal gain and his willingness to submit to the ancient custom of the son killing the father: a reversal of the Biblical myth which seems more atune to the rhythms of life itself. There is a progressive moral deterioration in succeeding tales, culminating in Earl Ransom (*King of Spades*), who hangs himself even though his father offers himself as a substitute, an offer which comes too late to undo the damage the father has already done the son; and in the coldly murderous Hunt Lawton/Link Keeler (*Riders of Judgment*), who becomes what he is because his father actually tried to kill him in order to secure his wife's obedience through fear.

The kingship motif suggests this moral deterioration as it relates to American history. In *Conquering Horse* we watch the transition of tribal chiefs from father to son who has proved himself worthy to lead his people, and we also read that the godlike stallion Dancing Sun is a king (*CH* 286);[8] the seed colt he fathers becomes a rejuvenating force for these people. In *Lord Grizzly* Hugh Glass grows from a stubborn, narrow-minded, insensitive individualist to a man aware of his own humanness and capacity for forgiveness, thereby enabled to free his surrogate sons from the threat of his retribution so that they can live and choose to "turn tramp or turn king" (*LG* 281). Scarlet Plume becomes "King" to Judith when they make love (*SP* 252): the power of love expressed through the primal energy of sex transforms her. But king becomes the crucified Christ, denied the chiefdom that was rightfully his inheritance and literally cut off by a vengeful whitewoman (*SP* 355). In *King of Spades* kingship is spurious, suggesting ties to British ancestry (the "old mother Europa"), uncertain in origins (possibly royal descent, but possibly the pretense of playacting—*KS* 3), and blinding in its effects. European-American kingship seems predicated on material wealth earmarked by gold which the Indians of *Scarlet Plume* scornfully call "goddung" and which tempts the son of Magnus King to forsake the promised wholeness of Erden and a nature paradise for gold and a destructively incestuous tie with his "mother" (both literal and symbolic). The last novel of the series, *Riders of Judgment*, portrays the demise of the cattle kings, making way for the small ranchers, then the farmers, then the depression and dust bowl—*The Golden Bowl* (1944).

This is the Year (1947) demonstrates vividly the post-mortem effects of Anglo-American nineteenth-century conquest of the West, the prairie, and the Indian. Pier Frixen may love the land, but he doesn't know how to love it and doggedly pursues old country farming methods which don't work on his prairie farm. His failures with the land parallel his personal failures with his wife, whom he also does not know how to love. The sexual life of Manfred's characters is always a good clue to their degree of wholeness. Even in *Green Earth*, which is a celebration of life, there is the dark strand of Ada's lack of sexual fulfillment in her marriage to Alfred. In many of Manfred's novels the men fail as lovers; but in *Milk of*

Wolves the approach is different: it is the woman (young Flur) who teaches the man (Juhl) a sexuality that transcends fulfillment through pleasure. The fact that she is half Indian is no accident, for Manfred is working here with the necessity that white Americans acquire a oneness with the earth, with the life principle, if they are to achieve wholeness both individually and culturally. The Indians had this connection; we can hopefully learn from them.

Juhl Melander is a sculptor from Hackberry Run in Siouxland who goes to Minneapolis-St. Paul, establishes himself as an artist, marries, fathers children, has affairs, becomes increasingly crude and cruel until he finally leaves his wife and family to become a hermit in the woods of a small island in northern Minnesota. Book One is titled "Villain in the Cities" most appropriately; it is difficult to feel much sympathy for Juhl during his last days in the city. Alone on his island, he meets neighbors on a nearby island: Wulf and Yvette, a happily married couple, Indian and white, who have twin teenager children, Flur and Faunce. Their lives seem to be idyllic, and Juhl envies their love that has endured and grown through their long marriage. Through their influence and that of nature itself he begins to become aware of his origins both in place and in time (lineage) (see *MW* 201). The spirit of place comes to him through his discovery of a giant red pine tree—a "king," "father of all red pines," "a great warrior," an "awesome wilderness hero. A tree of dreams. A tree of faithful love between earth and sun." This tree he finds in a place that seems to be "Eden itself" (*MW* 184-85). Juhl's human origin is the animal in him. Wulf the Indian has "the know-how of an animal" whereas "the white man had pretty much bred it out of his blood." Juhl recognizes that "Wulf was a superior human being because he still had that ancient ability. The stronger the animal in man the better the chance he had of getting the best of his blood into his civilized stratagems. That was why he, Juhl Melander, once of the Cities and before that of Hackberry Run, had chosen to become a shacker on Big Wolf Island. That he might, somehow, have the animal in him resurrected. Discover his blood. Instead of having the animal in him constricted and warped and made mean" (*MW* 207). This need to allow the animal within oneself to express itself but in constructive, life-affirming ways runs through all of Manfred's fiction.[9] It finds its fullest expression in *Milk of Wolves*. No wonder Manfred felt as he worked on this book that he was writing the great American novel (Interview).

Wulf is a mentor and example to Juhl; but he and Yvette die, leaving Flur and Faunce to work out their pubescent, incestuous relationship in an isolated island paradise that can threaten as well as nurture. Indeed, the reader becomes poignantly aware of how tenuous and fragile is this pastoral paradise, threatening human fulfillment through the indifferent forces of nature and being threatened by an ever-encroaching civilization. Historically, such an existence cannot endure; *et in Arcadia ego* (death is also in paradise).

But before death and seemingly inevitable change bereft Juhl of his paradise, he undergoes a transformation of character through the influence of Flur, who comes to him partly to escape her brother, partly because she is attracted to Juhl. Being much older than she and having sworn off women, he avoids any physical relationship. But Flur knows what she wants and pursues Juhl, even to the point of poisoning his pet wolf-pup who is her rival for affection. Then during a thunderstorm circumstances thrust them together; Flur is both bargaining woman insisting on marriage rights and wolf-animal, insisting that they mate in the "manner of the wolves," not in the "manner of the missionaries" (*MW* 222). Juhl becomes "king wolf" as they mate. This scene contrasts with Judith Raveling's plight, in *Scarlet Plume*, for sex with her husband had been perfunctory and she had resisted his desire to mate in the manner of Lucretius. She objected because she did not want to mate like an animal and because she sensed the hypocrisy in her husband, who went through the motions of a position supposedly conducive to conception, not because he wanted more children but because he wanted "the pleasure of pretending to want more" (*SP* 252,292). Flur's and Juhl's relationship exists at a different level of truth, not contradictory or either-or, but on a different plane. Flur insists on imitating the wolf-manner not only in lovemaking but in preparing to give birth to her child. She is animal, but also spirit, "swollen and spiritual both," awakening in Juhl "a profound respect for the sacred." He recognizes that although she does not have "the orgasm of the paleface," she seems to have "something equally thrilling. Just being swollen with the desire to have seed implanted in her was her true joy. Her love demands were not for her own selfish satisfaction so much as they were for something larger." For more than a month they make love in a frenzy of passion. Then she no longer seeks him; "womanly reverie, not radiant lust," impels her. He too no longer seeks her. "It was more than just being satiated. It was as though they'd both had to climb through the daily rains of a humid latitude to reach the clear air of a place of worship, a pyramid on a mountain plateau" (*MW* 224).

This primordial, animal-spiritual sexual experience purges and transforms Juhl. He is no longer simply the rutting stallion or the celibate hermit; he has been caught up in something bigger than himself and has learned from it.

The last stage of transformation takes place after Flur's death. Desperate to provide milk for their young son, he cuts his chest to give the child blood; repeated sucking stimulates his glands until he actually produces milk.[10] Juhl discovers one of the most basic experiences of motherhood. This androgynous development contributes further to his growth into wholeness. The novel ends only very tenuously optimistic. The child has died: although barrenness (typically the sign of despoiled human nature) is not the problem, no new biological line is established. Juhl is a man of sixty; it has taken him most of a lifetime to find himself, and he is alone. But he has no regrets; he is thankful for life itself; he has his work; he knows who he is and where he is from—his origins.

I am struck by the comparison-contrast possible between Pier Frixen at the end of *This is the Year* and Juhl at the end of *Milk of Wolves*. Pier too is alone; he has lost both wife and farm. But he is ready to begin again, confidently exclaiming, "I'm a young buck yit. My heart's still green" (*TIY* 614). What a world of difference there is between Pier and Juhl! To put it simply, Juhl has learned and Pier has not. Juhl's confidence derives from integration of mind and body, animal and spirit, past and present; Pier's confidence manifests the blindness of ego and an aborted soul. If there is any hope for the American self of the future, surely it lies in the direction Juhl has traveled. Back to the source. Back to the spring from the rock which becomes a river of life—and of death—and of renewal (see *MW* 249-50). Like Conquering Horse, Juhl will bring gifts to his people through his work; but unlike the youthful new chief, this aging artist will not lead his people. So far, the American self has not evolved a coherent and vital social structure.

Margaret Laurence and Frederick Manfred are both prairie writers seeking to reveal the dynamics of evolving selfhood. Wherein are the essential differences? Laurence's scope is more

THE LAND, HISTORY, AND THE SELF 119

personal and individual, whereas Manfred's is more national This difference stems partly from Laurence's novelistic approach, which contrasts with the romance mode of Manfred's Buckskin Man Tales, *The Manly-Hearted Woman* (1976), and *Milk of Wolves*. He seems to follow the romance tradition described By Richard Chase many years ago. However, in such works as *Green Earth, Sons of Adam* (1980), and *Of Lizards and Angels* (1992) he is more the novelist and more like Laurence. The romance may be typical of many American writers, but it is not the only viable mode.

Laurence and Manfred do seem to differ in their sense of a primordial past. Both writers portray the terror one can feel before the immensity of nature. Hugh Glass feels terror when he recognizes he is "completely alone in a wild savage country," severely wounded and desperately struggling to survive (*LG* 114). But for all the many outdoor scenes in Manfred, such terror is not common. Laurence seldom portrays characters out in the wild, but when she does, terror is keenly felt. Young Vanessa confronts a totally new experience when she sees a northern lake bounded by fossil footprints of primordial monsters. How to describe such a place? "No human word could be applied. The lake was not lonely or untamed. These words relate to people, and there was nothing of people here. There was no feeling about the place. It existed in some world in which man was not yet born. I looked at the grey reaches of it and felt threatened. It was like the view of God which I had held since my father's death. Distant, indestructible, totally indifferent" (*BH* I26). That she feels threatened, and that established views of God prove inadequate to combat the terror—this is what remains, not some avenue to sacred truth. Such a perception fits the "garrison mentality" described in Northrop Frye's analysis of Canadian literature (Frye 225). When the garrison of commonly held values begins to break down, terror is the natural result.

The appearance of the blue heron and its effect on Morag seem closer to Manfred's fiction, though such a scene is more the exception than the rule in Laurence's novels. Moreover, Laurence handles references to animals very differently from Manfred. The blue heron may suggest an appropriate response to place and time for Morag, but Morag does not identify with the heron. In one of Laurence's stories both a dog and a boy are conditioned in ways that make them suffer as victims while the real villains go free (*BH* 133-48). But there is no shared identity of animal and human being. Vanessa calls her grandfather "The Great Bear" because he wears a heavy bearskin coat and is surly. His commanding, controlled manner cracks once when his wife dies, giving young Vanessa a momentary glimpse of a feeling man behind a bear-mask. But the bear imagery does not function as it does in *Lord Grizzly*—or the wolf images in *Scarlet Plume* and *Milk of Wolves*. Laurence brings in a specific Indian reference at the end of her story, when an adult Vanessa sees the "Bear Mask of the Haida Indians" in a museum. As she looks, she imagines she "could see somewhere within that darkness a look which I knew, a lurking bewilderment. I remembered then that in the days before it became a museum piece, the mask had concealed a man" (*BH* 76). The imagery is appropriate and most effective for the kind of story Laurence is telling; but the meaning is a world apart from Manfred's. I simply do not find in Laurence that desire to connect with the primordial in us.

Both Laurence and Manfred focus a great deal on human relationships. One critic has stated that it is a truism that Canadian writers prefer to examine the relationship between generations rather than between individuals of the same generation (Jackel 48). This certainly seems to be true of Laurence's novels. One seeming exception, *A Jest of God*, portrays Rachel's first sexual relationship; but the real story is about Rachel's struggle to become a person separate from her dominating mother and to become herself a mother. In *The Fire-Dwellers* Stacey struggles with her destiny which is defined more by her responsibility to her children than by her relationship to her husband. The generational relationships typically focus on mother-child rather than father-son (as in Manfred). This is not simply the difference between a male and female writer. Dick Harrison's study of Canadian prairie writers, both male and female, reveals a consistent pattern of "the disappearing father" and, in Laurence's fiction, the emergence of strong and independent women. In the fiction of such writers as Laurence, Robert Kroetsch, W. O. Mitchell, and the late works of Sinclair Ross patriarchy has become weak or missing (Harrison 187-88). Manfred, however, works within a patriarchal framework both in his fiction and nonfiction: the shaping influence of fathers is the focus of his essays in *Prime Fathers* (1988), one of the last books he published.

Both Laurence and Manfred portray characters who seek a kind of paradise, attempting to find a place of peace and fulfillment. (Frye's notion of a quest for the "peaceable kingdom" seems to fit both writers—Frye 249-50). Both may utilize the formative influence of place and persons in any individual's quest for paradise; but those who find peace find it within themselves, not in any place or any relationship with others. Both writers show characters interacting with the past, either their own remembered past or primordial origins. That such ties exist seems implicit in the work of each writer. Laurence, however, seems to portray individuals involved in a struggle to separate themselves from a past that confines them; Manfred portrays characters who need to establish connections with the past in order to grow toward wholeness. Perhaps this difference stems from the contrast between a United States that formed its identity through a revolutionary process and a Canada that evolved through a long colonial history.

Laurence and Manfred are writers whose art was shaped by their common experience of the Great Plains, yet there are significant differences traceable to their distinctive cultural backgrounds. Ultimately, however, the similarities overshadow the contrasts. Frye concludes his analysis of Canadian literature by asserting that contemporary writers "have begun to write in a world which is post-Canadian, as it is post-American, post-British, and post everything except the world itself" (249). I would not go so far as that. Some differences traceable to national identities still exist. Nonetheless, the similarities are more prominent than the differences. Perhaps this is due to our evolving world-consciousness. More likely, however, it is due to the commonalities of human experience—regardless of one's historical roots or geographic location.

Notes

[1]For discussions of the role of place as well as people in the fictional regions of Laurence and Manfred, see Greta M. K. Coger, "Margaret Laurence's Manawaka: A Canadian Yoknapatawpha," *Critical Approaches to the Fiction of Margaret Laurence*, ed. Colin Nicholson (Vancouver: U of British Columbia P, 1990) 228-46; and Jill Gidmark, "The U-Land in Siouxland: A Minnesotan's View," *Midamerica: The Yearbook of the Society*

for the Study of Midwestern Literature 16 (1989) : 103-14. Nancy Nelson focuses on the role of sacred places in "Sacred Siouxland: Wakan Places in Some Novels by Frederick Manfred," *Heritage of the Great Plains* 28 (Spring, Summer 1995) : 40-51.

[2] Titles by Margaret Laurence referred to or quoted in the text are the following: *The Stone Angel* (SA) (1964. Toronto: McClelland and Stewart-Bantam Ltd., 1978); *A Jest of God* (JG) (1966. Toronto: McClelland and Stewart-Bantam Ltd., 1977): *The Fire-Dwellers* (FD) (1969. Toronto: McClelland and Stewart-Bantam Ltd., 1978): *A Bird in the House* (BH) (1970. Toronto: McClelland and Stewart-Bantam Ltd., 1978); *The Diviners* (D) (1974.. Toronto: McClelland and Stewart-Bantam Ltd., 1975).

[3] The sea and water imagery are especially important in the novels utilizing a Vancouver setting: *The Stone Angel* and *The Fire-Dwellers*. Western directionality receives only minor attention in Laurence's (and other Canadian writers') fiction; the direction of possible frontier beginnings would be north. Stacey (in *The Fire-Dwellers*) thinks of the Cariboo and points north as a possible avenue of escape from the responsibilities that burden and imprison her; she cries when one who has been there reports that he found a family deserted by the wife-mother who could not cope (*FD*, 159). The northern wilderness is no escape.

[4] Clara Thomas makes the point that "'going west' for [Morag] means a long journey through time." As her daughter moves westward geographically, she moves into her past, a journey that involves "the recalling of her former selves and gradually, a recognition and acceptance of their integration into her present self." ("The Wild Garden and the Manawaka World," *Modern Fiction Studies* 22 [Autumn 1976]: 405.) On one level, Stacey conceives of the north in similar temporal terms: she thinks of the Cariboo as a place that "always looks like Diamond Lake [which she visited as a happy teen-ager]. Like, I guess I mean, everything will be just fine when I'm eighteen again" (*FD* 155-56).

[5] See Thomas, "The Wild Garden and the Manawaka World," 401-11.

[6] See Margaret Laurence's comments on the relationship of freedom to survival and growth in Clara Thomas, "A Conversation About Literature: An Interview with Margaret Laurence and Irving Layton," *Journal of Canadian Fiction* 1.1 (Winter 1972) : 67-68.

[7] Mick McAllister has done a superb job of tracing Manfred's handling of these motifs in his paper, "We Sons of Jacob: The Procession to Apocalypse in the Buckskin Man Tales," presented to the Western Literature Association, October 1977.

[8] Titles by Frederick Manfred referred to or quoted in the text are the following (the first five comprise the Buckskin Man Tales, listed in historical sequence of the action) : *Conquering Horse* (CH) (New York: McDowell, Obolensky, 1959): *Lord Grizzly* (LG) (New York: McGraw-Hill., 1954): *Scarlet Plume* (SP) (New York: Trident Press, 1964): *King of Spades* (KS) (New York: Trident Press, 1966): *Riders of Judgment* (RJ) (New York: Random House, 1957): The Golden Bowl (Saint Paul: Webb Pub. Co., 1944): *This is the Year* (TIY) (Garden City: Doubleday, 1947): *Milk of Wolves* (MW) (Boston: Avenue Victor Hugo, 1976): *The Manly-Hearted Woman* (New

York: Crown, 1976): *Green Earth* (New York: Crown, 1977): *Sons of Adam* (New York: Crown, 1980): *Prime Fathers* (Salt Lake City: Howe Bros., 1988); *Of Lizards and Angels* (Norman: U of Oklahoma P, 1992).

[9] See Manfred's comments on "the Old Lizard" or "our primate nature" in *Conversations*, 43-45. For an excellent discussion of this theme in one novel, see Max Westbrook, "*Riders of Judgment:* An Exercise in Ontological Criticism," *Western American Literature* 12 (May 1977) : 41-51.

[10] When Manfred's first child was born, his body responded empathetically by producing milk in a swollen gland. He also used an episode from an Icelandic saga as a source for Juhl's successful nursing of his child. Interview with Frederick Manfred, 2 October 1981.

Works Cited

Frye, Northrup. "Conclusion to a *Literary History of Canada* (1965)." *The Bush Garden: Essays on the Canadian Imagination*. Toronto: House of Anansi Press, 1971. 213-51.

Harrison, Dick. *Unnamed Country: The Struggle for a Canadian Prairie Fiction*. Edmonton: U of Alberta P, 1977.

Jackel, Susan. "The House on the Prairies." *Canadian Literature* 42 (Autumn 1969): 46-54.

Kreisel, Henry. "The Prairie: A State of Mind." *Contexts of Canadian Criticism*. Ed. Eli Mandel. Chicago: U of Chicago P, 1971. 254-66.

Laurence, Margaret. "Sources." *Mosaic* 3.3 (Spring 1970): 80-84.

Manfred, Frederick. *Conversations with Frederick Manfred*. Mod. John R. Milton. Salt Lake City: U of Utah P, 1974.

---. Interview with Frederick Manfred, 2 October 1981.

Roth, Russell. "The Inception of a Saga: Frederick Manfred's 'Buckskin.'" *South Dakota Review* 7 (Winter 1969-70) : 87-99.

Manfred's Use of Language in *Riders of Judgment*

by Karol Brue Aeschlimann

In the Buckskin Man Tales, Frederick Manfred uses language expressively to tell a story about the West and those who have claimed it as their home. In *Riders of Judgment*, the last book in this series, we can examine more closely how this Siouxland storyteller effectively uses the language to weave an engaging tale about frontier Wyoming in the late 1800s.

First of all, Manfred uses the language to express an intuitive knowledge, one that is rather difficult to explain logically. As we examine the lives of the three brothers in *Riders*, we can see more clearly Manfred's view on this kind of intuitive knowledge. Secondly, Manfred employs the use of older stories and myths to suggest a connection to our historical/cultural past. And finally, Manfred ties us to the ancient storytelling tradition with his use of vivid picture-language and language that is pleasing to the ear.

Riders of Judgment centers around the Johnson County War of 1892. Cain, like biblical Cain, is a small homesteader, not a shepherd or a man of the open range. Unlike Cain of the Old Testament though, Cain Hammett does become his brother's keeper by sacrificing his life for the Wyoming small rancher's cause. Cain Hammett's character is based on the historical figure Nate Champion (McAllister 76).

Cain at first appears to fit the stereotypical model of a Western cowboy hero. He wears black, rides a black horse alone in the lush, colorful canyons of the Big Stonies. He is admired for his quick draw and for his integrity. But Manfred doesn't slip into easy stereotypes. His writing does not slide into a nostalgic wish for the good old days, nor does it read as escapist literature. Manfred is a master storyteller who uses detailed geographical and botanical information to describe the Bighorn country of Wyoming. His depiction of cowboy customs and mores, as well as his adherence to the historical fact, is authentic.

Perhaps the most interesting thing Manfred does in his writing is the way he hints at the Old Lizard. Manfred uses the language effectively to "get at" this rather elusive idea. Throughout the years Manfred has come to call his inner voice the Old Lizard (*Duke's*

MANFRED'S USE OF LANGUAGE 125

Mixture 120). The Old Lizard doesn't have much to do with the rational intellect, but has a lot to do with the unconscious, with the anima. This anima, or soul, is not an intellectualized piece of us, but a force beneath our outer selves (Westbrook, "Conservative" 14). It is connected to the universal; its power is generative, not empirical. Jung calls it the collective unconscious; Manfred calls it the Old Lizard.

In *Riders of Judgment* Manfred tells a story which includes references to the Old Lizard. In this particular book, the author calls the Old Lizard the "animal" or the "wolf". Manfred uses these words to create an image for us of that gut-level response to life. If he had tried to intellectualize this concept, he would have failed. The use of the word "animal," however, invites us to understand another way of knowing. For the typically rational American, this type of intuitive knowledge can be a new way of seeing. Manfred leaps the hurdle successfully, I believe, with this appropriate expression.

By examining the three brothers of this novel, we can see how Manfred develops the idea of the Old Lizard. The oldest, Cain, has a keen awareness of the animal within himself. He knows that when his animal signals, it is reliable; "one's own animal seemed to see better," Cain notes (*Riders* 66). Another time, just before the ambush at his cabin, Cain knows the animal "hardly ever missed. It always knew better than he did. Something was wrong" (292). And indeed, we readers know that Cain is in deep trouble. His animal is right!

When this primal energy is set loose, it is powerful, like "a grizzly tormented into one last desperate lunge and bite" (296). This energy comes to Cain when he is in imminent danger, or when he needs to summon a stronger voice to help another, as when Joey falls into the well, or when he "yelled for all he was worth, letting his animal into it" (306), to warn Harry about the cattlemen's ambush.

Cain seems to lose touch with this inner power when he gives into what he calls Rory's "onnatural" desire to avenge Dale's death. Westbrook says that at this point, Cain's "unity of human and animal is gone" ("Riders" 50). During this time, Cain not only rides Lonesome to his death, but he is unable to get Hunt to draw a gun on him. It seems that by not listening more closely to the Old

Lizard, Cain has become cruel and weak, out of touch with his "animal."

Dale, as youngest brother of Cain, really has no tie to his inner voice. Manfred gives no clues why this is so. Perhaps Dale isn't in touch with the Old Lizard because of an inherent weakness, or perhaps his whining, nagging wife drowns it out. Dale is shot in the back by Hunt as he rides home half drunk in a snow storm, crying over the chaotic conditions of Johnson County, over not being able to get Hunt to draw first for a showdown, and over being cut off from sex by his unforgiving wife.

On the other hand, Cain's other brother seems to be in touch with the Old Lizard. Harry is not particularly likable, since we know that he is capable of changing the brands on stolen livestock and that he is responsible for the cold-blooded hanging of an honest neighbor. But Harry is true to his inner voice. He knows that he is a "wild one," and prefers life as a Robin Hood to living tamely as a homesteader. He revels in the drunken fun of riding Old Blue on a bet, of having taken his own brother's wife, and of watching Mitch squirm uneasily at a hangman's joke at Cain's cabin.

It is interesting that Harry is the one who survives – perhaps he is most in tune with his life's source, however disturbing it may be. Three times he survives near-certain death: from hanging, from being ambushed in his sleep at Hidden Country, and, finally, from the cattlemen's ambush on the Shaken Grass. Three brothers, three ways of knowing the Old Lizard – these things we learn as Manfred unravels his story.

A good storyteller often enhances his tale by tapping older, culturally shared stories or myths and using them to give his story other dimensions; Manfred is no different. The allusions catch our attention so that we become more fully involved in the meaning; we wonder where the comparisons will lead. The name Cain, for instance, brings to mind the biblical Cain. But Manfred does not match Cain Hammett exactly to the Old Testament Cain. Neither does Manfred correlate exactly Gramp Hammett's idea of killing all firstborn with the biblical story. Gramp Hammett's brutal words connect us to that old, old story of Abraham and Isaac, but we do not expect Manfred to tell it in exactly the same way.

Another culturally shared reference Manfred uses is taken from the Psalms. When we first hear the plaintive words of Psalm 22, it helps us understand Gram's desire to join her husband in

MANFRED'S USE OF LANGUAGE 127

heaven. The words are haunting. When Dencil is found hanging from the cottonwood tree, these words come to Cain again, and their power commands our attention:

> My God, my God, why hast thou forsaken me? Why are thou so far from helping me, from the words of my roaring? But I am a worm, and no man. I am poured out like water. All my bones are out of joint. My heart is like wax. It is melted in the midst of my bowels. . . . Thou has brought me into the dust of death. (198)

These words now literally describe the condition of Dencil's rotted, mangled, maggot-infested body. As Cain rides away, the words also echo the plight of the entire Bad country. There is chaos and desolation everywhere as small herdsmen cry out for justice. The language of the old Psalm has been used effectively by Manfred in his storytelling.

Perhaps Manfred's strongest use of language is his ability to use words to create concrete images. This is especially apparent in his descriptions of the landscape. He knows the native wildflowers and the trees of the Big Horn country. Manfred isn't satisfied describing the vegetation in the sidedraw along the Crimson Wall with the use of only the word "red," for instance, but he sees the many tints and shades and hues of red when he describes how ". . . the chokecherries hung a ripened deep red, and the wild plums a turning red, and the wild raspberries a maidenlip red" (*Riders* 14). Or as Cain heads toward home, he rides "into the red maw of the Shaken Grass canyon . . . the brook ran red as if with spilled Indian blood, sudsing pink . . . streaming bloody . . . . Red sandstone and molten scarlet scoria glinted in the beaches" (33-34). The words of Manfred create a vivid picture for the reader.

Another poetic quality of Manfred's writing is the alliteration sprinkled throughout the story. The listening pleasure of his story is increased when we hear such phrases as "silver sage," or "magpies threaded through the trees," or "the gummy, gray ground." Even in the gun battle at Cain's cabin, Manfred uses language which has a pleasing sound to the ear: "He was immediately answered by a splintering shattering barrage of flying lead, from the barn, from the bridge, from the low bluff" (297). A good storyteller pays attention to how the language sounds, and Manfred has done that well.

Manfred uses repeated phrases or ideas to help unify the story, and to create a subtle rhythm. One scene which is unified with the use of a repeated simile is the one where Timberline is wounded and is trying to crawl back to the safety of Cain's cabin: "The stricken giant was still crawling slowly . . . leaving a sloughing rut . . . like the trail of a giant slug in mud" (294). This paragraph describing the wounded Timberline outside the cabin is followed by a description of what Cain is doing inside the cabin. Then Manfred shifts back to Timberline "still coming on, inching on, undulating like a wounded caterpillar" (295). Manfred cuts to action inside the cabin again, and then finally back outside to see that Timberline's "trail through the mud looked like someone had dragged a heavy log across the yard" (296). The repetition of differing similes describing what Timberline's trail was like is effective in unifying the scene, in letting the reader see both inside and outside the cabin.

And finally, an example of how Manfred uses a repeated image is one that seems to tie his book together and to suggest the cycle and sacredness of life. Some have come to call the idea that all things are essentially connected as Manfred's "long view" (Nelson 264). Near the beginning of the book as Cain is riding towards home from high in the Big Stonies, he stops with his horse and pack animal to drink from the stream. Manfred paints a peaceful picture of man and beast's connectedness as the horse, donkey, and man each on all fours sip from the clear waters of the mountain stream. Manfred frames this image with an ageless one describing how the pebbles in the bottom of that clear stream had come to be there:

> First wind and frost broke it off; then water washed it downhill. Night and day, while he was awake and while he was asleep, endlessly, the unraveling of the land never let up. Given enough time, the Big Stonies . . .would all someday wash down the Shaken grass into the Bitterness . . .and finally down into the Gulf, all of it drawing after itself until there would be nothing left but sea washing and washing over the whole rough earth. (*Riders* 34)

Manfred has essentially connected man and beast and the land in this scene. He describes the "unraveling" of the land, as it washes back to the primordial sea.

At the end of the book, Manfred uses the word "unraveling" again, but this time in referring to Cain's own "wearing away," his own death. "The terrible feeling that life was slowly unraveling out from under him. . . . Life was falling apart. . . was coming down on him like a sliding rockfall falling down on a man already pinned to earth" (296), suggests that death cannot be stopped, just as the erosion of the earth cannot be stopped; both are part of an ongoing cycle of life. These two passages offer a subtle unity which reflects Manfred's "long view". It seems a fitting way to unify his story, and to hint at the interconnectedness of all life.

Manfred is at heart then a storyteller who has given us a tale about the Johnson County War. He uses the language effectively to explain an intuitive reality, which he calls the Old Lizard. Manfred also effectively uses the language of older stories and myths to add another dimension to his tales of the West. And finally, Manfred is a master storyteller in the poetic tradition; he tells a good story by creating language that is vivid and pleasing to the ear.

Works Cited

Manfred, Frederick. *Riders of Judgment.* Lincoln: U of Nebraska P, 1982.
---. *Duke's Mixture.* Sioux Falls: Center for Western Studies, 1994.
McAllister, Mick. "The First Covenant in *Conquering Horse:* Syncretic Myth in the Buckskin Man Tales." *South Dakota Review* 20 (1982) : 76-88.
Nelson, Nancy Owen. "Frederick Manfred and the Anglo-Saxon Oral Tradition." *Western American Literature* 19 (1985) : 263-274.
Westbrook, Max. "Conservative, Liberal, and Western: Three Modes of American Realism." *South Dakota Review* 4 (1966) ; 3-19.
. "*Riders of Judgment:* an Ontological Criticism." *Western American Literature* 12 (1977) : 41-51.

From Mythic American Visions to a Shattered American Dream: Nature Expropriated in the Buckskin Man Tales

by Sanford E. Marovitz

In the five Buckskin Man Tales of Frederick Manfred, it is difficult to determine the romantic from the realistic, the mythic and legendary from the historical, the epic hero from the tragic antihero. With respect to the chronology of events they cover, this is as true of the last of the five—*Riders of Judgment*—as of the first—*Conquering Horse*. The five novels were published over a period of twelve years in mid-century, between 1954, when *Lord Grizzly* initiated the series, and 1966, when it concluded with *King of Spades*. The three interim novels, in the order of publication, are *Riders of Judgment* (1957), *Conquering Horse* (1959), and *Scarlet Plume* (1964). Like the Leatherstocking series of James Fenimore Cooper, the novels were written out of the chronological order of their settings, but unlike the saga of Natty Bumppo, Manfred's five volumes are not clearly related to each other by the reappearance of a single central figure in each. As Mick McAllister pointed out in his study of myth in *Conquering Horse*, the association among them is recognizable through theme and methodology rather than reappearing characters or common historical events.

Each of the five novels is self-contained, but read as a unit the series constitutes a panorama of the cultural transformation that occurred over much of the Great Plains during a period of approximately ninety years, from the beginning of the nineteenth century to 1892. In order of chronology, *Conquering Horse* opens the series sometime around 1800, probably before the Lewis and Clark expedition of 1804-1806; few whites had yet passed through the area covered, a broad expanse of territory that Manfred himself called Siouxland—that part of the northern Great Plains where the Sioux tribes dwelled—which provides the setting for most of his fiction. Siouxland extends outward, especially westward, from the point where Minnesota, Iowa, South Dakota, and Nebraska meet. Chronologically, the second and most widely read novel of the series is *Lord Grizzly*, set roughly a quarter century later when the early mountain men roamed the wide area stretching west from Siouxland into what is now Wyoming and Montana. The next of the novels in terms of chronology, *Scarlet Plume*, deals with an uprising of the Sioux in Minnesota in 1862; and the one that follows, *King of Spades*, opens at about the same time but centers on the rush for gold in the Black Hills of South Dakota in 1876. The last of the Buckskin Man Tales is *Riders of Judgment*, based on the Johnson County War of 1892 in Wyoming.

What this brief survey of the series connotes in terms of cultural transformation is that between the first novel and the last, the Indians have been pushed from the scene, and the whites have taken over the northern plains from the Mississippi River west through Siouxland and beyond. In representing this extended period of transition, Manfred not only drew from regional geography and history, but he also deepened his narratives with a pattern combined of biblical tales, especially from the Hebrew scriptures, and Greek myths. Though reared in the Christian Reformed Church and educated at Calvin College, Manfred rejected Christian fundamentalism in favor of a more liberal humanistic faith of his own, but he knew the Bible well and remained devoted to it as a source of ethical and spiritual guidance. As for Greek mythology, evidence of Manfred's long-standing interest in the Homeric epics and Classical tragedies is abundant in much of his fiction, including all five of the Buckskin Man Tales.

However, in creating his roman-fleuve of the plains, Manfred penetrated to a still lower layer, to the primal bedrock on which myth was founded, the depths of the universal unconscious where Old Lizard has its lair. When Old Lizard takes over, all restraints collapse, mind and body are no longer under the control of reason or emotion, both of which give way to irrepressible drives. But Old Lizard can be creative as well as destructive, for it drives the artist as it does the lustful, the enraged, the vengeful, and the maddened. Old Lizard gives the Buckskin Man Tales the raw power that pulses in them, but that throbbing force is more often latent than eruptive and predominant. As Emerson controlled Fate by working within its bounds rather than futilely attempting to assert himself over it, so Manfred nourishes his imagination with the facts of history and geography, then melds them with the forms and techniques of the artist and craftsman. Thereby he creates the artful components of his stories that keep Old Lizard at bay until some incident or graphic phrase in the fiction becomes the catalyst that stirs it into action. Then comes the ecstatic joy of existing in an American Eden or, on the other hand, the terror and blood that virtually explode through the pages of the Buckskin Man Tales and transform that dream of paradise into the chaos of nineteenth-century American reality.

I
Conquering Horse

Although Manfred was clearly sympathetic with the Native American culture, his only idealization of it in the Buckskin Man Tales is manifest in the character of *Scarlet Plume*. To be sure, in our own age of environmental awareness, Indian life prior to the twentieth century is often highly romanticized by writers inclined to celebrate the native acceptance of universal wholeness and unity, a central theme in *Conquering Horse*. Among the Indians, individually and tribally, this view constitutes the basis of their attitude toward nature and behavior among themselves; as Nancy Owen Nelson has explained with specific reference to the Sioux, the cultural concept of *wakan*—holy—is central "in all aspects of Sioux culture" (Nelson, "Sacred" 41, 42). Therefore, although Manfred would seem to be romanticizing the Indians in a conventional manner by emphasizing their affinity with nature, he was simply portraying them as he knew them historically to be, that is, as essentially and thoroughly religious. Like Henry David Thoreau a century earlier, Manfred's deep and enduring interest in the plains Indians led to his study of their history and culture; consequently, when he incorporated details of Indian life in his fiction, he made it throb with the vitality of truth, however romantic it may now seem to a largely secularized contemporary readership.

Although *Conquering Horse* is ostensibly an Indian novel, it is subtly universalized with thematic patterns drawn from the Bible and Classical literature. Structured in four sections—"The Torment," "The Vision," "The Chase," and "The Fathers"—it is basically an initiation story in which a young Yankton Sioux brave called No Name seeks the vision through which he may acquire both tribal recognition as an adult and a name appropriate to his new status. Typically American in this respect, he is in quest of his identity. The son of Redbird, chief of the tribe, No Name at seventeen is physically deft and courageous; an older brother he never knew died soon after being rescued from a fall between large rocks among which he and his friends were playing. Although the youth's death may easily be explained as accidental, the Sioux regard it as the result of his taunting the goddesses within the rocks, which are held to be *wakan*. Because No Name is now Redbird's only son, he is to replace his father as tribal chief if he has the vision for which he has long been waiting.

Meanwhile, he tells Redbird, "I walk at random. I wander without purpose" (Milton, 1980, 80). No Name has the attributes of a chief, but he is not perfect. He has seduced Leaf, one of the more desirable young maidens of the tribe, and because she has disappeared, he fears that she has committed suicide over her lost virginity outside of marriage. In taking the young woman as he did, he knows that he has broken the code of *wakan* and fears that his vision will not come because of it, but Redbird assures him that this action, too, is the way of the gods. Later he learns that Leaf has been kidnapped by the Pawnees, who leave her to die buried up to her chin because they discover that she is pregnant when they had initially accepted her as a maiden.

Before long, No Name undergoes a ritualistic preparation and sets off with a companion on a quest for his vision. He travels westward past the Missouri River to the Butte of Thunders, or sacred Thunderbirds, in what is now South Dakota. There, after four days of fasting alone on the large rock formation, the first part of his vision comes to him in the form of a phantom white mare who tells him that he must find and capture a white stallion with a scarlet mane in the land of the Pawnees. She tells him, also, that his father must die and gives him a charm to wear for help in time of need; then she walks off the butte into the air and disappears. With her instruction, No Name returns to his village, fearing that he must be the cause of Redbird's death. He suffers through the sundance ceremony, a test of courage and physical endurance; then he sets forth again, alone this time, in quest of the white stallion.

As No Name travels, he suffers many hardships through which he is aided in seemingly supernatural ways. Shrewdly, Manfred only presents these devices but makes no attempt to explain them; perhaps No Name is hallucinating, or possibly the guides are actually assisting him miraculously. At one point, for example, No Name finds himself in a surreal environment among actual dangers, wild dreams, and bewildering reality. He awakens from a nightmare in which he battles two eagles ravaging a horse and suffers through a terrifying storm. Then he sleeps and awakens amid a "gray, green sea" while overhead the sky is "all one vast continuous gray cover. . . . Whether he stood still, or spun around on a toe, it was all the same" (*CH* 180).

No Name requests assistance from his "Helper" in the charm given him by the white mare, but when none is forthcoming, he perceives guidance from two round, red "sacred stones" that are "about the size of buffalo testicles." Their spoken message to him anticipates the understanding of holistic unity that he will gain from the death of the white stallion and express when he returns to Leaf, whom he soon finds near death and rescues. The stones say: "We are round. We have no beginning and no end. We are related to the sun and the moon because they also are round" (*CH* 182). Their message is one of endless continuity, like the cycle of life and the natural cycles of the year, month, and day. Not only do the stones speak, but they also shift their position "as if pointing in a certain direction" (*CH* 183). "Now I have found the true path," No Name says (*CH* 184). He follows it directly to Leaf's "moon-like head" on the ground (*CH* 187), which astonishes him, for he cannot tell at first if she is dead or alive, ghost or mortal.

On being released from the imprisoning earth and restored to health, Leaf accompanies No Name on his search for the stallion, a horse reminiscent of the legendary "White Steed of the Prairies" about which Charles W. Webber and others—including Melville, in *Moby-Dick*—wrote in the early and mid-nineteenth century.[1] They find the stallion lording over a large herd, and by taking advantage of his consistent pattern of movements each day, they capture him and name him Dancing Sun. Though No Name can mount and ride him, he cannot break the fabulous steed, who finally leaps to his death from a cliff. No Name escapes dying with him only by jumping from the horse's back at the last moment.

Immediately after the stallion falls upon the rocks, No Name hurries down to him. He sings the death song over him and cuts hair from the scarlet mane; after slashing open the belly, he drinks blood from the horse's heart and eats a few slices from it to "bring [their] spirits together." The carcass is left on the rocks, susceptible to reabsorption by the elements, and over it No Name reiterates the central theme of natural unity: "Life is a circle. The power of the world works always in circles. All things try to be round. Life is all one. It begins in one place, it flows for a time, it returns to one place. The earth is all that lasts" (*CH* 286).

The dead stallion leaves a pregnant mare behind; she gives birth to a white colt, which No Name, Leaf, and their infant son bring with them back to the village. Upon their return, the young hero is denominated Conquering Horse, but the remainder of his vision, the death of his father, is yet to be fulfilled. At about this time, however, Conquering Horse sees "all life as one huge flow, with himself a streaming part of it. And being a part of it he felt the whole of it. . . . One part of the flow was exactly like any other part of it. It was all one and the same. Therefore he no longer needed to think about how his father's life would end" (*CH* 340). Although Redbird himself knows that his role in the vision of his son is predestined, he prepares to die fighting. But Wakantanka, great spirit of the Sioux, strikes the chief with a lightning bolt that removes him physically from earth before he can be slain in battle. Understanding what has occurred, Conquering Horse prepares to succeed his father as chief.

In *Conquering Horse* the gods of nature are all-controlling, and the Sioux tender them obeisance through a pattern of ritual and prayer. The Indians in this novel do not dissociate the beauty of nature from its sanctity, nor do they devalue any part of it because all things relate to the whole. No Name's maturation to Conquering Horse results from his identifying with nature and fulfilling his vision through it. His dream is not to own or dominate but to continue the tradition of Redbird and his tribal ancestors. In this novel, Manfred has brilliantly woven facts of social and natural history with mythic patterns from Native American and Euro-Semitic cultures into a poetic story of sensitivity and power.

II
Lord Grizzly

Within twenty-five years, much of the northern Great Plains had begun to evolve from wilderness to frontier as trappers roamed the mountains seeking pelts, and the Army pressed westward behind them. Although many of the plains tribes remained hostile to each other, the deepening incursions of whites into their territories brought them a new enemy to fight, a formidable one with an abundance of firearms, whose "gifts" and demands altered the original native way of life forever. Whereas the tribes were learning to regard the whites as invaders, a foe to stop before all that they held sacred was destroyed, the whites looked upon the Indians from the beginning as impediments that had to be overcome if not by persuasion, then by force.

Lord Grizzly is divided into three sections: "The Wrestle," "The Crawl," and "The Showdown." It opens in early June 1823 along the shore of the Missouri River, north of Ft. Kiowa in what is now south-central South Dakota. The novel is based on an episode in the life of the legendary Hugh Glass, already in his fifties and old for a mountain-man who has to rely on physical prowess and endurance to survive alone in the wild. While hunting apart from his companions—young Jim Bridger and John "Fitz" Fitzgerald, who is closer to Hugh's own age—Hugh is attacked by a female grizzly that he accidentally confronts with her two suckling cubs. Before he can shoot her, the huge bear knocks away his guns and sweeps over him. Though badly mauled, Hugh manages to kill her with his skinning knife before collapsing into unconsciousness. He awakens out from under the carcass of the skinned grizzly with his most severe wounds stanched and sewn, and the bearskin beneath him; his horse and rifle are gone, as are his companions.

Hugh determines to find his way back to Ft. Kiowa despite a broken leg and terrible, festering wounds where the grizzly had gnawed and clawed him. In *Lord Grizzly*, nature—including the Indians—is something to overcome and exploit in the quest for material acquisition and territorial control. But such matters are of little concern to Hugh Glass, an American hero only in the sense of his admirable self-reliance and physical accomplishments but surely not in terms of his values, which are entirely self-serving. Hugh accomplishes his immediate goal of reaching Ft. Kiowa, two hundred miles away, by crawling like a wounded animal, his broken leg dragging on a makeshift travois, over extremely rough terrain with little water and almost no food but roots and berries, insects and rodents as he struggles past the same Thunder Butte where No Name had had his vision a quarter century earlier.[2]

It is illuminating to compare No Name's relation to animal life with Hugh's. No Name gains insight toward maturity by capturing the white steed, then drinking its blood and eating from its heart after the horse has died; through this sacred act, a communion occurs in which the spirits of No Name and Dancing Sun merge. Hugh on the other hand, slays an immense grizzly in self-defense; then he eats the bear's flesh and uses its hairy skin for survival and protection. "Silvertip bearskin thrown over his back, bearhide guards on his elbow points and good knee, dried paws dangling from his neck on a deer sinew, he looked more like a wounded grizzly than a wounded human" (Manfred, *LG* 114). Later, as he crawls toward the Moreau River, he sees wolves feeding on the carcass of a bull calf, surrounded by coyotes and buzzards awaiting their turn. Nearly starved himself, he cries "Meat" and drives the animals away: "With a roar and a rush, silvertip grizzly bearskin lifting a little from the speed of his rush, dried grizzly paws bangling from his neck, . . . Hugh charged through the ring of coyotes and into the boiling mass of snarling white wolves. 'Whaugh!' he roared." "With bared teeth and clawing fingers, Hugh tore at the raw red partly mutilated flesh. . ." (*LG* 147). Afterward, as he moves away from Thunder Butte, "What amazed him was the way his body had taken to going on all fours like any four-legged creature of the wild. . . . It gave Hugh a peculiar insight into how the four-legged animals felt as four-legged beings" (*LG* 164). After his hair turns white from his travail, Bending Reed, his Sioux wife, calls him "Chief White Grizzly," a name he retains (but without "Chief") even among the Arikarees (*LG* 83, 230-41). Whereas No Name advances toward adulthood, Hugh reverts to bestiality, though he retains his human cunning.

Moreover, for No Name, the white stallion is wakan, but for the more pragmatic Hugh a living bear is danger and a dead one his source of protection. Earlier, however, when the mountain men talk of "the lonely grizzly bear" as "the lord of the American wild," Major Henry advises them that some Indians consider the great bear as "some sort of god" and treat it accordingly (*LG* 70, 73). Clearly, he has deeper respect for the spiritual element of nature than does Hugh, a shrewd observer of surfaces but one who cannot penetrate them. He acknowledges this himself when he thinks: "What this child don't see he don't know" (*LG* 249). To this extent, he is a child, indeed. His imperceptiveness in this respect becomes evident when he turns back toward Ft. Kiowa, seeking Fitz after his showdown with Jim near the Yellowstone River. On his way east along the White River he passes through the ghostly moonlit

Badlands, where he experiences a series of weird illusions that seem to evoke a spiritual cleansing. It, too, proves illusory, however, when Hugh senses another grizzly silently following him early one morning soon afterwards, perhaps a phantom; the silver shape stops when he stops and advances as Hugh does. Uncertain what to make of this creature, Hugh decides to kill it, but the bear hides and finally eludes him.

This decision to slay what he cannot control is typical of Hugh as Manfred portrayed him. One of the epigraphs to *Lord Grizzly* is a passage from D. H. Lawrence's *Studies in Classic American Literature* that describes the "dark, passionate nature" of "animals and savages" that Manfred often identified as "Old Lizard," a primal drive in man and beast. He might well have chosen another passage from Lawrence's text, one that depicts Cooper's Leatherstocking as "a man with a gun. He is a killer, a slayer" (Lawrence 69). Surely, this characterization is equally apt for Hugh Glass amid a herd of bison before his wrestle with the grizzly: "Hugh forgot himself, forgot he had a game leg, forgot he'd ever loved, forgot he'd ever killed Rees or any other kind of red devil, forgot he'd ever been a buccaneer killing Spanish merchantmen, forgot he was the papa of two boys back in Lancaster, forgot he'd ever deserted the boys because of their rip of a mother, forgot all, forgot he was Hugh even, . . . was lost in the glorious roaring chase, killing killing killing—all of it a glorious bloodletting and a complete forgetting" (*LG* 60). Here is a picture of Hugh killing not for money, land, or self-protection, but for the sheer joy of slaughter, and however he may feel at the end of the novel about his desertion of his family or the desertion of him by his companyeros, Manfred offers no clues to suggest that Hugh's predilection toward killing is ever remedied. Nothing in *Conquering Horse* is comparable.

With the assumed desertion of Jim and Fitz, all of Hugh's thoughts are on vengeance from that time forward, for he has convinced himself that he is as an agent of the Lord, chosen by Him to punish those who left him to die alone in the wilderness. To buttress Hugh's self-image as "one chosen," Manfred draws heavily upon the Hebrew scriptures. Hugh sees himself as a hairy Esau, "a cunning hunter, a man of the field" (Genesis 25:27). Esau was the first-born of Isaac and elder brother of Jacob, the Hebrew patriarch whom Hugh initially dismisses as alien to himself because he sees in Jacob's domesticity more of Rebekah, mother of the two brothers, than their strong father.

On reaching Ft. Kiowa and spending enough time there to regain his strength and health, Hugh sets forth again to find his erstwhile companyeros. Following their trail, he captures a mare that stands out among a herd led by a splendid stallion. When he notices her laden with milk, he reasons that she has foaled a male colt and that the stallion has "killed it as a rival" (*LG*, 201), an explanation that underscores the crucial desertion theme in Lord Grizzly, echoes the father-son rivalry in *Conquering Horse*, and foreshadows a central motif in both *King of Spades* and *Riders of Judgment*. By killing its own male offspring, the stallion rids himself of it, as by desertion a human expunges all responsibility for the deserted. In *Lord Grizzly*, not only does Hugh believe that Jim and Fitz have cut him off in this way, but he is fully cognizant of his own guilt as a deserter because many years earlier under the pressure of family obligations, he left behind in the East an old "rip" of a wife with their two children.[3] Desertion is central in the novel, then, because his own cowardice with respect to his wife and sons persistently throbs in his conscience, while his yearning for revenge against those he believes deserted him becomes a compulsion.

By the time of his showdowns first with Jim, then Fitz, Hugh has been pressed by consultation and example to forgive them—as Esau forgave Jacob—especially for an ethical trespass that they did not really commit because both men had watched over the presumably dying Hugh for several days until an Indian attack was imminent; then they had to flee or lose their own lives. Moreover, Hugh's constant recollections of his failure as a husband and father makes it clear that the essential showdown for which section three of the novel is named refers to the one he must have with himself. In Joseph M. Flora's view, Hugh fled west from his family "to escape the responsibilities of parenthood," and the "father-son relationship is at the heart of the novel" (Flora 31) His coming to terms with himself over his guilt, then, together with the horrifying accounts of other men who suffered through ordeals at least as bad as his own, lead him at last to accept the apologies and explanations of his companyeros and forgive them.

Although Hugh is no seer and has little insight into nature beyond what he needs to survive, Manfred inexplicably gave him the ability to anticipate what lies ahead for Siouxland in the decades to come. During his crawl south from Thunder Butte, he foresees that "the plains country was surely coming to a time when all of it would someday become settled too, just as the wild coasts of the Atlantic had at last become the States. . . . It was bound to come. It made Hugh sad to think on it, all the she-rips and their cubs coming in and destroying a hunter's paradise" (*LG* 161). Of course, for Hugh this is a melancholy thought, indeed, because to him "a hunter's paradise" is an arena of joyful slaughter.

III
Scarlet Plume

The Civil War was in progress in mid-August 1862 when Little Crow's hungry Santee Dakota Sioux rampaged against the white settlers in southern Minnesota, about a month before the battle of Antietam; it was "the largest Indian uprising in American history" (Huseboe viii) The Santees had signed treaties assuring them of food if they kept the peace, but the agent, Andrew Myrick, reneged because the money to pay for it had not come; allegedly it had been directed instead to support the Union war effort. Plenty of food was stored in the agency warehouse, but when asked what the Indians could do to assuage their hunger if it was not made available to them, Myrick said, "As far as I am concerned, if they are hungry, let them eat grass or their own dung."[4] A few days later when the Sioux attacked, he was slain and his mouth stuffed with grass (Brown 45). Manfred incorporated this and other facts from the uprising in Scarlet Plume, including the violent harassment of the captive Sioux by a group of infuriated women as the Indians were prepared for execution. Also, the figure of Scarlet Plume himself seems to be at least partially based on Chief Big Eagle, who did not participate in the initial attack. Ultimately, Little Crow's rebellion led to the death of over a thousand settlers, including women and children, many of whom were brutally tortured.

Evidence in all the Buckskin Man Tales testifies to Manfred's extensive reading of materials related to Great Plains history, including the tribal cultures and stages of white advancement that led to the transformation of wilderness into frontier and of that into modern civilization. Robert C. Wright has noted how closely he followed detailed reports on the Little Crow massacre, the central love relation of the historical red hero and white heroine, and the execution of the Sioux, "the largest single mass execution in the history of the United States" (75) But Manfred is principally a novelist, not a historian (qtd. in Milton 1974, 130), and in *Scarlet Plume*, his idealization of the eponymous hero emphatically overrides the grim, not to say shocking, description of torture and mayhem that illustrate the bitter side of our American past—with no racial exclusions. However, he does carefully distinguish between two major sub-tribes of Dakota Sioux, the Santees, led by Pounce and the renegade Mad Bear, who attack the settlement, and the Yanktons, headed by Whitebone with the counsel of his nephew, Scarlet Plume, a visionary and respected warrior of the same tribal heritage as Redbird and No Name in *Conquering Horse* two or perhaps three generations later.

Scarlet Plume is based on seemingly irresolvable contrasts between Indians and whites that generate searing heat and erupt in violent conflict. Lesser contrasts exist within both groups, but internal violence, though present, is limited despite what appear to be unbridgeable differences among the tribesmen and the settlers. The novel opens in a time of tenuous peace between the Sioux and a small missionary settlement in southern Minnesota a little south of Ft. Ridgely, but ominous conflicts are almost immediately apparent in the white community, and these both foreshadow and complement the chaos soon to occur. Disgusted with her spineless husband's drinking and sexual perversity, Judith Raveling persuades him to join the Union Army; soon thereafter she travels west from her home in St. Paul with her ten-year-old daughter, Angela, to visit her sister and family at the missionary community of Skywater. Judith had wanted a change, but she is edgy in Skywater because of the Indian encampments nearby, and she is less trusting than the settlers that the Sioux there have truly committed themselves to following the Christian gospel. Her uneasiness increases as she listens to steady drumbeats from the surrounding hills. When Scarlet Plume comes to the door and silently hands her a dead swan with a broken neck, she finds her disquiet justified in learning that his gift is a sign that the whites must flee or die. A breathless rider then stops and tells her that a settler has been slain and scalped.

As Judith runs to find her daughter and warn the other settlers, she is confronted by appalling scenes that reveal the shallow effects of Christian teaching even among those allegedly attempting to carry the Word among the Indians. First, she is shaken when she sees a settler skinning alive a trussed timber wolf on a "crude cross" (*SP* 14) while the tormented animal screams; he is torturing rather than killing the wolf directly because it had eaten two calves, as nature, of course, had guided it to do. Judith dashes to another house, where she watches in horror as a farmer and his wife chase each other in circles, he with a pitchfork and she with a heavy whip, yelling and cursing one another as they run. Not long afterward, when the Santees attack in full force, the savagery of their actions during the ensuing massacre has been anticipated by the bloodthirsty behavior of the whites among themselves for several of whom Christianity is but a facade and a justification for gaining control of the Indians and their land.

By the time the slaughter has ended, the outspoken agent, having expressed himself as Myrick did in history, is dead and mutilated with grass likewise stuffed in his mouth; Judith has been raped by Mad Bear, and Angela barbarously violated and slain. Before Mad Bear can take Judith captive, however, Whitebone, Scarlet Plume, and their Yankton tribesmen with bows drawn confront him and drive him off, keeping the women under their protection. During her long captivity Judith learns to appreciate the value of the Indian way of life, which is based on integration with nature in contrast to that of the whites, which is fundamentally exploitative. Through being forced into becoming a working member of the Yankton tribe, she comes to respect their culture and admire it, but even during the gradual course of this transformation of values, she longs to escape and return to her own kind in St. Paul. Finally, she does flee the camp under Plume's unobserved protection and with Whitebone's tacit consent. As Judith struggles to find her way home, Scarlet Plume makes his presence known, and the admiration she has developed for this heroic red plainsman evolves into love with a craving for physical union. For a time they live a paradisaical existence as if man and wife while slowly moving north toward Fort Ridgely, a trip she no longer wishes to make.

In terms of ethics and morals, the pagan Scarlet Plume is one of the most Christian figures in the novel along with Judith's missionary sister and brother-in-law, both of whom are slain. Scarlet

Plume, however, adheres devotedly to his own native faith, the same as that of Redbird and No Name before him. At once a sage and saint as well as a noble warrior, hunter, and lover, he is perspicacious enough to foresee by way of a holy vision the final conquest of his people by the whites. He willingly accommodates the teachings of Christianity and ultimately sacrifices himself for the sake of Judith, whom he loves and who loves him, because he is certain that the blood of red people and whites cannot run in the same veins: "My heart does not run with white blood," he tells her. "Nor does your heart run with red blood. The two can never beat as one" (*SP* 301). Here Manfred is clearly echoing D. H. Lawrence on Cooper's Leatherstocking Tales (Lawrence 61).

Scarlet Plume "remind[s] Judith of a Christ riding impassively to his fate," though it makes her "grimace to think that she could compare her red friend to Christ" (*SP* 349). Yet the comparison is apt, for she has learned that unlike her own selfish, grasping society, the Yanktons are a giving people; she is moved when Plume expresses a tribal code that would not be out of place adapted into the Christian scriptures:

> The white man makes his poor work for him. The poor must give him much gold to live in the houses he owns. That is not the way of the red man. When the red man returns from a raid with many horses, he gives them away and keeps only the poorest for himself. The more he gives away, the greater he becomes. (*SP* 301)

Scarlet Plume's words reinforce her love for him and arouse her passion, but committed to his vision of racial separateness, he rejects all possibility of further love-making and insists on hastening to return her to the white community despite her strong desire to remain with him and live as an Indian; his love for her cannot transcend his spiritual bond with his own people. Having had his vision, he accepts his role as a sacrificial agent of destiny, making no effort to defend himself against false charges when the time comes, determined only to restore Judith to her own white world.

Scarlet Plume is certain that in returning her to the whites he is subjecting himself not only to capture but to execution for his presumed role in the Sioux uprising. Judith is told by a missionary, "He has taken a fatalistic attitude toward it all. He believes it is fated that he should die at this time" (*SP* 361). Regardless of her insistence on his innocence, Scarlet Plume is jailed and sentenced to be hanged. On the way to the gallows, a German woman with a long butcher knife attacks the bound prisoners and slices off Plume's phallus, holding it high as a trophy before throwing it on the ground. The entire concluding episode of the novel closes the frame of deception, cruelty, violence, and death that opened it but with a racial reversal of assaulters and victims. The injustice intensifies Judith's resolve to leave her husband and white society for good and dwell for the remainder of her life as a Yankton with Whitebone's tribe among whom she will rear the child of Scarlet Plume she carries in her womb.

Although Scarlet Plume is the heroic center of the novel, the narrative point of view throughout is Judith's. Joseph M. Flora suggests that she is a more highly conscious observer of everything around her than an emotionally engaged woman: "Judith is never convincing as a mother in grief; she too soon views the Yanktons with a kind of emotional detachment" (Flora 33). Under the pressure of circumstances, however, hers may be a natural reaction as the best and only way to survive among a group of Sioux she still regards as savages, a culture then altogether untrustworthy and foreign to her. After time, she learns differently, of course, though one feels that the memory of little Angela—alive and lovely, ravaged and dead—remains very much with her, as is evident when she and Scarlet Plume pass through the destroyed settlement on their way back to the fort. She sees the scaffold he had built for her daughter's body and cries anew over this heathen treatment of Angela's remains. According to Arthur R. Huseboe, Judith "is Manfred's most fully realized woman character" (xi), a sound assessment in my view as well.

Scarlet Plume makes a strong case for Indian values and an equally severe one against most aspects of the white American culture of the time, from Christianity to exploitation and persecution. It is not the Christian faith in itself that Manfred faults any more than it was Melville's nearly a hundred and twenty years earlier in *Typee* and *Omoo*, but the hypocritical use of it to satisfy personal and material ends. Clearly, Manfred did not intend to provide a balanced view of sins and virtues among Indians and whites but to idealize elements of native existence through a red hero in whom the true Christian spirit is merged with that of nature, resulting in a humanistic ethic common to both. Unfortunately and one hopes wrongly—because the same ethic was largely in accord with his own way of thinking—Manfred implies that such an ethic cannot exist in exploitative white America as it can among the Sioux. Torn apart in 1862 over slavery and related economic issues, the United States was in turmoil because the moral structure and ideals on which the republic was founded less than a century before had lost their hold as ethical guidelines, and popular sovereignty had become a corruptive, divisive force instead of a benign, unifying one. The greed that fostered the War Between the States also increased malign treatment of the Indians, and that, in turn, resulted in the underlying truths of *Scarlet Plume*.

IV
King of Spades

The child fathered by Scarlet Plume and borne by Judith after she runs from Fort Ridgely to renew her life among the Sioux is brought to life as Erden Aldridge, an adolescent wild girl in *King of Spades*. Erden's white skin has been darkened by the sun, and as Blue Swallow she is dwelling alone in the Indian lands of the Black Hills when gold is discovered there by illegal prospectors. The implicit thematic and mythic connections with Scarlet Plume suffice to bridge the two novels (McAllister 31).

The satirical style and tone of *King of Spades* distinguish it strikingly from the other four novels in the series, but thematically the relation among them is clear. Moreover, the satirical mode in itself connotes ironic humor, and although comical incidents and phrasing are occasionally evident elsewhere in the *Tales*, chiefly in *Lord Grizzly*, *King of Spades* is the only volume of the five in which such humor predominates over a more conventional form of narrative development. The irony has a distancing effect that impedes direct engagement with the characters and events because these are necessarily regarded by readers and author alike as less indicative than representative, and the representation occurs on at least two primary levels—what is verbally signified and what is meant by it.

As Mick McAllister has observed, Manfred uses abundant animal symbolism in the Buckskin Man Tales; although he focuses on the bear and the wolf in *Lord Grizzly* and *Scarlet Plume* (31), other animals also carry symbolic weight, including the horse in *Conquering Horse*, the deer and panther in *Scarlet Plume*. However, these creatures are employed to represent mythic aspects of the deep unknown buried within the unconscious and exposed only symbolically outside of it, whereas the flat, stereotypical characters and site descriptions in *King of Spades* initially seem more specifically emblematic, suggesting such one-to-one associations as that of Earl Ransom with Oedipus and the meditative Hamlet. The plot is pure fantasy, the characters intentional stereotypes, and much of the narrative as a whole a parody of conventional horse-opera (see Flora 35-38). Yet Max Westbrook has perceptively examined the novel as a "*historical-rume*, the tale of realistic and individualist passions caught in primal currents of doom" (Westbrook viii).

Joseph M. Flora highlights the consciously literary reflections in *King of Spades*, all of which add to the depth and variety of its ironic connotations and relationships that deal basically with the escapades of Earl Ransom, erstwhile Alan Rodney King, who has no memory of his childhood in Des Moines with his British-born parents. His aristocratic mother, Katherine, is disinherited when, still in her early teens, she weds the lowborn Magnus King; they then immigrate to the Midwest, where he is educated to become a doctor. Roddy's botched Caesarean birth, executed by his inexperienced father, leaves young Katherine with a large abdominal scar and an inability to bear another child. As a boy, Roddy develops what Magnus believes is an unnaturally intimate relation with his mother; over the years, Magnus is increasingly troubled over this to the extent that he finally becomes so distrustful, jealous, and enraged that he shoots Katherine in front of Roddy, who in turn blasts his father with a shotgun and flees.

About ten years after this violent confrontation, Roddy reappears as Earl Ransom, an amnesiac in his mid-twenties, naive but handy with a six-shooter. He and a paternalistic crony are sometime prospectors approaching Cheyenne on horseback. Soon after entering the town, he kills a bully who has shot his partner in the barroom of a brothel. With the help of Kate, the young-looking madame who owns the place, he escapes and shortly becomes her lover, not yet realizing that she is the mother he cannot remember. After living with her for a while he learns of a gold strike in the

Black Hills and leaves to be among the first to stake a claim there, promising Kate that he will call for her. Although the Black Hills are still Sioux lands by treaty, neither he nor the horde of prospectors who follow him are daunted by this, for they rightly assume that the government will soon open the territory to them anyway, treaties or not.

Climbing into the hills, Ransom unwittingly wanders over the "mysterious" lair of Old Lizard. Among the forbidding granite shapes he sees is a ridge that "resembled an enormous sleeping lizard half-buried in mud" (*KS* 145). Momentarily, he distinguishes animal carvings in a red rock wall, one of which depicts a twelve-foot long reptile "with a terrifyingly long tongue," and descending into a gulch nearby, he notices "several holes resembling the raw broken mouths of lizards dug into the sides." With the symbolic appearance of Old Lizard, Ransom is open to primal experience, which comes to him two nights later after he finds flakes of gold and stakes a claim in the area. At midnight he awakens to see Erden Aldridge looking down at him, her hair braided Sioux-style, her eyes glossy black, and her skin dark but not dusky enough to be that of an Indian.

Ransom is charmed, then aroused: "He trembled to ravish her" (*KS* 158), which he does almost immediately as Old Lizard gains control, and the young virgin succumbs to his passionate advances. As they live blissfully together in a hidden cave through the winter, Erden shows Ransom a secret lode of pure gold and teaches him how to exist in relation to the land, as Scarlet Plume had taught Judith. With the coming of spring, an invasion of prospectors and miners occurs when the region is opened to them; they quickly create a primitive community and call it Deadwood. The proximity of these outsiders reawakens Ransom's desire for wealth, and as he works his claim, Deadwood rapidly grows into a town. Pregnant with his child, Erden disappears into the wilds, and Kate shows up some time later in a handsome coach to replace her. She has purchased a fine house in town, and again Ransom moves in with her, enjoying the luxury of fashionable clothes and a comfortable home, though his mind often turns to memories of his idyllic natural life with Erden. He is also tormented inside because he feels that something indefinable is wrong. He becomes hostile and irritable with Kate, then in a Deadwood saloon challenges another gun-slinging braggart, claiming to have a King of Spades in the hole; to this, the gunman, believing that Kate is Ransom's wife, responds that she is "the whore of hearts . . . old enough to be your mother" (*KS* 254). Ransom dispatches him with one quick shot; then on returning home, he argues again with Kate and kills her, too. Magnus had shot out one of her mismatched eyes, and Ransom shoots out the other. In the Deadwood trial that follows, Magnus reappears, searching for his lost son; Roddy had not slain his father after all. The ensuing dialogue reveals the truth of Ransom's identity. Learning that the woman he had lived with and murdered was his own mother, Ransom hangs himself instead of waiting for the court's verdict and leaves the missing Erden to be, in Magnus' closing words, "the perfect mother. A white girl Indian-raised" (*KS* 304).

It may easily be seen from this quick overview that the plot and characters of this novel are on one level pure fantasy; stylistically, it is closer to *Candide* than to the other four volumes in the series. However, as Joseph M. Flora has suggested, "Though Manfred wrote *King of Spades* with apparent zest and pleasure, the novel also has a serious part to play in the Buckskin Man scheme" (Flora 38). In addition to its mythic significance on another level, it represents the degradation of American promise through Ransom's rejection of the innocent Erden in favor of a debased Kate, mother and lover, madame in a brothel of her own, and preserver of the failed social schemes of Europe. From the latter perspective, the "nationhood" (Wright 85) and Oedipus themes combined suggest a young America's turning incestuously to the indurated roots of a dying past instead of blossoming afresh in the E[r]denic New World of possibility.

V
Riders of Judgment

By 1891 in Wyoming, the setting for the opening of *Riders of Judgment*, the "hunter's paradise" exists no longer; the Indians have lost their sovereignty over the land, the animals at issue are livestock, and nature has largely been domesticated, except in the hearts and psyches of the Hammett family and their foes. To be sure, although the land has been settled to the extent that Wyoming achieved statehood during the previous year, to Cain Hammett riding through a narrow canyon, the region around him looked like "paradise itself" (*RJ* 35) with the red rock walls looming over a creek lined with bright green vegetation and harmonizing with the purple slopes of the distant mountains.

But this lyrical description conveys only the appearance of paradise. Having murdered a man, Cain is hardly the person to find himself in Eden. In fact, his world constitutes a corrupted paradise; moments before taking in the beauty of the landscape, he notices in the distant sagebrush what appears to be a gray wolf. Immediately, he lifts his Winchester from its scabbard to fire at the creature as soon as it moves, but no movement comes, and upon looking more closely, Cain sees that he has been deceived, for the grayness is only "a dying clump of greasewood. . . . Too bad. He had felt like shooting" (*RJ* 34). Like Hugh Glass, Cain is ready to kill for the pleasure of killing.

Chronologically the last of the Buckskin Man Tales, Riders of Judgment is a fictionalized account of the Johnson County cattle war between the large stock holders and the homesteaders they were attempting to push out. The character of Cain Hammett is based on the historical Nate Champion, leader of the "Red Sash Gang," who died in April 1892, as Cain does, while defending the out-gunned settlers. The historical aspect of the novel is authentic. Before writing it, Manfred had spoken at length with cousins of Nate Champion, who provided him with many details of the cattle war while he surreptitiously took notes. He had become interested in the war while reading a contemporary account of it in Asa Shinn Mercer's *Banditti of the Plains, or The Cattlemen's Invasion of Wyoming in 1892 [The Crowning Infamy of the Ages]*, published in 1894. "That book is based more on reality than people know," Manfred said of *Riders of Judgment*, and Robert C. Wright has confirmed that "most of the characters have been based on real people and most of the events based on historical fact" (Milton 1974, 124; Wright 67). Among these actual figures were Cattle Kate and Jim Averill, who become Cattle Queen, or Queenie, and Avery in Manfred's novel, and their lynching occurred in history much as it does in the story.

The novel dramatically illustrates the American Dream turned nightmare. As paradise has been corrupted, so has the vision that drew eager young settlers to Wyoming's public lands to establish for themselves the mode of life that St. Jean de Crèvecoeur had described a century earlier in the third of his *Letters from an American Farmer* (1782). But the large cattle barons, unwilling to share the public range, tried to stymie the settlers' attempt to solidify their small land holdings. When persuasion, political influence, and contrived law did not work, the Wyoming Cattle Holders Association hired gunmen from Texas to drive the homesteaders out. By then Nate Champion and his Red Sash Gang had stepped in to help. As Manfred accurately depicted the war, although Champion was killed, the invading gunmen were arrested, and his cause was saved.

Priscilla Oaks has observed that Manfred took history and "molded the facts into a form of his own making"(v). The name Cain alone suggests that *Riders of Judgment* methodologically resembles the first two Buckskin Man novels discussed above, for it, too, combines history with myth. Whereas the mythic components of *Conquering Horse* and *Lord Grizzly* accentuate and complement the themes, however, in this final novel they become determinative, and Native American mythology has given way to Greek and biblical sources that underlie the history and give it a deeper level of truth. Like No Name, Cain is also seeking an identity, but for him it is not a matter of maturation; he is no seventeen-year-old on the path toward initiation. Also resembling Hamlet, whose name closely corresponds with his own, Cain Hammett tends to speculate upon matters that tie him as an individual to a world eroding under the inevitable effects of time: "endlessly, the unraveling of the land never let up"; eventually, all would be washed away into the sea till only the sea remained to wash over the entire earth. "It was enough to make a man shiver and think on God [or] even the Devil. . . . What was he?," Cain wondered. "Who was Cain Hammett?" (*RJ* 33, 34). The same pounding questions drives the Oedipal Roddy King, alias Earl Ransom in King of Spades, to suicide on the gallows after learning the answer.

When *Riders of Judgment* opens, Cain is "riding down through a cloud" high above the timberline in the Big Stonies. He is dressed entirely in black astride a black horse called Lonesome; wearing a black cartridge belt and holster nestling a Colt .45, he appears to be one of those "Riders of Judgment come down from the sky" mentioned in the first line of his favorite song (*RJ* 9). One can hardly imagine a more dramatic entrance for the hero of a western romance, especially—as told in the Hebrew scriptures—one who

FROM MYTHIC AMERICAN VISIONS 151

bears the name of the world's first killer. Riding alone, he descends along a trail that takes him through a glorious landscape, an idyllic open space "almost too good for grazing." Cain has often looked across this countryside as he does now, and each time he sees it "as a wonder again" (*RJ* 3, 5). His response to the natural beauty around him already suggests that Cain is more sensitive and profound than an ordinary cowman with a gun, but any doubt over his effectiveness with a weapon is soon assuaged when he unexpectedly confronts two men working for one of the largest cattle barons, an Englishman named Peter Caudle. The meeting is threatening, but it is immediately apparent that Cain can handle himself well, and the two men, Jesse Jacklin and Mitch Slaughter, Caudle's general manager and foreman respectively, are aware of it, too. Jesse invites Cain to work for Caudle and the large cattle holders, an offer that Cain immediately rejects. They are about to go their separate ways when Mitch wisecracks about Rory, the wife of Cain's brother Dale, and Cain lashes him across the face with his quirt, but Mitch does nothing more than glare at him with hate. He knows that Cain's gun is faster than his own.

Hence the stage is set for the moral tragedy to follow, but the psycho-mythic theme is still undeclared. *Riders of Judgment* is a complex novel in which the historical narrative serves only as a vehicle, though it provides the story that generates the excitement. Cain is the oldest of three brothers, all erotically attracted to their cousin, Rory—Rosemary—who was reared with them, and although she seems to have had affairs with Cain and his younger, wilder brother, Harry, whom he rescues from a hanging, she has married Dale, the youngest and weakest of the three. Their principal opponent in the tragedy is Link Keeler, alias Hunt Lawton, who has slain their grandfather and father, and is now gunning for them in the employ of the cattle owners.

Once more, the motivation is vengeance. Many years before, when Link was a child, Grandpa Hammett, his neighbor, advised the boy's father that first sons are nothing but trouble, and the best way to avoid it is to kill them. Link's father tried and failed, but Link's life has been dedicated to vengeance against all the Hammetts from that time forward. This recalls No Name's vision that he believes requires him to slay Redbird, his father; it echoes the assumption of Hugh Glass that the male foal of his mare was killed by the leading stallion of the herd to eliminate future competition for mates; and it follows Roddy King's attempt to kill Magnus. Mythologically, it builds on the stories of the Greek Cronus, the Titan who devours his own sons to avert possible threats to his rule; of Oedipus, who unwittingly slays his father and marries his mother, a myth that Manfred also employs to heighten the incest theme here as he does in King of Spades, and of the murderous curse extending through the house of Atreus.

The father-son opposition in much of Manfred's fiction may have an autobiographical source, for the death of his own mother when he was but seventeen was a severe blow for him, and he deeply resented the remarriage of his father that soon followed.[5] Cain's persistent vacillation over killing Link when he has the opportunity also tightens his association with the pensive Hamlet, who similarly delays over killing Claudius, and it leads to increasing bitterness among the members of his family, especially Rory. In a sense, Cain's moral strength is also his weakness, and in terms of the tragedy, his death is inevitable; for him, there is no other way out, but at least it makes a hero of him to the settlers, whose homesteads and economic lives he helps to save as he keeps their dream alive.

Nonetheless, on his way toward becoming a tragic hero, or perhaps anti-hero, trapped in a burning cabin and surrounded by the armed invaders, Cain falls into the same pattern as Hugh Glass after his mauling by the grizzly—he reverts to a bestial level as the primal "Old Lizard" assumes control. Like "a grizzly tormented into one last desperate lunge and bite, his animal came up and rose terrible in the back of his head, rampant" (*RJ* 341). Here is Tennyson's "nature red in tooth and claw" emerging to dominate Cain's sensitive, moral consciousness. Although the odds are greatly against him, he struggles to survive, but he is shot and killed running from the cabin toward safety. During his burial, a puff of vapor flies from his coffin "and vanishe[s] against the clouds over the Big Stonies" (*RJ* 368), which closes a kind of frame for the novel, for as Cain rides down through the clouds at the beginning, so he returns to them at the end.

* * * * *

The Buckskin Man Tales of Frederick Manfred are a remarkable performance. To a large extent, the major themes of all five novels are interlaced, though each of the tales has its own distinctions and merits. As a unit, they recount the metamorphosis of the West—of all North America—as it was transformed from a relatively primitive natural culture governed by a native ethos of myth into a relatively civilized unnatural culture guided chiefly by a written code of law. In the process, a noble way of life was lost, and the dream evolving from it, one that may yet be realized if Americans emerge from the pit of self-indulgence and moral lethargy, has been persistently darkened and forestalled by individual greed, perversity, corruption, and violence. This blight can be overcome but not without much pain and self-sacrifice, as the Buckskin Man Tales illustrate time and again. Here, then, is Fred Manfred's legacy, one that will remain a viable promise for which he would surely have wished to be remembered.

Notes

[1] See J. Frank Dobie, *The Mustangs* (Boston: Little, Brown, 1952) 143-70.

[2] For the sake of experience and authenticity, Manfred had walked at length over the same terrain; he forced himself to eat insects and small animals as Glass does, and he crawled over his own land using a travois, which he call a *slape*, to drag his own leg as Hugh does his broken one. He also climbed Thunder Butte but used the information he gained not in *Lord Grizzly* but in *Conquering Horse* (Milton, *Conversations* 70-71 and 70 n.4).

[3] Manfred possibly had Washington Irving's Rip Van Winkle in mind when he described Hugh's incorrigibility as a husband and father, and Mabel's shrewishness as his wife, but that is as far as the comparison with Irving's tale may be taken.

[4] Brown 40. Surprising historical and literary parallels are evident here. Joseph François Foullon, Minister of the household of Louis XVI in 1789, was almost universally detested in France for his wealth and callous indifference to the sufferings of the poor, exemplified in his possibly apocryphal response when reminded of their hunger: "If the people cannot get bread, let them eat hay." Carlyle referred to this statement in *The French Revolution*, and Dickens adapted it in chapter 22 of *A Tale of Two Cities* (1859); he dropped one "l" from Foullon's name and changed *hay* to *grass*. In the novel, revolutionaries capture Foullon, carry him to Paris, and hang him after stuffing grass into his mouth. When they jam his head on a pike, the grass is still there. Is it possible that Agent Myrick had read Dickens' novel three years after publication and quoted Foullon, only to suffer the same fate a few days later? I am most grateful to my wife, Nora, for reminding me of this incident in *A Tale of Two Cities*.

[5]Richard C. Wright, "Frederick Manfred," *A Literary History of the American West* (Fort Worth: Texas Christian U P, 1987); see p. 799 for Manfred's use of the archetypal mythos of Cronus and Oedipus, and p. 794 for Manfred's reaction to the early death of his mother and his father's short waiting period before remarriage.

Works Cited

Brown, Dee. *Bury My Heart at Wounded Knee: An Indian History of the American West*. New York: Holt Rinehart & Winston, 1970.

Flora, Joseph M. *Frederick Manfred*. Boise SU Western Writers Ser. 13. Boise: Boise SUP, 1974.

Huseboe, Arthur R. Foreword. *Scarlet Plume*. Frederick Manfred. Lincoln: U of Nebraska P, 1983. v-xiii.

Lawrence, D.H. *Studies in Classic American Literature*. 1923. Garden City: Doubleday, 1951.

Manfred, Frederick. *Conquering Horse*. Boston: Gregg Press, 1980.

---. *King of Spades*. Boston: Gregg Press, 1983.

---. *Lord Grizzly*. Boston: Gregg Press, 1980.

---. *Riders of Judgment*. Boston: Gregg Press, 1980.

---. *Scarlet Plume*. Boston: Gregg Press, 1980; cited textually as *SP*.

McAllister, Mick. "The First Covenant in *Conquering Horse*: Syncretic Myth in the Buckskin Man Tales." *South Dakota Review* 20.3 (Autumn 1982): 76-88.

Milton, John R., moderator. *Conversations with Frederick Manfred*. Salt Lake City: U of Utah P, 1974.

---. Introduction. *Conquering Horse*. By Frederick Manfred. Boston: Gregg Press, 1980. v-xii.

Nelson, Nancy Owen. "Sacred Siouxland: Wakan Places in Some Novels by Frederick Manfred." *Heritage of the Great Plains* 28.1 (1995): 41-51.

Oaks, Priscilla. Introduction. *Riders of Judgment*. By Frederick Manfred. Boston: Gregg Press, 1980. v-xiv.

Westbrook, Max. Foreword. *King of Spades*. Frederick Manfred. Lincoln: U of Nebraska P, 1983. v-xi.

Wright, Robert C. *Frederick Manfred*. Boston: Twayne, 1979.

Frederick Manfred: The Quest of the Independent Writer

by Delbert E. Wylder

In May of 1979, the National Endowment for the Arts announced a new program—Senior Fellowships for Literature—which will result in a few one-time grants to individuals "who have made an extraordinary contribution to American literature over a lifetime of creative work." These fellowships, however, are not to be awarded to "those whose work has had great commercial success." Frederick Manfred, the Iowa-born author of eighteen novels, two volumes of short stories, and one book of poems, seems to fit neatly into these requirements. Born on a farm near Doon, Iowa, in 1912, just six years after the birth of Robert Penn Warren in the small town of Guthrie, Kentucky, Manfred has devoted his life to writing and has made an outstanding contribution to literature in America. His production has been large in volume and significance; yet, he has not received either the financial success or the general acclaim of the Kentuckian. The list of accomplishments—and awards—on the back cover of Warren's latest volume of extraordinarily fine poetry, *Now and Then*, is overwhelmingly impressive. As more than one individual must have already noted, he has little left to win but the Nobel Prize for Literature. On the other hand, American literary committees and organizations, with the exception of the Western Literature Association, have been more than reluctant to recognize the merit of Frederick Manfred. It should also be stated that the academic community as a whole has given little recognition to Frederick Manfred and his works, again with the exception of those scholars interested specifically in Western American literature.

This is not to suggest that the world is out of kilter and that the Eastern publishing establishment has once more failed to recognize a Western writer, nor is it to denigrate in any way the accomplishments of Robert Penn Warren. It is to suggest, however, that both careers have developed along different lines, with different interests, and with different visions, and that both writers have contributed much over their lifetimes of creative work. Manfred would be the last to complain of Warren's awards and fame, nor is he, himself, impatient. What is important to Manfred is his art, though, like any human being, he could not help wanting some recognition for it.

Manfred and Warren have lived quite different careers. Warren left Kentucky for Vanderbilt University, one of the more prestigious universities in the South, and then went on to receive a master's degree from the University of California. He did further graduate work at Yale University and was a Rhodes Scholar at Oxford. For much of his life, he has been associated with the academic community as a teacher of literature and creative writing. To the contrary, and in contrariness, Manfred enrolled in tiny Calvin College, in Grand Rapids, Michigan, a school supported by the Christian Reformed Church. By the time he had graduated, in 1934, he had not only lost his Christian orthodox beliefs, he had also lost any interest he might have had in teaching. During the Depression years of 1934-37, he hitchhiked around the country, ending up in Minnesota as a sportswriter for the *Minneapolis Journal*. From 1940 to 1942, he battled tuberculosis in a sanatorium. In 1942, recovered, he joined the staff of *Modern Medicine* before becoming an assistant campaign manager in Hubert Humphrey's unsuccessful bid to become mayor of Minneapolis. He continued to work on a novel—the dust-bowl novel *The Golden Bowl*—and its publication, and his credentials won him a University of Minnesota Regional Writing Fellowship. From then on, writing has been his life and his livelihood, and his tendency has been to write from his native area—his Siouxland. In 1960, he was able to move to his house, Blue Mound, north of Luverne, Minnesota. He was home. For the most part, he has maintained his distance from the academic community. He spent one year, 1949, as writer-in-residence at Macalester College, and recently he has had an arrangement with the University of South Dakota to teach creative writing—as a writer not-quite-in-residence, since he drives back and forth from Luverne. He has, on numerous occasions appeared as guest speaker or to give readings at writing conferences in colleges and universities, often with little or no pay, and he regularly attends the annual meeting of the Western Literature Association, a group he finds both receptive and amenable. For the most part, however, he shuns academic gatherings and spends little time with New York publishers. He is more content to be writing and working in his home place. His traditional and emotional ties are with the people and the land of his region; thus critics have generally considered him a regionalist.

In a sense, Manfred is a regionalist, since most of his novels and short stories are set in the Dakotas, or Minnesota, or Iowa. But he is a regionalist only in that sense. Unlike a Herbert Quick, for example, his themes transcend the region. More like Faulkner, he has attempted to limit his fictional exploration of the human condition to that area he knows best and to the people whose lives and traditions he knows best. And, unfortunately, there has not been a Midwestern Renascence in which he might have been "discovered." Few people think of Fitzgerald, a fellow Minnesotan, or Hemingway from Illinois, as midwestern writers. Furthermore, Frederick Manfred is a "maverick." Alan Swallow appropriately included him in a 1959 essay called "The Mavericks," and Joseph M. Flora explained the term quite succinctly in his Western Writers Series *Frederick Manfred:*

> The mavericks are serious writers who have pursued their themes without much recognition from the Eastern press, partly, Swallow felt, because the Eastern press has not understood the Western themes or techniques or has been too contemptuous to make the effort.

But even to many Western critics, Manfred remains a maverick, primarily because he simply is one. Manfred reads critics, he listens to them, he has close friends who are critics, and he probably wouldn't even mind if one of his children married one. However, he will no more listen to a critic tell him how to write than he will listen to an editor who tries to make changes in his manuscripts. Manfred has his own voice, and he has his own concept of structure. For the most part, the little critical evaluation that has been done on Manfred has not been descriptive, it has been comparative. Critics have, for the most part, expected him to adjust to the dominant techniques and structures of the time. His differences from these expectations are seen as faults. Such a position is easy to take, particularly with some of the earlier novels. But as Manfred continues to publish, he makes little or no effort to correct these "faults," and it is becoming more and more apparent that Frederick Manfred's growth will be on his own terms, and that it is, indeed, growth. Manfred's last three novels, and especially the last two, should convince the critics that this growth should be recognized, and that Manfred's voice deserves to be heard.

Perhaps the first critical articles to bring Manfred's works to the attention of the "literary establishment" (rather than the book reviewers) were two articles by John R. Milton, now a colleague of Manfred, but then a professor and chairman at Jamestown College in North Dakota. The first was published in *College English* in 1957; the second was published, in 1958, in Ray B. West's *Western Review* at The University of Iowa. In that "Examination of New Writers" essay, Milton discussed *The Golden Bowl* (1944), *Boy Almighty* (1945), *This is the Year* (1947), *The Chokecherry Tree* (1948), *The Primitive* (1949), *The Brother* (1950), *The Giant* (1951), *Lord Grizzly* (1954), and *Morning Red* (1956), and added a "postscript" on Manfred's novel based on the Johnson County War, *Riders of Judgment* (1957). Milton, using *The Golden Bowl* as a base, discusses Manfred's concept of the "long view" which, he concedes, at least appears in, although is not necessarily central to, all of Manfred's novels. The main character, Maury, Milton asserts, learns "the long view, the lesson of the land: hope is based on the roots of tradition, on brotherhood, and on the necessity of continuing the species" (Milton 1958, 182). He also suggests that, in Manfred's attempt to present the "full truth," the novelist has a tendency to provide literal transcriptions of the real world at the expense of the artistic concept of economy. Milton believes that "an overwhelming mass of detailed material tends to smother artistry" (Milton 1958, 184).

In discussing the trilogy *Wanderlust* (consisting of *The Primitive*, *The Brother*, and *The Giant*), Milton charges that it

> suffers from a lack of selectivity, from personal prejudices, from moralizing, from uncontrolled excursions into the bypaths of autobiography, from an inconsistent tone, and from a childish ineptness in some matters of taste. (Milton 1958, 187)

Furthermore, in Milton's opinion, Manfred's

> love of "things," his themes, and his uncontrolled passion for life all contribute to his frequent lack of conciseness, to his

apparent lack of concern for artistic craftsmanship. What he must learn, above all else, is his proper relationship to his readers. (Milton 1958, 187-88)

Though most of these comments seem derogatory, Milton treats Manfred and his works with respect, and he sees a promising future for the writing if Manfred can successfully blend his heart and his craft and can show some artistic selectivity and restraint.

To some degree, Joseph M. Flora's Western Writers Series *Frederick Manfred* elaborates on some of the same problems in Manfred's fiction, although this critical pamphlet is less negative than Milton's article. In one short passage, for example, Flora, discussing *Morning Red*, is concerned with structure, selectivity, craftsmanship, and taste:

> The counter pointing of plots is not the major difficulty, nor is the problem even necessarily the great number of characters. The stumbling block is that Manfred suggests that some characters are going to be more important than they are. The reader gets too much detail about characters who do not matter. There is also too much specificity—for one example, in menus—a carryover from the autobiographical trilogy. Too, Manfred has seldom refrained from presenting the homely realities of any bodily functions, and in *Morning Red* he presents those realities at the expense of the tale. (Flora 21)

Flora includes, in his discussion, the novels written between *Riders of Judgment* and *Milk of Wolves*, which had not been published: *Conquering Horse* (1959), *Scarlet Plume* (1964), *The Man Who Looked Like the Prince of Wales* (1965), *King of Spades* (1966), *Eden Prairie* (1968), and many of the short stories, as well as the short novels in *Arrow of Love* (1961). An interesting task, then, is to look at the most recent publications of Manfred's to see whether he has indeed improved in artistry and taste.

For a reader coming upon Manfred's work for the first time, the answer may well be "No." Particularly for a critic who has been schooled in Percy Lubbock or in "the modern novel" based on an almost classical control of structure, symbol, and language, the answer may still be a rather vehement "No." Manfred is not a Hemingway nor a Fitzgerald—that is not his temperament. His sensitivity is basically rural rather than urban, close to the earth rather than sophisticated, and definitely not cosmopolitan. His literary tradition has derived from the Greeks, from the Bible, from Chaucer and Shakespeare, and from Mark Twain. He has not, as John R. Milton has hoped, learned his proper relationship to his reader. Like the stonecutter (not sculptor) hero of his *Milk of Wolves*, he is content to carve out his works and to let his readers, particularly the sophisticated ones, learn their proper relationship to his works. Given time, this miracle may happen, for Manfred is a gifted storyteller who may be forgiven for what many critics seem to see as artistic faults.

Approaching a Manfred novel, the reader should first note that here is a distinct sensitivity at work. First, Manfred is unashamedly male, and he sees the male principle as the major creative force. He does not espouse the macho image for its own sake, however. Like the American Indian, or the American farmer, or like any people oriented to basics, he sees the regenerative force as both a blessing and a threat. The male's function in the continuum is to sow the seed for the next generation—to guarantee the continuum. But the social animal needs to control that sex drive or he becomes, like the trickster in Indian myth and legend, a force that can destroy the society. Like the new-biologists, Manfred sees man as an aggressive predator. Second, Manfred is indeed rural, and this is not to say that he writes of the sensitive small-town youth who, like Sherwood Anderson's Winesburgians, must leave the crudeness and restrictions of the small midwestern towns for the culture of the cities. Manfred and his characters revel in the unsophisticated life. His characters may hate, at times, the work of the farm, for instance, but they take pride in the work, they take pride in fulfilling their responsibilities, they relate to the animal world with awe, curiosity, and humor, and seem crude in their expression of life. Especially the youthful heroes are torn between this sense of responsibility and their desire for freedom, just as they are torn between their sexual desires and the societal restrictions on them. Finally, Manfred's narrative perspective is distinctly his own. He makes little attempt to narrate with distance and objectivity. As writer, he often stands within the novel, blending his voice with those of the characters, moving into and away from them so that, at times, the reader has difficulty distinguishing between the voice of the character and Manfred's own voice. To the contemporary reader, this may be anathema, but it is Manfred's method. Such a method is less evident in his historical novels of the American West, which is one reason why most critics find these his most successful novels.

They are not, however, *necessarily* his most successful works. Manfred, as novelist, continues to improve, and that improvement comes more from a maturity of vision than anything else.

The first of his last three novels, *Milk of Wolves*, was a long time waiting to be published. Because his editor had moved from one publishing house to another, there were complications. *Milk of Wolves* was too long and needed editing. Manfred was adamant. The maverick found himself a maverick publisher, and *Milk of Wolves* was finally published by the Avenue Victor Hugo Publishing Company in a columnized newspaper-type format, and was not, therefore, edited and cut by a New Yorker. The novel is the long, rambling story of Juhl Melander, who leaves his home after graduating from high school to find his way into the world of stonecutting. He leaves the village of Hackberry Run, his sister, and his mother, who has hoped he would continue as a blacksmith like his father. By the end of the novel, Juhl has moved full circle and is back in Hackberry Run to live in his father's house, where he will continue to cut stone. But it is the circle he has moved in that is important, even more than the coming home. The circle has been his life. How successful or satisfying that has been is reflected in his answer to his own self-questioning at the end of the novel, "Listen, if you were to tell me I had only one more minute to live, no more, I'd still say it was a great life. I don't regret one minute of it. All of it, the good with the bad, was wonderful. The whole river of it was worth having'" (*MW* 250).

That whole river has been the life of a male artisan. He has seduced women, carved stone (or rather found the forms waiting to be released from the stone), married, fathered children, and battled the world to maintain his freedom on his own terms. As a stonecutter, he has thumbed his nose at the "culture" of the city. He has married one of the daughters of the rich, but he has remained the working man, the masculine hero who tests himself in the world of back-breaking toil as a stonecutter and lumberjack, and then has finally tested himself in the wilds on an island in the Lake of the Woods on the Canadian border. On the island, he returned to the primitive, and his statement at that point in the novel not only sums up Juhl Melander's attitudes about the male principle in art and life, but Frederick Manfred's as well.

> The stronger the animal in man the better chance he had of getting the best of his blood into his civilized stratagems. That was why he, Juhl Melander, once of the Cities and before that of Hackberry Run, had chosen to become a shacker on Big Wolfe Island. That he might, somehow, have the animal in him constricted and warped and made mean. Because he had done some mean low boorish things to his friends. Even villainous. Though of course that he'd remained the ruttish stud was perfectly all right. The genius in him was located in that. The whole point was to allow the genius stud in him to paw naturally for the white bird fluttering and singing just above him. (*MW* 207)

The truth of the matter is that Juhl *has* acted boorishly and villainously not only to his friends, but to his wife and family as well. He has paid in guilt and suffering for what he has done, though he spends little time in complaint. The stud-genius, the artist-hero, adapts well, however, to a primitive environment. He marries a young Indian girl, fathers a child, and finds his own "sacred" tree that puts him completely in touch with "place"—or the source of his being.

> He spotted it across an open space and in the lowest part of the depression. It stood alone, apart from the others, as if the others had withdrawn in deference. . . .
> He went over and tried to put his arms around it. Lord God in heaven. . . . It was four foot through. It was the king all right. The monarch. The father of all red pines.
> He pressed his cheek against one of the flakes of its tannish-red bark. The flake was as big as a plate. He placed his ear on the more solid part of the bark. With the top of the tree running in the strong wind he could hear profound anguishing sounds of live woods sliding over each other deep inside.
> God.
> In all his life he'd never heard anything like it. Heartwood music. Earth, without tongue, was here clearly humming a hymn to the sun. Or was the whole majestic tree the tongue? In

THE QUEST OF THE INDEPENDENT WRITER 163

any case, here at last was the true sound of a place. It came up out of the earth and rose through the vast trunk of the rooted monarch father. (*MW* 185)

Although Juhl Melander has found "God"—for the exclamation in the preceding quotation is not only Juhl's surprised response to his discovery of the source of power through place, but it is also his recognition of that supreme power—he is not allowed to enjoy his idyllic retreat. He is defeated by man and nature. Starting out for civilization to try to stop the encroachment of government and real estate men who wish to develop the area into a park and tourist attraction, Juhl suddenly realizes that he has left his wife and son at the mercy of her incest-crazed brother. He returns immediately, only to find that the brother has already killed his wife. But his son is not dead. Juhl cuts into his own nipple to bring a flow of blood to nourish the child and, after days of feeding the child on blood, a tiny milk-sac develops in his breast. Juhl gradually develops a supply of milk to sustain his son. He has become both father and mother, incorporating both male and female principles in one body.

But he knows that he cannot withstand the combined efforts of state and local government, and he decides to return to civilization with his son. Crossing the lake, they are caught in a sudden storm and, though he ties his son to his back and manages to swim to the shore, his son has been drowned. At the end of the novel, he returns home but, as has already been indicated, with a sense of what his own life has been, and the power of it.

Such a simplified review can not, of course, give any suggestion of the depth or the complexity of the novel—its themes and its structure. Superficially, the artist-hero in working man's clothes and distrustful of the educated and the sophisticated may seem to resemble the artist-hero of Ayn Rand's *The Fountainhead*, but the resemblance is only superficial. Juhl is sought after by women, he is the independent artist, he is a man of the working people, but he is also a boor and a villain, and Juhl himself, as well as the reader of the novel, is aware of his failings.

Nor does this hurried review of the novel indicate any of the "faults" that Manfred's critics will find with his artistry. As only one example, Manfred's treatment of sex is hardly conventional.

In an era when writers, both male and female, can delineate with great detail the sexual organs and the variety of sexual activities of both heterosexuals and homosexuals, Manfred remains something of an enigma. The problem is one of "voice," which has been mentioned earlier. Manfred as narrator, as well as his characters, views sex from a complicated and confused perspective. There is a certain air of Victorian puritanism and prudishness in the descriptions, and at the same time a rather adolescent romanticism that idealizes and spiritualizes sexual activity. Added to this is the crudity and boorishness of the farm youth who has grown up watching the coupling of mares and studs, bulls and heifers, boars and gilts—even roosters and hens—and who has watched with natural curiosity, empathic delight, and even ribald but perhaps self-conscious humor. Here is neither the phenomenological descriptions of an Updike nor the "discovery" descriptions of Erica Jong who, in her own sophisticated way, always seems to write as though she has, standing on a peak in Darien, been the first to see the Pacific. In Manfred, there is, without apology, the early-twentieth-century Protestant, adolescent, barnyard views combined.

With all its literary "faults," however, *Milk of Wolves* is a strong novel, and it is particularly important for an understanding of Manfred's concepts of the artist and of Art.

Having completed *Milk of Wolves*, Manfred began work on a large autobiographical novel that once more would examine the world of his youth, but from a new perspective he had gained from his experiences with Juhl Melander. Somewhere during the composition of what would finally be *Green Earth*, Manfred felt the pull of another novel about the Indians and about the strange relationships between male and female, and the internal conflict of male and female within the individual. In a burst of energy and inspiration, Manfred completed this Indian novel, *The Manly-Hearted Woman*, which was published by Crown Publishers in 1975, the same year as the delayed publication of *Milk of Wolves*.

The Manly-Hearted Woman a simply told, seemingly simple novel of two young Indians of opposite sexes whose lives cross momentarily but significantly. The first plot is the story of young Flat Warclub, who has never been on the warpath and who thus receives little respect from his own people. However, after a vision, he joins a war party which is leaving to help a sister band of Yankton Sioux against their mutual enemies, the Omaha. His vision is a tragic one. He is to lead his people to victory, but he will die in the battle, an accidental victim of one of his own men. Before he

THE QUEST OF THE INDEPENDENT WRITER 165

dies, however, the gods give him the right to "talk to" (or sleep with) any of the women of his sister tribe, for the band needs the regeneration of new seed. For a few days, he lives with a strange couple—both females, but husband and wife—while he "talks to" a variety of women, young and old. Finally, he is allowed to "talk to" only one of the couple, the wife Prettyhead. On the appointed day, he leads the war party against the Omaha and is killed as the gods had prophesied. His body is returned to the camp in honor.

The second plot is the story of Manly Heart, a girl who grows up in the Blue Mound band and whose early sexual experiments seem conventional except for her incestuous attraction for her brother, Stalk, although most of the Indian boys shame her because of her experiments with a youth named Hollow Horn. She is not only sexually precocious, she is also far too interested in the things boys do: riding horses, hunting, racing. Most important, she is fascinated by the concept of the Vision and its importance to the male. Her first marriage is to an aged widower, He Is Empty, and she changes from a "sit-beside" to a wife who sleeps with her husband and, in the process, rejuvenates him. At his death, however, she is left alone, and suitors once more begin to seek her out. Her second marriage is to a middle-aged widower, Red Daybreak, who is a sadist. As they have intercourse, he chokes her. Finally, she overpowers him and then shames him. She divorces him, and once more she is alone. She tries to find happiness with a young lover, Sunny Day Walker, but he is too involved with himself, and his lovemaking is unsatisfactory. As she explains it, his song is too soon sung. She learns in these years that many women of the tribe are sexually unsatisfied.

One day, she goes alone from the village and has a vision. She is given a new secret name (Point from the Clouds), and she is told that she may live like a man, that she can go on hunts with the men, and that she may even take a wife. In short, she is now being allowed to be a man. Her helper is to be an ancient arrowhead that she must wear hanging between her breasts. She is also told that she will do great things and be renowned. As a woman, she continues to question the gods. "But, but, but," she questions, until the voice in the vision is almost exasperated. However, she returns to the village, takes a wife, and proceeds to live the life of a man with full acceptance by the men. She and Prettyhead, however, live in the lowest status-position in the village. It is in their tepee that Flat Warclub finds a temporary home.

On the day that Flat Warclub's helper tells him to stay with Pretty-head, Manly Heart, who is supposed to guard the horse herd, returns to the tepee despite the warning of her own helper. She questions her helper, disagrees with it, accuses the gods of being unfair, rationalizes her need to return to the tepee, and disobeys. As she leaves, the arrowhead drops to the ground, changes to a lizard, and disappears into a crevice. When she finds her way back to the tepee, she peeks beneath one side and watches Flat Warclub and Prettyhead in their lovemaking. She is amazed, almost thunderstruck, at the sight. She then guards them against any intrusion by others. She has fallen in love with the male—with Flat Warclub.

She has not only fallen in love with Flat Warclub, she has also found that they are closely linked in the other world, for she has found that his secret name, given him through his helper, is Stone from the Clouds. When the warriors bring his body back from the battle, she jealously assumes all responsibility for it. She does not allow the women with whom he has talked to touch the body, and she mourns alone. After a time, she returns to the village to live alone, divorcing Prettyhead. Once again, she must spend five days each month in the separation hut. Having become a woman again, she begins to menstruate. She no longer speaks to anyone in the tribe, and the rest of her life she is known as the Silent Woman.

Beneath this simple tale, however, lie many complexities. Before he dies, Flat Warclub realizes that he should have mated with Manly Heart, but it is too late, and the gods did not ordain it. By giving him the pleasures of his last few days, the gods have made him more aware of life, and thus of what he is about to lose. The sense of heroic-tragedy has been increased; and Flat Warclub becomes a martyr for the tribe. Further, the fates seem to have made the very battle in which he is killed almost unnecessary. When the Sioux ambush the enemy, the Omaha are starting on a peace mission to the Sioux. They have decided to share the buffalo run that has been the subject of the quarrel. Only the uncontrolled fury and sexual desire of Bitten Nose (an antagonist of Flat Warclub who had years ago killed his own brother) toward the beautiful maiden who is to be offered as a peace offering to the Sioux chief prevents the interruption of the gods' predictions. When the girl looks contemptuously at Bitten Nose's disfigured face, he pulls her from her horse and attempts to rape her. His actions, the actions of a true trickster character, start the battle. Thus, the novel deals with fratricide, with incest, with heroism, with spirituality, with life and death and sacrifice. It is perhaps Manfred's most compact, most tightly structured novel.

And it is told in the most simple of terms. On the surface, the novel reads like a warrior tale from one of the works of George Bird Grinnell, or like the simple novels of Indian life by James Willard Schultz. The rhythms ring true to Indian legends, and Manfred's sparing use of natural detail makes all of the story believable. Such a minor detail as the hide of a horse giving a "rippling shudder" immediately charges a scene with reality, and Manfred is as successful in describing the spirit world of the helpers as he is in evoking the realities of Indian life. Because of his restraint, his concern for structure, and his success in blending myth and reality, this will probably be viewed by most of his critics as his most successful novel.

Yet, as fine an achievement as it is, *The Manly-Hearted Woman* is not Manfred's best, for Manfred then turned to the completion of *Green Earth*, and this novel is Manfred's finest achievement to date. *Green Earth* is another autobiographical novel, in which Manfred returns once more to the Siouxland of his early years, the years preceding those described in *The Primitive*. The novel is divided into three books, each dedicated to a family component. The first book of 148 pages, "Lady of the House," is dedicated to "ALICE: mother;" the second, of 335 pages, "Lord of the Barnyard," to "Edward John, Floyd, John Garret, Abben Clarence, Henry Herman: brothers;" and the third, of 257 pages, "Angel Country," to "Henry Van Engen and Herman Van Engen: uncles." This is a more than appropriate dedication since *Green Earth* is a novel about family and its relationship to the land from which it gains a living, to its Christian and national heritage, and finally and particularly, that family's influence on the life of its children, in this case, of "Free Alfredson," the son of Ada Engelking Alfredson and Alfred Alfredson.

The novel begins:

> It was the Sunday before Christmas, 1909. The Alfred Engelkings were having supper. It was a simple meal: rice with

milk and brown sugar, black rye bread with butter, and green tea.

Almost from the first, Manfred has begun to detail the eating habits of the characters in the novel. And detail piles up in this novel to the point where many critics may find it obstructing the progression of the action. Yet, *Green Earth*, without the details of midwestern farm and country life of the teens and twenties would be, to some degree, like Irving's "The Legend of Sleepy Hollow" without the details of the Pennsylvania Dutch community. Detail in this novel does not impede as it does, say, in the novels of Thomas Wolfe. Detail establishes the way of life: the work, the way of living, the religious practices, the games, the attitudes, as well as the eating habits. The relationship of men and women to the farm animals, for example, and especially to the horses, is as important in this novel as it was to the people who farmed in Iowa in those days. The harness is described with an accuracy that recreates a historical period—and Manfred knows the difference between a checkrein and a crupper. The relationship that resulted from man's life with the horse is depicted not only in such scenes as planting and corn picking, but also in the relationship that made the death of a favorite buggy horse like a death in the family. In a technological age, in which a large segment of the population gets no closer to a cow or steer than a waxed carton of milk and a plastic-wrapped steak, such detail is necessary, for this novel is a hymn to an older way of life.

Most importantly, however, Manfred does not sentimentalize "the good old days." If readers feel nostalgia for those more pastoral days, that feeling will be conditioned by Manfred's delineation of the hardships of the way of life of that time. The back-breaking labor is there, and both men and women have their own variety of work. The plight of the renter, who moves from one farm to another, trying desperately to become a landowner, is part of the novel, but there are no Marxist overtones to the descriptions. The system is accepted by the farmers as their way of life. There are good and bad owners, and people live within a way of life without thinking about a "system," and the narrator does not impose an economic concept upon the materials. Manfred is not writing a political novel; he is presenting a human document.

THE QUEST OF THE INDEPENDENT WRITER 169

That document certainly may appear to be flawed artistically. The novel begins with Ada Engelking and her first "romantic" courtship, and then moves on to a more mundane courtship by, and marriage to, Alfred Alfredson. Their first child, a male child named Alfred and nicknamed "Free," becomes the central character in the last two books. Once he is born, the focus of the book begins to shift to the problems of young Free and his attempt to adjust his own free and rebellious ego to his family and the society around him. Manfred, however, shifts focus carefully, almost as life itself shifts the focus from one generation to another. What is important is that the forces that operate in the first book remain as influences on the growing, developing boy. The individual, the novel seems to suggest, is shaped by the past and the environment into which he is born. Gradually, Free becomes the central character, but always in the background is the family and the way of life on the land, and the heritage of religious training.

Free grows, commits errors, feels guilt, and learns. His progress is neither a pilgrim's nor a hero's. He sees the world's hypocrisy and is made to feel his own. In short, Free Alfredson grows up, learning about the world that surrounds him, including the mysteries of sex. And throughout both Book Two and Book Three, there is the pervading sense of the shaping influences of his father and mother, and especially the mother. In particular, the mother is always there, and the novel ends with her death in 1929, on the same day as the death of Manfred's own mother.

Once more, with such a close autobiographical connection, there is the possibility of sentimentality, but Manfred carefully avoids it. The death scene is almost coldly realistic, with death coming as a matter of course after a detailed history of medical difficulties.

The novel is too long for a detailed analysis here of any of its parts. Unfortunately, for many critics Manfred's love of "things" will still be very much a part of this novel, his voice remains the voice that has disturbed many critics, and there will be those who will fault the structure of this novel. In some scenes, Manfred's taste may be questioned. He has not developed into a "sophisticated" writer, as some critics have hoped. What Manfred has done, however, has been to bring his "voice" into its most perfect expressions of the people he writes about, and he has carved out a tremendously realistic novel about the development of a personality within the family context.

Manfred's growth as a novelist is most evident, however, in his vision of mankind. Much of the rebelliousness of his earlier novels, as in his attacks on hypocrisy and hypocrites, is muted in this fine novel. There is a mature vision of humanity in which divisions between good and bad are not so easily seen. There is a tolerance, a compassion, an understanding that values and celebrates life and seeks to reveal it in all its aspects, from its most ribald and humorous episodes to its most solemn. It is a vision different from that of Faulkner and Chaucer, but with the same involvement in mankind. It is important that critics learn to read Frederick Manfred in his own terms, for the rewards are great. Whether they do or not, Frederick Manfred will continue to write. He will, like Juhl Melander, in *Milk of Wolves*, keep trying to catch that "white bird fluttering and singing just above him." Just as Alfred Alfredson continued to farm, Manfred will continue to write, for that is his way of life, and that is his world.

Notes

[1] Nineteen novels is the correct number if *Wanderlust* (the revised trilogy including *The Primitive*, *The Brother*, and *The Giant*) is considered as a separate work.

[2] Manfred is an omnivorous reader and is particularly interested in the works of Robert Audrey, Desmond Morris, Konrad Lorenz, Lionel Tiger, and other "new-biologists."

Works Cited

Flora, Joseph M. *Frederick Manfred*. Boise: Boise S U P, 1974.
Manfred, Frederick. *Milk of Wolves*. Boston: Avenue Victor Hugo Publishing Co., 1976.
Milton, John R. "Frederick Feikema Manfred." *Western Review* 22 (Spring 1958): 181-99.
---. "Voice from Siouxland: Frederick Feikema Manfred." *College English* 19 (December 1957): 104-11.
Swallow, Alan. "The Mavericks." *Critique: Studies in Modern Fiction* 2 (Winter 1959): 88-92.

Part III

Returning to Siouxland: The Later Novels

Seduction, Betrayal— and Redemption: *Flowers of Desire* as a Modern Sentimental Novel

by Christy Rishoi

Admirers of Frederick Manfred's fiction may be surprised by his 1989 novel, *Flowers of Desire*. The hallmarks of many Manfred stories—American West settings, man-against-nature themes, and Native American allusions—are entirely absent in *Flowers*. Instead, Manfred's readers are introduced to fresh-faced, Midwestern teenager Carla Simmons, who lives in a small, conservative, lily-white town in the 1940s, and whose major concerns are clinging to her virginity and pondering a career as an artist. Carla has the requisite sexually promiscuous girlfriend, and she meets the requisite nice, slightly older man who promises to marry her in a conventional attempt to persuade her to have intercourse with him. Although she doesn't yield to his persuasive tactics, Carla is physically attracted to Oren Prince, and so, true to the times, she pressures her parents into giving their permission for her to marry before she turns eighteen. When they finally agree and she sets happily off to the big city to marry her ironically-named "Prince," she finds he has betrayed her by getting another woman pregnant and marrying her instead. Stunned and stung, Carla wanders the streets of St. Paul and somehow ends up having intercourse with five different men the very night she learns of Oren's betrayal. Only through the intervention of several more men does she escape prison time for juvenile delinquency and even attempted murder, and is finally returned—safe, but pregnant with twins—to her home.

Aside from a surprising and radical shift from thematic concerns of his earlier work, Manfred's novel is noteworthy in its choice of genre as well as its adherence to the political project of many twentieth-century women writers. First, it bears a remarkable resemblance to the sentimental fiction genre exemplified by America's first best-selling novel, *Charlotte Temple*, published in 1791 by Susanna Rowson. At the same time, however, Manfred "writes beyond the ending," to echo the title of Rachel Blau du

Plessis' book, to free his heroine from the only two acceptable outcomes—marriage or death—for the sentimental heroine, allowing Carla instead to establish her identity outside of marriage as a single mother as well as continue her previously repressed quest for self-fulfillment.

Written primarily by, for, and about women, sentimental fiction was once widely read and hugely popular, but it also performed critical social and political tasks during its heyday in the 18th and 19th centuries. The most famous example of this, perhaps, is Harriet Beecher Stowe's *Uncle Tom's Cabin*, which set the nation on fire with its indictment of slavery, but which was in turn indicted by the literary establishment for being a melodramatic, manipulative tear-jerker. The sentimental novel itself, however, was well established long before the publication of *Uncle Tom's Cabin*. Many early American novels, such as Rowson's *Charlotte Temple*, *The Coquette* by Hannah Foster, and *Emily Hamilton* by Sukey Vickery all implicitly argue that a "woman must take greater control of her life and must make shrewd judgments of the men who come into [it]" (Davidson 113). The key to greater control, according to sentimental ideology, is through education and self-sufficiency for women.

Vilified by critics for its focus on the domestic, the local, and the feminine, the genre of sentimental fiction was well ensconced in the trash heap of American literature by the time the New Critics had their say. In recent years, though, the reputation of American sentimental novels has been radically rehabilitated, due in large part to the ground-breaking scholarship of Cathy N. Davidson in her work *Revolution and the Word*, and Jane Tompkins in *Sensational Designs*. Tompkins in particular argues that "this body of work is remarkable for its intellectual complexity, ambition, and resourcefulness; and. . .the enormous popularity of these novels, which has been cause for suspicion bordering on disgust, is a reason for paying close attention to them" (124). Davidson writes that "[i]mportant social matters are reflected in sentimental plots, including the preoccupation with extramarital sex and the social and biological consequences of sexual transgressions (115). Taken together, Tompkins and Davidson are among the foremost proponents of the view that sentimental fiction, far from being trite and trifling, actually reflects and shapes social mores.

While the literary community might have reassessed its opinion of sentimental fiction, few serious contemporary writers have shown a parallel interest in reviving the genre for modern readers. But Manfred revises the formula to reflect the mores of 1940s middle America, making a significant departure from the earlier formula by allowing his heroine to reinvent her life, which helps to reinforce Tompkins' point that sentimental fiction is "a political enterprise, halfway between sermon and social theory, that both codifies and attempts to mold the values of its time" (126).

Those values, of course, transcended the early national period and serve to privilege the couple over the individual, reinforce marriage and heterosexual bonds, as well as delineate a gendered division of labor well into the twentieth century. Du Plessis notes that

> In nineteenth century narrative, where women heroes were concerned, quest and love plots were intertwined, simultaneous discourses, but at the resolution of the work, the energies of the *Bildung* were incompatible with the closure in successful courtship or marriage. Quest for women was thus finite; we learn that any plot of self-realization was at the service of the marriage plot and was subordinate to, or covered within, the magnetic power of that ending. (6)

Perhaps the most famous example of this dynamic occurs in Louisa May Alcott's *Little Women*, where questing Jo March is transformed from a free spirit who means to be a literary spinster into a docile wife and mother who writes in service of family ideology. In du Plessis' formulation, there was literally no other possible outcome for Jo's *bildung*. Dominant ideology required that Jo's quest be repressed in favor of her "true" calling.

The specific social mores articulated by sentimental novels (and carried forward into the domestic novels of the nineteenth century) have of course been problematized and deconstructed in both literature and feminist theory in the twentieth century. As du Plessis argues, "[t]o compose a work is to negotiate with these questions: What stories can be told? How can plots be resolved?" (3). In large measure, the work of feminist critics has been to challenge received notions of the acceptable teleology of women's lives. Sentimental fiction, a product of social ideologies like all literature, sought to repress the heroine's conflict between *Bildung* and romance by limiting her fates to either marriage or death. In *Flowers of Desire*, Manfred challenges the conventions of acceptable plot resolutions which, according to du Plessis, "separates love and quest" (5) by positing a third outcome involving a reinvention of womanly fulfillment. Carla's "natural" instinct for mothering essentializes her somewhat, but, combined as it is with worldly ambition, represents a significant shift.

Social mores have changed a good bit, but women still struggle with the age-old conflict between personal quest and love; the desire for self-fulfillment is still at odds with the powerful ideology prescribing fulfillment through incorporating identity into a marriage. In *Flowers of Desire*, Manfred takes care to allow some of these social changes to alter the fate of his protagonist from that suffered by Rowson's Charlotte, who dies while giving birth to her illegitimate daughter, or even that of Alcott's Jo, who wishes to avoid marriage, but is helpless before social convention. Not only does Carla avoid marriage, the plot line reflects contemporary society's more accepting stance toward girls who become pregnant, and argues that only a mistake in judgment has occurred in such cases, not a major sin. Carla's story moves from unquestioned faith in the primacy of love as the zenith of womanly ambition to a deepened understanding that, unless she achieves a fully realized identity on her own, the promises of romantic conventions are empty. Even more critical, she asserts that she's intended to prove that "you really don't need a husband to raise babies" (240). Carla Simmons is not finally condemned to die for her sexual experience, and, furthermore, she is able to resume her quest for self-fulfillment after her disastrous attempt to adhere to social conventions of romance and marriage. Here is a male author with admittedly strong opinions defiantly suggesting that a disapproving, judgmental society needs to realize that mistakes are only that—mistakes, not sentences to eternal damnation, nor even sentences to conventional gender roles.

Although Manfred goes against genretype with the final message of *Flowers of Desire*, he nonetheless follows his predecessors by strongly suggesting that young women need to be warned about men's true motives. Early sentimental fiction tended to portray romance and marriage as fraught with possibilities for disappointment and worse for women, and it encouraged young women to take control of their lives by showing the woes suffered by girls who fail to make critical judgments about the men they encounter. Manfred's novel follows this tradition by putting an assortment of seducers, cads, and other depraved specimens of manhood in Carla's path. Like her 18th- and 19th-century counterparts, Carla falls prey to their false charms, and she pays for her indiscretion in the way women have always paid: she gets pregnant. Manfred portrays most men as unscrupulous and exploitative, willing to deflower a maiden without a second thought, and he implicitly warns female readers to be on their guard and never trust a man's promises. That warning comes by negative example, of course, so we learn from Carla's fall.

The fallen heroine is a recurring motif in American literature, both in canonical and popular fiction, from Charlotte Temple to Hester Prynne to Carla Simmons. As Wendy Martin writes, "American [literary] heroines are destined to dependency and servitude as well as painful childbirth because...they have dared to disregard authority or tradition in the search for wisdom or happiness; like Eve, they are fallen women, eternally cursed for eating the apple of experience" (329). Carla Simmons is a fallen heroine, too, and like her fictional antecedents, she was raised to know right from wrong. Indeed, Manfred begins the fourth paragraph of the book with the fact that she's a virgin. The cult of virginity looms large for Carla, who gets conflicting messages about sex; her mother makes it clear that sex is something women have to just endure, while her friend Tracy describes her addiction to the lovely "swoons" she experiences with her various lovers. Carla has been raised to value her virginity, and to save herself for her husband, but, being a normal adolescent girl, she has plenty of sexual urges. She represses her desires fairly successfully, although she doesn't accept her mother's notion that women aren't destined to enjoy sex. Her sense of herself as a sexual being coincides with her meeting with Oren, but that side of her is at war with the strict morality of her family. In spite of his unabashed emphasis on physical desire, Carla believes he also loves her and wants to marry her, and that is why he desires her sexually. It's clear he *does* want to have sex with Carla, but Manfred also suggests that marriage would not have been mentioned at all if Carla had just been willing to have sex with Oren. As a result, when Oren is able to have sex with another woman, his ardor for Carla cools considerably.

SEDUCTION, BETRAYAL—AND REDEMPTION 177

The story line is by now a cultural archetype: Boy meets girl, boy wants to have sex with girl, girl is saving herself for love, boy promises love to get sex from girl. The fact that this story continues to be played out over several centuries is testimony to the enduring nature of the predicament. But Manfred adds a different twist to the archetype by stalling Carla's downfall. In spite of competing pressures from parents and society to remain virginal, and from Oren to give in, Carla remains true to her upbringing and arrives to marry Oren with her virginity intact—no fallen woman, she. Only when she finds him married to another woman who is pregnant with his child does Carla lose her compass, and only then does she fall. And she doesn't just stumble; she falls into an abyss. Wanting revenge somehow, Carla decides to act as her friend Tracy would. But while Tracy's response would be simply to find someone else and have fun anyway, Carla isn't in the right frame of mind for that approach. As a result, when she meets a man in a uniform with a missing leg, panhandling outside a restaurant, she falls prey to a different sort of line from a man who wants to sleep with her. Thinking him a war hero, Carla decides to give herself to him, only to discover he is a petty con artist who owns an assortment of uniforms to wear for panhandling (depending upon the service branch he's hanging around). Leaving him and heading to a restaurant, she meets three real soldiers just back from battle, for whom she also feels sympathy, but each of whom, in turn, rapes her.

Dragging herself away from that ordeal, Carla meets yet another serviceman and falls yet again for the same line. But this time, she reaches orgasm and finally understands what Tracy had meant by the sexual "swoon." Unfortunately, she is also arrested during this encounter—the fact that the female minor is thrown in jail, rather than the adult male seducer, is an ironic commentary on the plight of the fallen woman. Carla has been wronged, perhaps due to her naiveté, but because society expects women to uphold its morals, it is she who must be punished.

Up to this point in the story line, *Flowers of Desire* remains true to the sentimental genre, demonstrating as its predecessors did that women are victimized by what Davidson terms the "verbal chicanery of men" (111) and arguing that young women need to have a strong center, and to hold to that. But Manfred simultaneously turns *away* from genretype and brings sentimental fiction forward in a new form. In its heyday, most sentimental heroines ended up depressed, degraded, disgraced, and eventually—usually—dead. Having made some mistake in judgment, these heroines must bear the brunt of those mistakes by suffering social punishment and ostracization. They might have fallen through no direct decision of their own, but rarely for them was there redemption. Once lost, lost forever.

Here we see Manfred engaging in what du Plessis defines as a "transgressive invention of narrative strategies...that express critical dissent from dominant narrative" (5). Although Carla makes a series of bad sexual choices, she is not punished with a life sentence; rather, she is freed to pursue her vocation which had been subordinated in favor of the romance quest. Surely her situation would challenge the most forgiving of 1940s parents—she is seventeen and pregnant, but doesn't know who the father is because she slept with five different men on the same night. An earlier rendering of such a plot line would have cast Carla out in the world to fend for herself, and she would have suffered the rest of her life for her error, if indeed she even survived the ordeal of childbirth. Subverting convention, Manfred's tactic is to return Carla to her family and allow her to decide for herself if she wants to raise her babies with the help of her parents and indeed, her entire community. And it's clear by the end that Carla's life isn't ruined because of her fall: she dreams of going to school and of reviving her art career ambitions while raising her children. She is, in fact, *redeemed* as a direct result of her ordeal.

Of course, it is never possible to write or act outside ideology, and hegemonic discourse will only sanction a degree of resistance to dominant norms. Thus, Manfred is unable to script truly alternative outcomes for his heroine. But because hegemony must gain consent from those it controls, there is a constant evolution in social conventions, allowing Manfred to revise the social construction of women and posit a different trajectory from the conventional "fallen woman" story. Tracing female literary heroines from Charlotte Temple to Jo March to Carla Simmons, we also find the shifting ideologies of womanhood as they are played out in the larger culture. In answering the question posed by du Plessis, Manfred answers that the old stories about the price and place of female sexuality can be told with a different ending, thus participating in a significant movement among (mostly) women writers of the twentieth century—the project that tells the untold stories of women's lives. The dominant ideology of womanhood will only change when men join women to insist that women's lives are equally rich in variety and desires. With *Flowers of Desire*, one of his last major works, Manfred joined this enterprise, and while the end result isn't flawless, it stands no less as testament to the strongly individualized creative force he brought to all of his work.

Works Cited

Alcott, Louisa May. *Little Women*. 1868. New York: Dell, 1987.

Davidson, Cathy N. *Revolution and the Word: The Rise of the Novel in America*. New York: Oxford UP, 1986.

Du Plessis, Rachel Blau. *Writing Beyond the Ending: Narrative Strategies of Twentieth Century Women Writers*. Bloomington: Indiana UP, 1985.

Manfred, Frederick. *Flowers of Desire*. Salt Lake City: Dancing Badger Press, 1989.

Martin, Wendy. "Seduced and Abandoned in the New World: The Image of Woman in American Fiction." *Woman in Sexist Society*. Ed. Vivian Gornick and Barbara K. Moran. New York: Mentor, 1971. 329-346.

Tompkins, Jane. *Sensational Designs: The Cultural Work of American Fiction, 1790-1860*. New York: Oxford UP, 1989.

Baseball as Passionate Preference in *No Fun on Sunday*

by Joseph M. Flora

Those who knew Fred Manfred or those who have read much of his fiction could not be surprised that he would write a novel with baseball at its center. Although Manfred is remembered for his endeavors on the basketball court at Calvin College, baseball was his true sports love. His conversations and letters teemed with references to the game. His fiction from the early *The Chokecherry Tree* (1948) to the later *Green Earth* (1977), both of which depict memorable Siouxland contests, prepared readers for *No Fun on Sunday* (1990) and its celebration of country baseball.

The word *celebration* is not excessive. The narrator tips his hand in the opening paragraph:

> In May, when the grass turns green, and the lilacs fill the air with purple perfumes, and the orioles tell of orchards bursting with pink blossoms, then the boys, old and young, get out their bats and balls and run to the pastures and play the wonderful game of baseball. (3)

The sentence echoes the opening lines of *The Canterbury Tales*, one of Manfred's favorite works, a work that is concurrently religious and earthy—and celebratory.

The literature of baseball is vast, but signs are scant that Manfred's novel has found many readers. Reviews of the novel were few, mainly brief. Not even Manfred enthusiasts have given the novel much attention. Although it received a positive review in *Western American Literature* (Martin 286-87), no papers at the Western Literature Association meeting have focused on it. If the novel makes its way, it will do so slowly.

We may guess that the novel was problematic from the beginning, that Manfred had to struggle to find a publisher for it. Although in his long career, Manfred was published by some major houses, no single house was wed to him as, say, Scribners was to Hemingway or Random House to Faulkner. Alan Swallow had good reason to identify Manfred in mid career as a maverick writer (74-92). The appellation remains apt. Manfred would continue to search for the "right" publisher. Crown, Manfred's last major commercial house, published three Manfred novels between 1976 and l980. There would be no Manfred novel after Crown published *Sons of Adam (*1980) until 1989, a large span for so prolific a writer as Manfred. Crown doubtless saw *No Fun on Sunday.* In his late career, Manfred was again beset with publishing problems. In 1989 Dancing Badger Press published *Flowers of Desire,* a novel that saw Manfred focused on sexual desire as determinedly as William Butler Yeats had been in his late work. This small house produced an attractive paper edition of the novel but could not give the book the promotion that a large commercial house could.

For *No Fun on Sunday* Manfred turned to a university press, one that makes Western American literature a major strength of its list.[1] In the past two decades or so, several university presses have published original fiction and poetry and have reissued work of important writers that had been difficult to find. The academy has benefited from the presence of publishing houses less commercially driven. Occasionally a university press finds that it has a best seller on its hands, as Louisiana State University Press did with John Kennedy Toole's *Confederacy of Dunces (*1980). But that is rare. With original work, the presses are attempting, rather, to give good work some audience, to encourage talent. In Manfred's case, the University of Oklahoma Press was paying tribute to a senior writer who had found his most lasting audience in the Midwest and West, but a writer unable to find the national readership that once seemed to be within his grasp.

If Manfred's depiction of sexual themes played a role in the failure of *Flowers of Desire* to find a large commercial house (as seems likely), that depiction would probably keep many university houses from the novel. In his review of *Flowers of Desire*, Dexter Martin recognizes that Manfred's treatment of sex there is somewhat problematical; he describes the novel as Manfred's "all-out answer" to those who had criticized his previous depictions of sexual themes.[2] And although sex is on Manfred's mind in *No Fun on Sunday* (how could it be otherwise? Manfred recognized sexuality as pivotal in human life), nothing in its treatment would likely cause a commercial publisher to turn away. Reviewers might even have wished for more explicit treatment of sexual themes. Why no takers for so wholesome a book?

The reviewers doubtless asked, who is the audience? Manfred seems not ever to have worried over that problem. In his late career, he had many stories to tell, but they tended to be stories set in the past—the America of his youth and young manhood, an America of the upper Midwest, rural and remote, America in the teens and twenties. Hemingway gave readers life "in our time," and most successful fiction writers have followed that lead. (It is a truism that Hemingway's protagonists aged as he did.) Even Faulkner when writing his masterpiece centered on the Civil War framed it from the contemporary anguish of Quentin Compson. Readers who recalled the time Manfred depicts in *No Fun on Sunday* (a diminishing number) or those who grew up with stories about it would seem the most likely to be attracted to Manfred's baseball story. What interest would his story have for city youth, for those who grew up in America since World War II? As the century draws near its end, it isn't even clear that baseball any longer deserves the designation of the great American pastime. Professional football occupies American attention for as many months of the year (with more intensity many would argue) than does baseball. With television, NFC and AFC games are accessible virtually throughout the land. Boys—and increasing numbers of girls—are growing up with hoop dreams rather than baseball dreams. The commercial reviewer may have been skeptical about the appeal of the book for younger readers. The novel, after all, describes a large number of baseball games in some detail—acceptable in film sequences, perhaps, but problematical on the printed page save for the aficionado, or so reviewers may have judged. (Although it might be argued that there is too much baseball in *No Fun on Sunday*, we do well to recall that many readers have found too much whaling in *Moby-Dick*.) Furthermore, the dilemma over whether or not to play baseball on Sunday will be quaint to most Americans living in the latter half of the century. Reviewers might also draw back from Manfred's style, judge it rural to a fault. Poetic in the opening paean, the narrative is decidedly plain, flat, oral, and often punctuated by clichés.

Manfred, however, was not driven by the agenda of a commercial house—though he probably argued for the sales potential of a baseball book that had done what no other had done, make central the drama of country baseball. If something more contemporary might appeal more to publishers, Manfred recognized what his true subject was—his Siouxland, especially rural Siouxland. (I have

BASEBALL AS PASSIONATE PREFERENCE 183

always found Manfred more convincing with his rural folk than with his city folk.) He also argued that his prose style was the right style for the place and time that he was describing.

When Manfred's novel was at last published, baseball had a much tarnished image. Fans were disgusted with player strikes, with what they saw as extravagant greed: many judged that baseball now embodied a corrupted national dream. From that perspective, Manfred's novel came at an appropriate moment. Baseball needed a good word to be said for it, needed a look at its connection with the land, its connection with country folk. Bernard Malamud's classic *The Natural* (1952) had begun by affirming that connection; Manfred would make country baseball the whole of his novel. His protagonist would dream about going to the major leagues and almost make that step.

Manfred's plot is simple, perhaps deceptively simple. We explore the dream (and its near fulfillment) of Sherm Engleking to play short stop for the Chicago Cubs. We meet Sherm, age thirteen, as he begins junior high school in a conservative Christian academy of Siouxland, discover his extraordinary devotion (and ability) for baseball, and follow him through age nineteen, when he loses three fingers in a farming accident, his baseball dream ended. Over half of the book is given to Sherm's nineteenth year, a year that finds him successfully courting Allie Pipp and playing a series of baseball games that lead to an invitation to join the Chicago Cubs training camp. Were Sherm to make the Cubs, he would have to confront the issue that has from the beginning been problematic: he would be playing games on Sunday, something opposed to the religion of his family, fiancée, and community. Knowing Sherm as we do (Manfred stays close to Sherm's point of view throughout the novel), we may feel fairly certain how he would have resolved the issue of conscience, but he never has to decide. His hand gets caught in a corn-picking machine, ending his dream. Sherm will spend his life on an Iowa farm.

Manfred's title is a clue to the complexities that lie behind that plot. It does, of course, highlight the scepter of the moral dilemma Sherm faces. His hoped-for career comes into sharp conflict with the values of his community, a community that puts great emphasis on the traditional meaning of Sunday. Sherm attends Christian Academy, named for his denomination, but also for centuries of a religious faith that demands much from its adherents. The title *No*

Fun on Sunday smacks, however, of an oppressive Puritan heritage that denies the pleasures of this world. Nothing would please Sherm's mother more than to have her youngest son enter the ministry of his denomination. At thirteen Sherm gives passing attention to the possibility, but primarily as possible leverage for his goal of getting permission to play school sports, though it is clear that he does not intend to enter the ministry.

Manfred never allows us to remain over-serious about that title, however. For it embodies one of the novel's sexual jokes. Told that baseball on Sunday is wrong, Ted Herman, manager of the Hello Homebrews looking for a rematch with Sherm's Bonnie Boys, observes that those who hold that view probably have sex on Sunday. If that pleasure, then why not the pleasure of baseball. Manfred's characters are not really the stern folk that we often find in depictions of Puritan New England. Although we indeed find some hypocrisies among them, they are, by and large, earthy folks who take amused looks at country matters. Along the way, the reader is frequently invited to chuckle over sexual innuendo and direct sexual references. Like his brother John (who has a vigorous sex life with his wife), Sherm is likely to have a fulfilled sexual life with Allie even if he will not play baseball.

The title does, however, accent the dominant gender issues of the novel. If the dictum against Sunday baseball comes from the church pastor and elders, it is carried out by the women of the novel. In *No Fun on Sunday* baseball brings to the fore the tensions that exist between the world of women and the world of men. Sometimes those tensions appear perilous.

Protagonists of sports novels usually face antagonists other than opponents in athletic contests, sometimes several, as in *The Natural*. In *No Fun on Sunday*, Sherm's chief antagonist is his mother. She dominates the action of the first movement of the novel; then Manfred removes her from the scene until the last movement. At age thirteen Sherm had fled her roof, living first with one sister, then with his brother. But "Ma" threatens Sherm's plans throughout. (Until he is twenty-one she has legal authority.) We are always aware of his sustained effort to keep her at a distance. Presumably Sherm has seen her from time to time in the years of his adolescence, but the reader does not until late in the novel. She arrives during the action of the last game that Sherm will ever play, the game that convinces the Cubs' scout to invite Sherm to spring practice. In what may count as the most embarrassing moment of Sherm's life, his mother rushes onto the field at the top of the ninth: "an old woman's shrill voice pierced through everything" (258). In her accented English, the Frisian-born woman cries, "Sher-mee! Sher-mee!" Sherm is, of course, nonplused. Manfred's use of cliché may be double-edged as he takes us into Sherm's mind: "Speaking of the devil." Ma's message is clear: "My boy, you playing baseball on Sunday? In this godless city?" (258) —and so is the chief issue of the plot, though Ma is led from the field and Sherm finishes his game (and, alas, his baseball career) with a rare feat, an unassisted triple play that wins the game for his team and his invitation to appear at the Cubs' spring practice.

Manfred's decision to keep Ma at a distance was a wise one. He could not let her ruin Sherm's *annus mirabilis* that portrays the complexities and realities of country baseball. He may have sensed, too, that Ma's dialogue, her broken English, might seem exaggerated or comic to contemporary readers—one way of viewing her presence at Sherm's last baseball game. But comedy is scarcely the intent behind Ma's presence. She is well-meaning, yes, but well-meaning in the way that Mrs. Adams is well-meaning in Hemingway's Nick Adams stories. Portraying Mrs. Adams less in *In Our Time*, Hemingway knew he was portraying her more. In "The Doctor and the Doctor's Wife," this woman, ever eager to control, says to her husband (whom she has once more defeated in a conflict of wills), "If you see Nick, dear, will you tell him his mother wants to see him?" (Hemingway 26). The words are chilling to the attentive reader. As the story ends, Nick chooses his father over his mother. Hemingway is careful to keep Mrs. Adams out of sight through the rest of *In Our Time*, though her presence may be felt in the surrogate Mrs. Krebs of "Soldier's Home." In "Big Two-Hearted River," the last story of Hemingway's composite novel, Mrs. Adams is surely one of the things that Nick has a need not to think about (Hemingway 134).[3]

If Mrs. Adams provides the reader with an enduring chill, Manfred uses Ma to give the reader a similar sensation. Significantly, it comes at the very end of the novel. After Sherm's stepfather has died unexpectedly, Sherm departs to help support his mother in her grief. He had been genuinely fond of Garland, who had (unsuccessfully) tried to use his influence to get Ma to be more understanding about Sherm's love of sports. Ma behaves well at the funeral service for Garland, but at the cemetery her propensity for over dramatization comes to the fore. Laertes-like, she jumps into the grave and throws herself on the coffin. Although the reader's immediate reaction may be (as at the Le Mars baseball game) one of amusement, amusement and surprise dissipate. With Sherm and the family, we come to sense Ma's great grief. Neither of her sons is able to console her, though they would like to, a fact that stresses the strong gender division of the novel. But Allie, "with her loving patient hands," is able to do so. Allie is able to speak the right word for Ma, but a somber one for the reader: "Now, now, it's all going to be all right. Time, Mother, time. Sherm and I will always be here to comfort you. Together we have him at least" (287). There it is: "Together we have him at least." Those are the haunting last words of the novel.

Although Allie has agreed to let Sherm try out for the Cubs, she has been full of misgivings—misgivings about playing baseball on Sunday, misgivings about having to leave Siouxland for godless Chicago. Following that memorable Le Mars game and his invitation to Sherm, the Cubs' scout cautions him that the issue of Sunday baseball is one he will have to work out with his conscience (266). But because of the accident (fortunate in most respects for Ma and Allie), Sherm never has that battle of conscience. Hemingway's Nick says to his father, "I want to go with you" (Hemingway 27), a choice with implications not just for the moment but for Nick's life and for our perception of *In Our Time*.

Sherm's mother and Allie have noticeable support in Manfred's heavily gendered novel. Sherm's sister Joan, with whom he first lives after leaving home, dislikes baseball and has accepted her mother's view on Sunday play. Sherm greatly prefers his sister Ada, who does not like baseball either, but Ada, mother of his nephew Free, is more tolerant of this male passion than her sister Joan. Nevertheless, she tells her mother that Sherm is going to play a Sunday baseball game at Le Mars, leading to Ma's dramatic invasion and the fierce reassertion of women's will that comes at the novel's end.

Ma has had a major ally, too, in Matilda, John's wife—major because Sherm has been living with Matilda and John for over five years. Sherm cannot help but notice the tension in their marriage. Matilda enjoys nagging, and John admits to Sherm that he feels that he had been trapped by sex into the marriage. (Sex has been, however, an important conduit to restoring humor and vitality in the marriage.) Matilda regularly mocks John's and Sherm's love of baseball. It's a boy's game, she keeps reminding them and the reader. It is surely significant for Manfred's theme that women's world conflicts with men's in the reversal that makes Sherm's moral dilemma moot. John and Sherm have just begun to master the new corn picking machine that is increasing the farm's productivity when at noon dinner on that crucial day, Matilda "told" John to take a couple of hours off in order to drive her to the Ladies Aid: "You boys are doing so well with the expensive machine you surely can bend a little and let me have some fun too" (270).[4] The reader should note both her destination and the play on the novel's title as they underscore the division between males and females.

Matilda's request almost leads to Sherm's death. While John is away with Matilda, Sherm operates the machinery by himself, but without sufficient attention. Playing imaginary baseball games as he drives horses and the machine, he reaches into the husking rollers to break up a jam. The machine grabs his hand. The reader senses that another "machine" has been waiting for just such a moment. "Together we have him at least." For the attentive reader, it is a telling line, dripping with irony, when Matilda says as John and Sherm depart for the Hello Hospital, "You men . . . the way you get into these awful accidents!" (278).

Yet the pervading gender conflict of Manfred's novel is never so sharply disturbing as it is in *In Our Time*. Manfred is always pulling back from Hemingway's dark (di) vision. Sherm's mother does not chill us as Nick Adams's mother does. Manfred's narrator knows that Ma has been shaped by her culture, an old-world culture. She has not yet become American; America's language is only partly hers. She prefers the ways of her native land. Baseball is the great American game, that game in which every player gets his turn at bat, the chance to become the hero, to save the game and the day. How could she understand its dynamics? Resistance to the game is less keen in her daughters. The reader is meant to see the cultural conflict as well as the gender conflict. There are, after all, many women attending those baseball games that Manfred so lovingly describes. Partly, they are indulging their "boys." But the games are also part of major community rituals. The first baseball game to be described in the novel takes place during the annual Decoration (Memorial) Day church picnic. The marrieds face the singles. The day is a civil holiday celebrated in this Siouxland (highly homogeneous) community in the context of the church's life. For most Siouxlanders, church and community are inseparable. That the game be between married and singles underscores the community focus on marriage and family, on the community's vital interest that sexual drive serve the interest of the community. The later games of the novel are rooted in intense rivalries between neighboring towns (like our prehistoric ancestors, we remain tribal). Baseball games help Manfred's people define themselves.

Thus it is that Manfred gives us an ambiguous ending to *No Fun on Sunday*. The reader is meant to feel the pain of Sherm's loss, to regret that he will not have the chance to realize his ability as a baseball player. But how different his plight is from that of Roy Hobbs at the end of *The Natural*. There Roy has been beaten by the forces of money, greed, evil; his baseball career is over and he retreats into loneliness, obscurity, and bitter tears. In *No Fun on Sunday*, on the other hand, Sherm has a place eager to claim him—indeed, a place that he has never left. It is not just that Ma and Allie have Sherm at the end of the novel: Siouxland has him, and that is, the novel conveys, a good place to be. The community, not the individual, is the victor.

Eudora Welty observed, "fiction depends for its life on place," a dictum to which Manfred would give full assent (Welty 118). In *No Fun on Sunday* the reader approaches baseball through the lens of place. A reader who takes the descriptions of the several baseball games of Sherm's career as some indulgence on Manfred's part would do well to consider them in this light. Each game plays an integral part of Manfred's careful structure.[5]

The first game finds the Bonnie Boys uniformed for the first time ever. When the uniforms don't fit, "the lady of the house" has to make alterations. Free's mother "sighs over wearing special clothes for what was a boy's game. . . but with a forgiving sigh" (146). The gender theme persists, then gets a new complication, for the sexual orientation of the Hello pitcher is suspect; the community is homophobic, we are not surprised to learn. Because Bonnie wins after falling behind 11-0, the Hello Homebrews understandably want a rematch. The issue of Sunday baseball (and Manfred's title) emerges from these dramatic circumstances.

Bonnie plays its second game at Hazard, aptly named as it turns out. The fates are against Bonnie from the start. Wimp

Tollman can't make the trip because his father wants him to help put up alfalfa hay, and Jimmy Wales has to work late at the bank because the state examiners are in town. Before the game starts, pool hall bums have "to scoop up the cowplops and the horseballs" on the diamond, usually a pasture (168). One umpire can't make it; so the burden of calling the game falls on a single official. Hazard has secured Swede Risberg for shortstop: Risberg was one of those who had played for the White Sox in 1919 and was suspended from baseball for throwing the world series (country baseball is full of such surprises, as Manfred keeps reminding us). Owing to Risberg's skill Bonnie loses this game, but Sherm gets a huge reward at the end of the game. Risberg tells Sherm that he has the skills for the majors. But before that important spur to Sherm's motivation, he had been taken anew by the sheer fun of the game, and looking back at it the reader may wonder if Sherm in the majors would ever have found the game this much "fun."[6]

The third game is memorable for the high quality of the play and for a more important reason. The opponents are the Tennessee Rats, a black team. Because in the 1920s African Americans were not allowed in the major or minor leagues, they had to form their own leagues; they also sought white teams willing to play them. Thus the Rats arrive in Siouxland. Manfred not only reminds us of the conditions of the time, he also makes clear that Siouxlanders shared the racism prevalent throughout the nation—though they seldom if ever saw a black person. Bonnie and the country around it were scarcely a melting pot. Manfred also shows us black men with the passion for baseball that we find in Sherm. The game indeed turns out to be a humanizing experience for the Siouxlanders, who must acknowledge the exceptional ability of their opponents. They reach out to them so that the Rats will not suffer economically after losing the well-played game when Sherm homers. The "American" pastime here shows promise of being a means to greater opportunity for blacks and for a greater humanity for whites.

The game against Amen is a pitching duel, memorable because Sherm's young nephew Free Alfredson opposes Smokey Joe Lotz, who once pitched for the St. Louis Cardinals. By this time in the novel, Free has become almost as important to the reader as Sherm is. Fond of using doubles or twins in his novels, Manfred has paired Sherm's dreams for playing in the majors with those of Free.[7] Free has developed a good "screwball" pitch—good enough to take Bonnie to a 4-3 win over Amen. When word of Free's skill reaches Deacon Blake, the Cubs' scout, he makes plans to see him play in the rematch against Hello. Because of Free, manager Garrett Engleking has the chance to tell Deacon about Sherm. Two futures will be at stake in this game, as chapter 13, the shortest chapter in the novel, highlights—but ominously, in content as well as chapter number. Deacon is alerted to the possibility that Free, still in his mid teens, has pitched too many innings, his arm damaged.

The glory of the Amen game will not be repeated in Hello, as the reader has strong intimations even as the teams take warmups. Bonnie's second baseman arrives stinking of homebrew beer; two of his teammates are also half-drunk. Their play shows the effects. Free on the mound is extended far beyond what should have been allowed; his arm fails. Despite homers by both Sherm (disgusted at the drunkards, he protests that this is the last game he will ever play for Bonnie) and Free, Bonnie loses, 9-4. Deacon tells Free to rest his arm for a whole year, and he will look him up again. (Free will not, of course, go to the majors. The reader senses a very different life for him—and one in Siouxland.)[8] Deacon wants to see Sherm play one more game before submitting his report—hence Sherm seizes the opportunity to play for Le Mars in a Sunday game against Rutherland. As we have seen, the Le Mars game returns us pointedly to issues of gender and religion and community.

For all that the reader encounters of the intricacies of games and strategies, baseball is a means as well as an end in *No Fun on Sunday*. The novel teems with metaphorical implications. The game is sweet and wonderful to Sherm because it reflects his life philosophy. Baseball is not time driven, as basketball and football are. One does not battle the clock. The chance for the hit, even the victory is there until the last out in the ninth inning—no matter how far behind the team—as that first game with Hello exemplifies. Sherm frequently applies the lessons of baseball to life. Trying to help his brother-in-law bring in a crop before the storm hits, he admonishes, "We want to win this ball game, don't we? . . . If we hurry we can still pull her out in the ninth" (55). Some years later, he tells his fiancée, "You can't go through life with defeat always in your head. When you walk on the diamond you've got to figure you've already won. If you don't, you're licked before the first pitch of the game" (185). As a young man fighting tuberculosis, Manfred followed a similar philosophy, and Sherm's lines embody Manfred's faith every time he began a new novel. Thus it is that at the end of *No Fun on Sunday* the reader views Sherm's future with some confidence. His baseball playing days may be over, but the poetry of the game will continue to inspire him.

Baseball is not, after all, the only means Manfred uses to make Sherman a very winning protagonist; baseball is not the only vocation that Manfred considers with some detail in *No Fun on Sunday*. The reader will learn as much about farming as about baseball, as much about rural life as about country baseball. For many late twentieth-century readers the pictures of farming will seem much more remote than the baseball games, but Manfred's presentation of pre-industrial family farming is an important ingredient to his creation of "place."

When Sherm at age nineteen makes plans for a professional baseball career, he has already had extraordinary success as a farmer. That career began at age thirteen when he ran away from home in protest to his mother's tyranny. He goes first to his sister Joan's because he is aware that Pete Waxler, his brother-in-law, is a poor farmer. But Pete is smart enough to welcome Sherm's services. In town Sherm gets pamphlets from the county agent and begins to transform the Waxler farm. At thirteen, he is doing a man's work and doing it well. By late-century standards, Sherm would be a victim of child labor abuse. Siouxlanders of the time, however, would not find much to raise an eyebrow over. Sherm shows his mettle when he learns that his sister has stolen from him. (All of the early scenes have shown an independent Sherm, one who makes quick decisions, and makes them work.) Disgusted at the perfidy, Sherm quickly departs for his brother John's. John welcomes him; Sherm again quickly proves his worth and eventually becomes a partner on the farm. As was common in nineteenth-century America and into the twentieth century (especially on farms), Sherm had left most of his boyhood behind by age thirteen. (Manfred shows his reader a time and a society where the word *adolescent* has no meaning.) We know, consequently, that he will also respond capably to the farming accident that takes him from baseball. The reader has been made to feel the pleasure in farming that is well-done.

This is not to say, of course, that everything is even at the end of Manfred's novel. It is not. Sherm has been denied a choice and a conflict that he should have had. One of the several things that makes Sherm so attractive a character is his early commitment to baseball, his "passionate preference." I borrow here from Robert Frost, quite naturally, since Manfred is usually thinking of writing when he describes baseball. (It is significant that Sherm admonishes Free to "just pitch us a good poem of a game" 148). Late in his career, Frost observed, "The time for a young artist to begin to be an artist, to have a passionate preference for art come over him, is somewhere between the ages of fifteen and twenty-five. . . . The tenderest thing you can have as a patron of the arts is a sense of that, almost unexpressed in the young person . . . his first passionate preference" (Banner 10). Sherm had discovered his passionate preference earlier than fifteen, and Manfred portrays it very convincingly. By the time he is in the junior high years, Sherm thinks baseball year around, and he practices batting all by himself using an old broom handle for a bat and stones for a baseball, often pretending that his Cubs are beating the Pirates. In winter, frozen horse apples make a good substitution for a ball. Imagining that isolated batting practice, one might be reminded of Frost's narrator in "Birches" as he sees the bent birches after a winter storm. He would prefer that some country boy had bent them: "Some boy too far from town to learn baseball,/ Whose only play was what he found himself,/ Summer or winter, and could play alone." Manfred's boy has not been too far from town to learn the game, and he has also learned to play it alone. Similarly, of course, Frost has been thinking about the writing of poetry as much as about birch swinging. He echoes his earlier reference to baseball in his wonderful last line: "One could do worse than be a swinger of birches." So Sherm has found; so the reader of *No Fun on Sunday* should discover.

Frost's comments about the glory of the passionate preference were occasioned by his concern for how that passion was nurtured (mainly not nurtured) in the academy. For some time Frost had been disturbed that colleges and universities had not done that very well.[9] A large part of the drama of Manfred's novel results from a failure of sufficient nurturance. Sherm's school and community provide some opportunity for him, though the hand at school could be heavy. His mother, sisters, and sister-in-law clearly do not understand the creative drive that baseball represents in Sherm and in Free. Had his mother even been neutral about his passionate preference, Sherm's whole life (and hers) would have been different. Instead, his mother tries to make Sherm's career decision for him. She reflects the values of the community that the ministry is the most exalted possible profession. A teacher at school recognizes that Sherm has intellectual abilities that exceed those she usually finds. She encourages him to continue in school, to have big dreams; he could become many things she admonishes. But Ma refuses to see the implication of her injunction against sports. Denied that outlet in school, especially the chance to further his passionate preference, Sherm leaves school for farming, claiming a measure of freedom and opportunity in it—and the chance for country baseball. How many mute and inglorious Miltons might there be in Siouxland? Sherm might be included among them. Manfred and Frost are certainly one in celebrating the creative impulse, the special gift of a "passionate preference," the love of the deed for its own sake. They admonish as well that a caring society will seek to nurture such gifts.

We must acknowledge, however, that his passionate preference denied him, Sherm is more fortunate than many who have been denied theirs. His second choice has at least been his choice, and he is very good at it. He will be surrounded by a caring family and community difficult to duplicate in the late twentieth century. The community is imperfect to be sure. Some of its flaws we've noted; others are not hard to find. But it is solid and has many strengths—largely because it is fairly uncontaminated by the industrialized twentieth-century. In *No Fun on Sunday* there are almost no references to events in the outside world. Indeed, the characters distrust that world. Their rhythms are still the rhythms of nature—planting, harvesting, replenishing. Their preferred game is played outdoors. Few citizens leave Siouxland—to most the very thought of doing so is threatening—and few newcomers arrive.

Place in Manfred's Siouxland ends up by being rather like place in the Morgana, Mississippi, of Eudora Welty's *The Golden Apples*, though her place is created in large part by a rich texture of myth and his by realism. In Morgana also, the artistic souls are frustrated, and only a few escape. Many who wander away from Morgana make their way back. Morgana makes large claims on its citizens, in part because it is also closely identified with nature. Time moves slowly there, as it does in Siouxland. Morgana's power is often immense, especially if it censures or excludes. If it does not know how to nurture adequately its most creative youth or to recognize its heroes, it provides most of its citizens a sustaining identity. So, too, does Sherm Engleking discover the strength of Siouxland in *No Fun on Sunday*.

Notes

[1] The University of Oklahoma Press also published Manfred's *Of Lizards and Angels: A Saga of Siouxland* (1992).

[2] Martin characterizes the book as "sex on nearly every page, sex at its worst as well as at its best, sex as it really is, not just 'a beautiful gift from God'" (286).

[3] Sherm recognizes that he does well to keep his distance from his mother. When she tries to reassert her influence through letters, he spends little time with them. Instead, he drops them into the privy.

[4] It is fair, however, to contrast the difference in men's fun and women's fun. Baseball is played for its own sake. "Ladies Aid" may be a social event, but it traditionally involves the practical as well: sewing, quilting, or other projects to further the humanitarian outreach of the church. (The word *aid* should not be overlooked.) The women of Siouxland attend the games of their men; they may feel some resentment that the men undervalue their own efforts or need for "fun."

Manfred has made conflicting ideas of fun a recurring theme, always with gender implications. Preceding Sherm's *annus mirabilis* of country baseball and his courting of Allie, Sherm, Free, and Harm Joly present the program for the church's young people, a shadowgraph. (Movies have not yet come to this part of Siouxland, mostly because the church frowns on them.) The three teenagers have a joyous time practicing for the event. When they present their pantomime behind a sheet, they get a response they had not anticipated. Reverend Tiller stops the show because of the audience's response. Taking shadow violence for reality, the females are weeping and crying; the males are cussing and swearing. Later, Free reports on the reaction of his parents to reports of the uproar: "Oh, Pa heard about it but he didn't say anything. Only Ma got a little excited. She didn't mind us having good fun; she just didn't like it that we scared the girls so. She said we should have remembered the the local gals ain't all that up on things. And, she was a little worried that we were aping one of the Devil's clever inventions, the movie" (132).

[5] Manfred anticipates the movement of the whole novel in Chapter One. It establishes Sherm's love for baseball, his cleverness at school and his ability to get out of a difficult dilemma, and Ma's opposition to baseball (we hear her call "Sher-mee," as she will in his last game), and it ends with his disappointment when the principal rules against a proposed baseball game. Sherm is caught by another machine.

[6] Clumsy Peter Harber, who has been having his difficulties in the game, spots a rabbit sitting under a thistle, laughing at him he imagines. He throws

a ball at the rabbit, knocking him out, then tosses him into the lap of a woman watching the game, inviting her to make a rabbit stew. The dazed rabbit recovers and hops away. Sherm is highly amused. "There's nothing like the fun of country baseball" (174). In the first Bonnie-Hello game, a "gopher ball" is the source of similar amusement (158). In the Le Mars-Rutherland game, a huge riot between the two teams and their fans occurs on the field, stopped only after four fire engines arrive and hose down the participants (262-63). From her distance, Ma must have been convinced that the sport was indeed Satanic.

[7]Sherm has already been paired in chapter one with his dead brother, a rival who appeared to be moving toward Ma's preferred profession.

[8]In *Green Earth* Free is eager to escape Siouxland, to find a larger world—unaware yet of its claims on him, his feeling for it.

[9]Frost delivered his remarks at a lecture and reading at the University of North Carolina on March 14, 1961. After reproaching America's colleges and universities for the failure to nurture creative efforts adequately, Frost sought for solutions: "It's a stern thing. It's one of the sternest things of all. It's sterner than learning . . . it's sacrificial. And you mustn't be with people that make a slighting, a triviality of it, a mocking way with it. . . . The tenderest thing you can have as patrons of the arts is a sense of that almost unexpressed in the young person between fifteen and twenty-five, his first passionate preference.

Belief . . . comes with this passionate preference, this dream of something to be. You know, you believe yourself into what you're going to be. You don't know yourself into it, you believe yourself into it. At the age of twenty, you can't go before a committee and tell them what you're going to be, not very well. It's going on all the time, but how crude a thing it is, that's the secret, sacred secret. It's a very, very precious thing." Through his novel, Manfred late in his career expresses a similar conviction.

Works Cited

Banner, Leslie. *A Passionate Preference: The Story of the North Carolina School of the Arts*. Winston-Salem: North Carolina School of the Arts Foundation, 1987.
Frost, Robert. *The Poetry of Robert Frost*. Ed. Edward Connery Lathem. New York: Holt, Rinehart and Winston, 1969.
Hemingway, Ernest. *In Our Time*. 1925. New York: Macmillan, Collier, 1986.
Manfred, Frederick. *No Fun on Sunday*. Norman: U of Oklahoma P, 1990.
Martin, Dexter. Rev. of *Flowers of Desire* and *No Fun on Sunday* by Frederick Manfred. *Western American Literature*, 25 (Fall 1990) : 286-87.
Swallow, Alan. "The Mavericks." *Critique: Studies in Modern Fiction* 2 (Winter 1959) : 74-92.
Welty, Eudora. *The Eye of the Story: Selected Essays and Reviews*. New York: Random House, 1970.

Part IV

Assessing a Legacy: Notes of Appreciation

Hypnotized By a Reptile: A Student's Account of How the East Was Won by a Giant's Dusty Roar

by Olga Klekner

I was born and raised in Socialist Hungary and came to these United States of America in the autumn of 1973. I was a twenty-one-year-old budding poet, deeply in love with an American young man whom I had married a few months earlier. Thus, I bet my future on a single card with handsomely painted hearts on it. I was just unable to understand, and thus ignored, the English writing on it.

Upon my arrival my vocabulary consisted of "Hello," "Thank you," and "I love you." Looking back, I am quite amazed that even the most essential, obviously crucial swearwords were missing from my lexical knowledge. I should have known some. My father spent long months in American prison camps during World War II, and after a glass or two of "palinka," a Hungarian alcoholic insane concoction whose mere vapor could help annihilate chemical warfare danger, he fondly remembered his friendly prison guards, who were willing professors of obscenity. I quickly realized that in this strange, new American reality, an immigrant does not have to speak English to survive comfortably in the United States. Ethnic cultural islands flourish everywhere with peace and stubborn willingness to survive in their own unique ways. They are imbedded into the body of the American landscape and offer their newcomers a virtual, pain-free, and comfortable metamorphosis into a new hyphenated American personhood. Unfortunately, even with time passing, some are reluctant ever to leave this comfort zone.

So it was with me. In the next five years, following my initial culture shock, which left me uncharged and even mildly despondent, I refused to learn English. I spent the small amount of energy I had on hating the language. When one does not understand a language, the impenetrable sound of it takes over, and we judge it and respond to it from the waves its strange sounds create. To me English sounded rather cocky, and it seemed that people were singing it right out of a badly written, unintelligible ballad. I had no desire to sing it. I had no desire to read it.

In a desperate search to express myself non-ethnically, but still within a creative form, I enrolled to study art at Henry Ford Community College in Dearborn, Michigan. I also registered for English 131. It was not a sudden, lotus-filled enlightenment or a love-attack for the language. With considerable pain I learned that obtaining a degree even in basket weaving required two courses in that much cursed, godless tongue. Of course my opinion of the language had not changed drastically over the years. I had simply learned to tolerate it. With happy satisfaction, I still wrote only in Hungarian. I had published my poetry in countless Hungarian literary and political publications and also in a Canadian anthology—all in my blessed, beautiful native language. Over the years, English stayed cold and distant and required lead-weight effort to read. I was joyless when I found myself to be forced to speak it. Then one hot summer morning in 1991 I found myself sitting in a required English composition class. I was scared to death. My professor required the reading of books by authors I had never heard of. Little did I know that the professor of English 131 I practically crawled to register for, Dr. Nancy Owen Nelson, had a clandestine contact with the force of universal literature gods and had me under her secret spell within the very first week of classes. That she had me read a book titled *The Golden Bowl*, which to my satisfaction I was able to purchase "used" before classes began. Little did I know that a simple saga of an infertile morsel of the United States would forever make me fall in love with a language that I had detested; now I found it more and more poetic, rich in beauty, zest, and deep in harmony with each passing day.

When I registered, I found out that I had 93 unusable credit hours from my college years from Hungary. With bitter silence I waved "good by' to a career in writing and decided to indulge in another love of mine, art, and the study of behavior, psychology. "The unfortunate who are forced to speak a language like this will need me some day," I must have said to myself. I still didn't know that an author named Frederick Manfred would shake the living hell out of my Hungarian comfort and destroy my doubts about ever enjoying this language. I didn't know that he would help me to fly on the delicate, new wings of this amazing language that grows stronger on my lips, on my mind, on my fingertips each time the taste of a new word left me breathless.

Oh yes, *The Golden Bowl* and his author had an enduring, profound influence on my life. Of course immediately after I purchased the novel, my remarkably "high" level of interest didn't even nudge me to peek into its pages until my professor with her ominous intonation specifically requested her class to do just that. The length of the book seemed surmountable, and it didn't feel heavy in my carefully judging hands, unlike *The Dollmaker*, the other assigned novel, which sent the slow shivers of terror down my spine.

From the very beginning, there was something about my woman professor that made a sleeping interest toward the English language awaken in me. The more she talked and the way she talked about the life and passions of Frederick Manfred, the more I needed to know about him. I remember watching a video of this man who liked running around stark naked on his Siouxland. He enjoyed lying on top of rocks, to feel the rhythm of life from the abyss. Among other things, I like tasting old bark of trees to have their intense soul merge with mine, so I instantly felt to have found in him an earth-particle of organic intelligence that was predestined to be within my conscious experience. Thus after reading *The Golden Bowl* I began a letter dated November 21, 1991, which I later sent to Frederick Manfred; I opened with the following exclamation: "It is a privilege knowing you! Yes, to a certain unexplainable angle I really believe that I know you."

The Golden Bowl . . . how I loved reading this magnificently powerful story of a land and her simple, questionably volunteer prisoners whose invisible umbilical cords kept them faithful to a dustscape that offered only memories of abundance! To compare Manfred's style with anyone else's would be like comparing fresh-picked, hard-muscled apples to lukewarm meatballs on leftover spaghetti. His zesty, rhythmical and exuberant sentences keep the reader intense and angry about something unjust that hovers above the wind-raped land like sea gulls circle above the exquisite depth of the ocean that holds secrets and surprises. One longs to dip into this pure poetry of intense motion, to be touched by the unknown, and to steal the secrets that are told many times but still possess the magic of newness and private pain.

Manfred's stubbornness to stay with Siouxland and tell its story is his private pleasure and private pain, for the lush stories are also rooted in dry lands and some of the past unproductive crumbs of earth touch the poet in his soul and convince him to sing his marvelous songs year after year, not for a second resting on yesterday's laurels.

One needs to be possessed by unyielding intensity to be a poet, and Manfred is a poet who is blessed with an inner vision that reflects past, present, and future on raw, vibrating landscape that tastes like rhythms on fire:

> East of the house gate, where a washout, or gully, turned with the Highway, the roots of a tree-stump hung octopus-like from the gully's upper fringe. The skull of a cow, a broken box-wagon, an old bedspring, and other metal scrap littered the floor of the gully. (12)

I don't know if there is such a thing as love at first sight, but the moment I started reading *The Golden Bowl* I was touched by the endless magic of this magnificent language and now I am forever lost in its breathless wonder and exciting possibilities. Manfred's powerful words described the Bad Lands I have never known, yet have felt, I have never seen, yet have heard of; land that would have slowly rusted into infertility under the people of Hungary. I remembered rich, ripe fields from my childhood travels as well as stunted, dried-out corn fields. For me, as an immigrant, abundance has always been a hard-earned gift and forever in transit.

From the beginning, the reader feels Manfred's stubborn anxiousness about something that returns in every thought and every lavishly painted picture. Only a poet's feverish, slashed soul can offer such uneasiness that a reader prays for a miracle, wishing for an apple tree to grow into this Garden of Dusty Evil. But apple trees do not blossom in a desert and women have been punished for Eve's sin of curiosity ever since she had the need to know more. With a poet's bold creating powers Manfred's heroine Kirsten becomes the only blossoming promise.

Manfred's anxiety stems not from the not-knowing, but from being aware of the truth of the Bad Lands' historical reputation. Prior to writing his sagas, when he dealt with subjects that touched the pages of history, he took painstaking time and effort to research the truth. By choosing heroes who are unable to win against destiny, he courageously crosses over to unsafety: he refuses to offer his readers a magnificently positive ending where

Maury, his bride and her parents would dance in a rain that offers to wash away past doubts and unhappiness and would nail a rainbow the size of South Dakota across the sky.

There are no rainbows in *The Golden Bowl*, not in an after-rain sense anyway. Manfred's rainbows are grainy dustbows tossed over the land by choking, moistless winds that break those who are unable to bend:

> The wind drove and the sun burned, drying and cracking and breaking the land.... The great wind roared with greater fury. Dust drifts wavered around and over the buildings, the machines, the homes, the chalky bones of cattle, and the path to the privy in the leafless orchard. (9, 10)

Like a cradle padded with thorns and dust, the thoughts in italics rock us into a hypnotic sense of understanding a solidly painted surreal reality. If Manfred is a poet, he is a fantastic painter too, who dips his magical brush into hues of dusts, winds and earth tones. He holds his vast pallet with a strength of a Greek god who was never punished but rather praised by Zeus for giving mankind this inescapable future in *The Golden Bowl*.

The poet-painter is unmerciful. He is not holding our hands to gently guide us over the hopeless unpleasantness of infertile lands. He is putting the readers in charge of their own panics and feelings of uncertainty. Manfred should be sued for placing his unsuspecting, gentle readers in his microwave mind. His thoughts, rhythms and colors are not native for the non-poet reader, and I suspect the stress could become real and constant.

All living organisms are under swelling stress in *The Golden Bowl*. Because stress does not permit growth, they are heroically transformed to grow side roots, forcing those delicate new growths into land which is cursed to move by the violent commands from boisterous winds and wrinkling wills. Life on dry earth is a lonely life for all. In the center of that loneliness Manfred puts the land itself that is abandoned by those who lost faith in dreams. He places the loyal, lonely children of God, the Thors, on the land; for them, time and space did not provide more than stillborn opportunities. Only predestination and the brilliant young mind of the poet controls, and the reader starts to long for rain long after it becomes painfully clear that God has only dry tears for the land. Manfred chooses an end that begins with the unmerciful middle. With seemingly gallant ease he finishes the story with the moist dreamland of a farmer's heart:

> In the hidden country of a pilgrim's heart, rains are falling. The sun shines there, and men go into the fields and work, and believe in the work of their hands. And sow grain, and broadcast the seed of grass for their cattle and horses. And plant corn and melonseed in the gray-black loam.
> And the land trembles with multitude of germinant sprouts growing and leaping in the sun. (225)

Hence, Manfred cradles us into his most poetic dream with the help of a silent power, the Old Lizard, which he believes to be an inner-guiding, universal unconsciousness. If not in the midst of a too chaotic, loud life, all writers hear a voice, a calling that demands response to a longing of fingertips to connect with the minds and spirits that dictate that which can never be learned. The Old Lizard is the much-welcomed, primal power behind the poet. The ancient reptile's "pardon me while I give a damn" attitude guides Manfred's dreams and awakenings. The Lizard plants a seed in the poet's bloodstream that makes his grateful miracles happen, and every year is "The Year" for him: Manfred is committed and tireless in his writing. It seems that for him every finished project offers another beginning. Manfred's uniqueness partly stems from staying free and naked in spirit as his Lizard dictates him to be. He is a grateful and obedient, never an opposing, instrument in his Lizard's hands. His pains and joys and hopes and loves are etched into old stones and rocks of a land he became a giant part of, and Manfred salutes that underlined unorthodox bond with fifty years of story telling. According to some old, wise saying, behind every successful man there is a great woman. Behind the success of the poet-storyteller Manfred lies a wide-awakened sage, the unrestrained Old Lizard. This Old Lizard had to be created with the first intelligent life and holds the spark of wonder of ancient collective understanding.

Long ago, when Manfred found his voice with *The Golden Bowl*, he found his Lizard as well. Forty-five years later his reptile succeeded in hypnotizing me and helped to open a gate to new understanding. He succeeded in helping me love the English language. I am grateful for *The Golden Bowl,* I am grateful for Frederick Manfred, whose poetry in prose awakened the seed of interest in me toward the English language and its magic.

*****

Years have passed since I first read *The Golden Bowl.* I feel like a born-again poet, if there has ever been one in me. I am the product of a ringless literary marriage between a powerful writer and a magnificent teacher-scholar of his brilliance. She encouraged me to try my wings in new highs. I often hear the roar of winning, and I love to hear my own wings slashing the wind. A raw, primal roar to succeed created Frederick Manfred and Frederick Manfred's call upon the Old Lizard keeps recreating the perceivable, yet magical presence of him and his dream world.

The letter I sent to the author of *The Golden Bowl* three years ago ended with my very first poem in a language that keeps me awed and feeling fulfilled in my hyphenated Americanness. I used to think that I would never be free again—I am, after all, a Hungarian-American. The hyphenation kept me in a horizontal prison, in a political coma, pulling my identity in two directions, never allowing me to break free from this strange, one-hundred-eighty-degree gravity. The hyphen in its brokenness suggested a brokenness in me. Now I no longer feel like a prisoner. In a sense, I have become the hyphen, the controlling force. I am pulling closer a golden past while I bathe in sunshine streaming from the bursting buds of explosive new growth. Golda Meier once said that "those who do not know how to weep with their whole heart don't know how to laugh either."

I thank my life, maybe even my own Old Lizard, for teaching me how to laugh with all my freed soul and all my restless heart.

Manfred

Your thoughts are
like the wind's wild,
free blows.
Your Lizard licks off
yesterday's sensual woman's touch
from your lips.

Your heart forgets to beat
then madly rushes you
to the next word
your feverish soul creates.

You are tasting earth
with your heart
and instead of modern day's
cholesterol
inside your artery
LIFE itself
builds up
and will kill you
when you will be exactly
  one hundred,
and you will experience death
with deep, quiet laughter
  and
a soft breast pressed
  against
      your
          wondering
              hands

*****

Dearborn, December 15, 1997

    I was wrong. Fred Manfred didn't live to be one hundred years old. His Old Lizard stretched in his soul one more time before it pulled on itself the satisfied blanket of immortal peace on the bed of a place without true human understanding, a place without lies and fear, heaven or hell. Frederick Manfred was not a man who wore his knees out in any kind of church rows. Neither am I. Thus I refuse to claim that I sense two huge, naked, invisible-to-mortals feet dangling off of a cliff of a fluffy little cloud. He wasn't a fluff-loving kind of man. His threads of human existence sewed his entire being tightly to the landscape of blood and reality. The altar where he worshipped left dust and grass stains on his elbows, thistles on his eyebrows and the taste of a woman on his lips. He stood his ground as a dreamer all his life, nurturing the curiosity of an immense, disheveled child within. His vast soul was filled with wonders. The Old Lizard was surrounded with earthly beliefs and wheat-smelling dreams, with a frame of a man whose skin and bones, flesh and blood were of honor. When he knelt, it was to taste an ant or to scrape his knees to feel the pain of a hero he would endow with life in a novel, or to plant seeds in his garden as well as in his mind, or cradle and love a woman who smelled of elder-flower, sweat and curliness.

I don't know where he went. . . . where his soul went. I don't think he went anywhere. His heart stopped and just stared when his brain could no longer send billows of passions and dreams. If there is God, she lets his soul stay on earth where he belongs. On earth, where dozens of books testify about the essence of his dreams. I wish he would have after-life needs and opportunities to peek through rain-splattered windows, walk through good mud with naked, laughing feet, bathe in the smell of a woman. But I know of no opportunities like that in death. Yet there are other ways....

I have a confession to make. I talked to Fred the other day. I called upon a filament in his soul, upon the whisper of his Old Lizard to enter my own Inner Meadows. I wove that night, and now I still have some waiting, empty nests made out of cinnabar leaves and tender moss on tall maple trees, where he can watch lions roam through winter snow or lie on rocks a million years old with lines of poetry embedded in them. There is one rock in there, with a passionate imprint of a tall man's naked body. Passion is known to melt into rocks. With awkward handwriting, as if scratched there with petrified maple twigs, the Old Lizard can read four lines he dictated long ago:

> So what about it, boy?
> Is your work going well?
> Are you still lighting lamps
> Against darkness and Hell?

Since Carl Sagan passed away and lit his last lamp to take a closer look at the sky, I look in amazement at the constellations and celebrate the stars above for both of us. Since Frederick Manfred died, God help me, I am pregnant with a wrinkled Old Lizard with a crooked smile and crooked teeth that loves the hell out of the bites I take for both of us, from the flesh of life. I can tell you, we are compulsive overeaters, and the dance we do in The Meadow, lit by candles against darkness and wrong, fills the Black with light as Fred conducts us to do more and more attacks to blast, and blast, and blast... to blast in his name, in the name of Life, for the glory of love, language and poetry.

Works Cited

American Grizzly. Video. St. Paul: The Center for International Education (CIE), 1983.

Manfred, Frederick. *The Golden Bowl.* Brookings: South Dakota Humanities Foundation, 1992.

I read a part of this essay at the Twenty-Sixth Annual Dakota History Conference on Friday, June 3, 1994. Frederick Manfred was in the audience. "Well done," he said afterward, smiling. His invitation to see his home, the opportunity to be around him for three days, to observe Manfred closely, and just to listen to his voice was one of the most powerful experiences of my life. He died three months after I met him. He was a magnificent man of honor and passion who could have walked into a forest full of legends and need not feel outnumbered.

"What would they do?": The Narrative Integrity of Fred Manfred

by Max Westbrook

During the early 1970s, I visited Fred Manfred. In his characteristic state of youthful energy, Fred began telling me about a tribal custom of the Yankton Dakota Indians. He was like a happy explorer who had found an ancient treasure chest full of diamonds and emeralds.

With his enormous hands out front, drawing the story in the air, Fred described a Yankton Dakota custom employed under desperate circumstances. They were a very small tribe, and their enemies were the Omaha, a much larger tribe. Indian warriors, Fred explained, try to kill the leader first. If the leader is killed, his followers usually flee. What martyr, then, or what fool would be willing to lead the small tribe and die in a hopeless cause?

According to Fred's research, the brave who agreed to lead the small Yankton tribe would be bribed, in advance, by the gift of any woman in the village for four days, the women, of course, having no say in the matter. When this tribal custom was put into practice, the women had to obey and submit, while the men would grind their teeth in bitterness, sulk in their misery, and keep silent.

Fred said he was making a novel out of this. To motivate the doomed leader, Fred made him unusually strong, handsome, and conceited. After four days of masculine gratification, Flat Warclub (Fred knew no shame) would lead the charge and die gloriously.

Battle, I reminded Fred, is often weird. Improbable things do happen. What if Flat Warclub somehow survived and came back?

Fred did not write *The Manly-Hearted Woman* that way—he kept to the more realistic odds—but for the moment he was intrigued with that possible turn of events in his plot. His eyes opened wider, as if to wonders never seen before. "What would they do?" he asked out loud, then promptly answered his own question: "Why they'd kill him, of course."

I have used this exchange dozens of times when trying to explain to my students a fundamental principle in the process of creating stories. I urge them to notice what the story-teller did *not* question. He did not ask, What idea would I illustrate if I wrote the novel that way? What personal belief would I illustrate?

"What would they do" states graphically what critics mean when they say a story-teller is a person who can "think people." William Faulkner, for example, once remarked that he did not tell his characters what to say; they told him, and he listened (120). Manipulating characters and events to illustrate the author's ideas leads to slick fiction or propaganda.

Attempts to prescribe what artists must or must not do are repeatedly shown to be foolish; but, based on what we have seen so far, artists who hope to achieve the integrity of narrative—as distinguished from the partisan distortions of characters and events—need to discover and create characters and a time and a place and then to let happen what would happen. If the story doesn't end the way the author wants the story to end—and this often happens—it may be hard on the author's emotions, but so be it.

Nonetheless, good writers have a convincing record of showing that the critic's principles of creativity are actually prescriptions and therefore false. Perhaps there are other ways of achieving literary integrity. Perhaps art can be born with a free-spirited flash that creates its own objective power.

For Fred Manfred, however, as for legions of others, the method of discipline begins with the seminal question, "What would they do?" In fact, the brief moment during which Fred reconsidered the fate of Flat Warclub reminded him of another time he had followed the trail wherever it led.

When he got to the end of *Riders of Judgment*, Fred told me, he developed a high fever and had to put the manuscript aside and go to bed. Once recovered, he returned to the last few pages needed to finish his novel and again came down with a high fever. As I recall, Fred said the sudden high fever came upon him three or four times before he realized he simply had to write with a raging temperature to finish the novel. That was the way it had to be.

Was he wishing Cain Hammett had not waited too late, or could somehow pull off an impossible miracle? Was the story of Cain's doom too painful to write in a normal physical state? During my visit, Fred did not speculate about the why, but the novel itself shows that Cain had allowed his chances to slide. Cain's ill-fated negligence and the story of what made him that way are—to put it in one oversimplified sentence—what the novel is about. To achieve narrative integrity, that was how the story had to end, whatever may have been the wishes of Fred Manfred.

Narrative integrity is just one of the ways in which Manfred went beyond the primitive powers he is often credited with. True enough, he sometimes wrote with a merciless sledge hammer, and the indelicate and obscene were often, for him, funny and real. After all, the culture he was born and raised in thrived on barnyard humor. But a powerful swing without art will strike no fire. Manfred's art, apparently, was so strong it could drive him to fever pitch.

To claim that a story has its own independent integrity, however, is not to say that literary art is pure. There has to be something we critics clumsily and inadequately try to name, a vision, a world view, perhaps just an attitude toward life.

For Manfred, I think that underpinning of content is best described as American sacrality, "American" because it includes reason *and* realism, "sacrality" because it is primarily that universal belief Mircea Eliade analyzes in *Cosmos and History: The Myth of the Eternal Return.*[2]

Eliade contrasts Christianity and sacrality. For Christians, God has made His one physical appearance on earth in the person of Jesus Christ. For several decades after the time of Christ, a child could talk to a parent who had seen God. After several more decades had passed, a child could talk to a grandparent who had seen God. But what about a hundred years later? Two hundred? A thousand? Christ has appeared only once, and Christianity, says Eliade, becomes more intellectual than felt, at best a faith based on the word of others. How many partake of the Lord's supper and actually feel they are drinking blood and eating flesh?

Sacrality is strikingly different. Manfred, American Indians, and probably the earth's majority see God (Wakan, the sacred) in the rising sun, in birth and death, the four seasons, in unexpected moments when the eternal is glimpsed in an ordinary bush, rock, whatever. Religion is neither a conviction based on the intellect nor a faith based on the testimony of people who lived two thousand years ago. God is seen and felt in daily lives.

Since critical comments on Manfred and any other writer are always suspect, it is good to hear from the writer. Unfortunately, I cannot date this one, and I cannot claim it is verbatim. What happened is I was teaching *Conquering Horse* in a western literature course, and, realizing I would be seeing Fred at the upcoming meeting of the Western Literature Association, I invited the class to give me a few questions they would like the author to answer.

One question concerned religion. Was the religious material in "Conquering Horse" from Indian culture, were there Christian parallels, did it come from both Indian and Christian sources, or were there other sources?

Fred's answer, according to my notes and *without* his reviewing them for corrections, went something like this: "The religion is Indian. They saw all (everything) as religion. The real was spiritual. The actual was merely a manifestation. The spiritual might at any time speak to you (so you should always listen) through the actual. When it did, the actual through which the spiritual spoke was Wakan."

Fred Manfred was Frisian, not Indian, but he obviously had a deep affinity for Indian religions. The actual was a good deal more than "merely a manifestation" for Fred, but seeing the world in a sacred way was personal to him and heartfelt, not just an attractive viewpoint to use in stories about Indians. Sacrality, Manfred believed, is basic to the world we live in, Indians, whites, all of us.

When writing of white and modern Americans alive in a sacred world, Fred kept to narrative integrity by including many who would not listen and could not see, some able to glimpse without understanding, and a few who achieved—but rarely lived up to—a high level of sacred wisdom. The real does not change to accommodate the current beliefs of a given time and culture; and modern society claims that reason has a monopoly on knowledge. What often happens to Fred's white Americans is they get into trouble because they misappropriate primal energy into the pursuit of money or some other ambition. Temptations of the profane world may be stronger than the unguided individual living in a civilization that is indifferent to the miracle of the daily rising of the sun.

In *Riders of Judgment*, Cain Hammett has the ability to sense a sacred presence: "Gooseflesh pimpled out over his arms and body. He felt it. He looked down at the bumps. When the animal in him roused up it was time to take notice. It hardly ever missed. It always knew better than he did. Something was wrong (337)." Cain, however, is hamstrung by jealousies and Hammett, like Hamlet, balks before the God-like role he has been assigned by fate: the duty to be judge, jury, and executioner.

Fortunately, Fred himself did better. Once in New York, he told me, walking through a long tunnel, he felt his own "gooseflesh pimple" over and immediately scrunched his neck up tight, just in time to prevent an assailant from tightening a wire around his neck. His being six feet nine and farmer-strong helped make him a difficult target, but it was the warning in the skin that saved his life.

In literature, however, failure, especially a glorious failure, makes for better reading than a story of success. Good writers remember that the subject of the most exciting book in *Paradise Lost* is the rebellious angel, Satan. The subject of the least interesting book is Jesus Christ. Good writers know that gods may be perfect, but a perfect human being belongs in a comic book. Flawed and struggling mortals are the cast of characters in the actual world and in literature that is faithful to the actual world.

Perhaps the most fundamental cause of the protagonist's failure in Fred Manfred's fiction is that following the sacred way is difficult for those who are raised in a sacred society but far more difficult—even dangerous—for moderns who tap into primal energies without being guided or educated in sacrality. There is no ritual exercise in the city, no modern shaman or wise old man to consult, and no history of living in a world that is Wakan.

Juhl Melander in *Milk of Wolves*, for example, is a talented sculptor with a creative drive too powerful for the profane world. He leaves his wife and children and their city-life, marries an Indian, fathers a child, but does not realize that his white-man version of the primal has no history. Having attended no school of sacrality, Melander is too uncivilized for the white world or the Indian world. He brags about having discovered his "blood," his "stud . . . genius" (207, right column), but there is no wisdom to accompany the energies thus invoked. The animal inside warns him, just as Fred Manfred's animal warned him, but Melander, like Cain Hammett, does not listen, and the result is that his wife Flur is killed. Later, he kills his own Indian son in a boating accident when he drives—without purpose—at a reckless speed.

Melander's sophomoric abuse of his artistic talents is demonstrated early in the novel, when he designs a statue of a friend's wife so that rain would make it seem to urinate. As a delinquent student of sacrality, he is worse than sophomoric. He is destructive and shows no grief for his dead son. Human energy and creativity are potentially powerful, but dangerous when abused.

The best explanation I know of the sacrality of energy is Heinrich Zimmer's analysis of the ancient tale of Abu Kasem in *The King and the Corpse* (9-25). Abu Kasem is a miser who puts all of his energy and passion into making and hoarding money. A very rich man, Abu will not buy himself some new slippers in spite of the fact that he wears a pair so patched and stitched they are a public disgrace, and yet—even when urged by a friend—he vigorously defends his tattered slippers and refuses to spend money for a new pair..

In a series of apparent accidents, the worn-out slippers get him in trouble, and each time he has to pay a fine. A fine, of course, is unbearable agony for a miser, but poor Abu cannot escape from his ill-fated slippers. He throws them in the river, buries them, burns them, and throws them in a lake, but they always come back and always cause another apparent accident and another fine. Finally, Abu appeals to the mercy of the court, he is released from the slippers, and the story comes to what seems a lame ending.

Zimmer then analyzes what has happened. Simply, Abu Kasem put all of his energy and passion into making money, a fanaticism that located itself in his disgraceful slippers. He could not get rid of the slippers because he would not purge himself of his miserliness. The slippers became an autonomous force because what we devote ourselves to usurps our energy and becomes an independent power, like a habit that seems stronger than we are. Thus Abu is controlled by his slippers as surely as harsh drugs control the addict. When the slippers get him in trouble, it is not by accident. When he cannot rid himself of the slippers, the cause is not some supernatural or fancied power. The slippers keep coming back because Abu has empowered them with all of his energy and passion.

Eden Prairie is one of Manfred's many tellings of modern energies and passions in a sacred world. The misplaced energy of Karen Alfredson is Edenic innocence rather than Abu Kasem's miserliness, but Manfred is telling an original, mythic version of the same archetypal paradigm that underlies the ancient tale of the miser.

The original innocence of Karen makes her look like a Victorian prude, but she has no other available language she can use to express her primordial drive for a life that is pure and childlike. Unlike prudes who are fueled only by the intellect or by denial, Karen is capable of spirited action that is both brave and comic. When she catches two students making love, her primordial innocence is outraged, and she battles fiercely to separate them. She is outlandish in her pure rage, but her passion is born in the same primal breeding grounds as the passion that fueled the young lovers.

Edenic innocence cannot find a context in the modern world. Kon Harmer, a version of the Biblical Adam, is not strong enough to inherit what his father has achieved, and his brother is ambitious to commercialize the family's Garden of Eden. For Karen and Kon, then, there is no inheritance, no continuity. They are modern-day Adam and Eve in a world of hustling Babbitts and rutting school children.

Primordial energies are repeatedly shown to be essentially the same for moderns as for the ancient. Thus Manfred includes the comic, dirty jokes, farming lore, art, baseball, science, sex, weather, books, the land, the city, and hundreds of other subjects that characterize modern America. Usually the primal is too powerful or too alien. Becoming strong enough to keep on struggling is a rare triumph. Still, it is possible to see and to learn in Manfred's fictive world. Lord Grizzly does. And becomes a better man.

Most, however, fail to live in a sacred way. They cannot live in harmony with both sides of the brain: the right (holistic, creative) side and left (abstracting, logical) side. They cannot keep in touch with both the primal powers and the actual world. Primal energy is displaced and becomes a self-destructive stubbornness so fanatic it destroys that which is most desired.

Sherman Engleking, for example, the protagonist of *No Fun on Sunday*, is a hard-working farm boy whose only chance for success is to do what he loves most: play baseball. He is remarkably talented and has signed with the Chicago Cubs, meaning he has a chance to make it in the major leagues.

Before it's time for him to leave, he is working on a new farm machine, a corn picker. The machine becomes clogged with corn, he reaches his hand down toward its deadly gears and barely escapes serious injury to his hand. Having been warned both verbally and by his own experience, Sherman then insists on working the machine alone, which is even more dangerous, again reaches in toward the gears to clear the machine, and this time loses three fingers, thus ending his chance for a career in the major leagues.

Just before the accident (if it can be called an accident), Sherman reflects on local baseball games: he starts "remembering how he [and the other two good players on his team] used to will and will to win, will so hard they actually would win. Mind hot in their skull, rampant like a bull about to mount a heifer, they'd win despite wretched fielding by the rest of the team" (271). Foolishly matched against the machine, that fierce energy loses.

Primordial energies are also misappropriated in *Of Lizards and Angels*, a novel in which warnings over the years continue to be ignored, which explains why incest is repeated from generation to generation. Like Cain Hammett, Juhl Melander, Sherman Engleking, and others, the characters in *Of Lizards and Angels* cannot learn from what they see, or embody successfully the talents they have been given.

Clearly, Manfred writes of people caught between sacred realities and their own profane values. But it is also clear that his most memorable characters are stubborn and contrary, filled with abounding energy, and excited to be alive. "What would they do?" is answered by actions that are heroic, cowardly, outrageous, even fatal. Thus Fred Manfred—obedient to his genius—faithfully tracked his characters to the end of their story.

Notes

[1] Manfred makes a similar remark in *Duke's Mixture:* "There's an interesting thing that goes on when characters start showing up and you think they should go this way and they have their own notion. You always follow where they want to go. Never force it, cause then it's wrong" (237): or, more simply, "I'm just a clerk, taking it down" (236). Commenting on the writing of *King of Spades*, Manfred says, "Nights when I went to bed I couldn't wait until morning to find out more about what was going to happen . . . [next]" (79-80).

"Listening" to one's own characters, of course, represents a peak in the creative process, but it is neither the exclusive nor the absolute mode of creativity. Manfred, like other writers, also talks about plotting, selecting characters to introduce, and various devices and stages included in the more conscious part of developing a narrative. See, for example, *Duke's Mixture*, 82.

[2] See especially xi, 63-73, and 141-147. Eliade's *The Sacred and the Profane* is also essential to an understanding of sacrality.

Works Cited

Eliade, Mircea. *Cosmos and History: The Myth of the Eternal Return.* New York: Harper and Row, 1954.

Faulkner, William. *Faulkner in the University.* Ed. Frederick L. Gwynn and Joseph L. Blotner. New York: Random House, 1965.

Manfred, Frederick. *Duke's Mixture.* Sioux Falls: The Center for Western Studies, 1994.

---. *Milk of Wolves.* Boston: Avenue Victor Hugo, 1976.

---. *No Fun on Sunday.* Norman: U of Oklahoma P, 1990.

---. *Riders of Judgment.* New York: Random House, 1957.

Zimmer, Heinrich. *The King and the Corpse; Tales of the Soul's Conquest of Evil.* New York: Meridian Books, 1960.

"Love, Dad"
from *The Wonderful Life and Death of Frederick Manfred*

by Freya Manfred

My father rises at six a.m. before the rest of the family and devours three bowls of Special K cereal drenched with skim milk and topped with gobs of extra-large California raisins with seeds. (After years of eating the same breakfast, he learns these huge seeded raisins are to be discontinued, and stocks up to make them last another year.) When his coffee is ready, he inhales a soup-bowl sized cup of it, whitened with milk and three spoonfuls of sugar. He stares out the window while he eats, his sky blue eyes dreamy and unguarded, wide open and ready for anything, like the eyes of a sensitive child—already zeroing inward toward what will become reality when his fingers hit the keys of the old black Remington Seventeen typewriter in the cabin 200 feet from the house.

At six-thirty a.m. he puts on his old wool coat and his tall fur hat, and strides out to his tiny 8 X 10 cabin, a remodeled chicken house with whitewashed boards inside and out, a small heater, two small windows, and a door. Inside: a plank desk, an oak swivel chair, a narrow cot with a big pillow and a little pillow and a maroon and gold Calvin College basketball letter blanket folded at the end of it, two walls lined with books, and a small curtained-off closet where he stacks papers and manuscripts. His rugged 6'9" frame, giant muscled shoulders, long legs, size 16 feet, and shock of reddish-brown hair make the room seem very small if you stop by to visit. He's wearing old jeans, an old flannel shirt, and a long brown smock tied at the neck with wide pleats on each side.

"Daddy, why are you wearing a dress?"

"Dress, ha! It's an artist's smock. I wear it to keep the ink off my clothes while I write. Someday, if you become an artist, you'll have one just like it."

I spy a black leather cup filled with dozens of odd-sized pens and pencils beside the Remington. "Daddy, why do you need all those pencils?"

"To make corrections, Dolly. Writers need to make corrections. And to write poems, if one strikes me."

"Can I have a pencil, Daddy?"

"Of course, Dolly. Choose one. Then you can write your own books."

Morning is the quiet time. Dad hunches in his cabin, typing, concentrating, intense, "because when you write," he says, "you burn, you burn at 100%; you give it all you have, and more. That's why I hate to get sick. I can't write at 60% or 80%. I end up with pap, just pap." He writes hard for three or four hours, especially hard for a man who almost died of tuberculosis less than a decade earlier. When he left Glen Lake Sanitorium in Eden Prairie, Minnesota, after two years of complete bed rest, Dr. Sumner Cohen told him that writing fiction was too passionate and emotionally stressful a task for a man with half of one lung and a quarter of the other missing. He suggested Dad find "part time work in other venues. Don't become a writer, or raise any children, if you want to live." This is why Dad stops writing around eleven a.m. and takes a walk to the end of the driveway to get *The Minneapolis Star* and have some lunch. And then takes a nap with a pillow over his head.

All morning in the summer we can hear the clacking of the typewriter keys. My sister, Marya, and my brother, Freddy, and I mustn't shout or fight or laugh too loud when we play in the sandbox or on the swings in the back yard. If we do, we'll get into trouble. "Thwack!" his cabin door flaps open and hits the outside wall, and he jumps out roaring, face red with passion, "Dammit, I told you kids to keep quiet! I'm trying to write here!" We scatter like blackbirds, and later, if he remembers, which he usually doesn't, I get scolded because I'm the oldest and should keep the others quiet. It's best to stay in the front yard, roll down the hill into the prairie grass; set up lemonade parties for my dolls, and look for bugs and flowers. But what in the world can he be doing for such a long time? When I sneak up and peek inside the cabin window—I'd better not make a sound!—he's bent over the Remington, tapping away with his forefingers, the small finger on his left hand permanently crooked because the tendons were cut when he slipped and flung his hand through a window on Gramma Shorba's icy back steps.

I didn't question how my father spent his mornings, but my friends did. Diane Pond, whose father owned a successful car repair business, and Lois Linder, a farmer's daughter, and Nemo Beach, the son of Northrup Beach, our pediatrician, made frequent comments: "What's your dodo Dad doing in that old shack? How come he doesn't go to work like a normal person?" "What do you mean, 'writing stories'? Why doncha ask him to tell us a story, for once?" And then, "How tall is he, really? Did he honestly, truly, cross-your-heart, pick up one end of Mr. Brown's Ford all by himself?"

I used to stare intensely at my father the way my sons now stare at my husband and myself, as if my *body* was trying to absorb the essence and truth of him through unselfconscious five-year-old eyes. Did Dad's stories appear in the air above his head, where only his piercing blue eyes could spot them? Could my eyes learn to see stories too? Or did his stories come out of the black spaces underneath his typewriter keys, clicking and clacking like teeth, spewing forth long rolling white sheets of paper covered with letters and words? How did he know which letters between A and Z to type? And later, at six, I asked myself, "Does he know what he wants to say when he wakes up, or does it come to him during the pauses, when he stops typing and stares without looking at the whitewashed wall of his cabin? Or is he saying what God tells him? And if it's God, is it the same God who covers our hill with grass in the springtime? The God who sometimes asks me to comb his hair and the hair of his wife with a black comb as I crouch near the wet earth smelling God's smell: loam, sand, stones, wheat grass, water, sun, all glittering, sweating, breathing into me? Or is there some other God inside Dad's cabin—a colorful story-telling God speaking with many voices? Or is it just Dad, long tall Dad, banging words onto the page, the same old Dad who tells stories all the time to my mother and brother and sister and me, to the milkman, the dry cleaner, the plumber, and all the neighbors. Just our regular Dad, who leans one elbow on the top of Mrs. Linder's refrigerator and opens a beer and sips it once or twice and then starts a story about the time when his Dad fell seventy-five feet off a windmill and survived....

Although I teach creative writing workshops, I still find it difficult to tell my students entirely *in words* how writing works, perhaps because I was first exposed to the process so young. I believe I absorbed what writing was kinesthetically, even before I learned words, certainly before I learned words to explain the process. I watched my mother write too: poems at first, and then book reviews, and tried to absorb, understand, even memorize what she was doing. I drank my parents in—being writers—the way I drank in the honeysuckle bushes thrusting out buds in the spring, opening their pink flowers to the sun, permeating the yard with scent. The writing Dad did in his cabin suffused our house and yard as if it were a kind of plant life, growing and changing and natural as weather—a day in, day out, physical outpouring of his own blood and bone turned to black bits on a white page, which, when read, made a kind of music. His face, while he wrote, was distorted with ferocity, exhilaration, exaltation, and exhaustion. And this stormy and sunny weather pattern in which I grew up encouraged me to write my own first stories when I was six.

*****

Despite endless money worries, Dad is most optimistic every year or so when one of his books is published. A big cardboard box from New York, Denver, Utah, Nebraska, Oklahoma, etc. is delivered to the house with 100 copies of just one book, Dad's latest: *The Golden Bowl, Boy Almighty, The Chokecherry Tree, This is The Year, The Primitive, The Brother, The Giant, Conquering Horse, Lord Grizzly, Riders of Judgment, Green Earth:* over the years thirty-four novels, two books of poetry, and the conversations, essays, and letters. After his work is done for the day, Dad gets a sharp knife and carefully cuts the box open, and inside we discover sleek new covers, strongly woven backs, pure white and black pages. Dad's face swells with pride as his big hands stroke the books. He picks one out, eases it from the box, and opens it slowly. He smells it.

He shows us how to "break in" a book so you won't crack it's spine. A book with a broken spine doesn't "last." You hold the book upright and closed, with the spine down on a table. You take hold of the stiff outer back cover and press it down, lightly and carefully, and then do the same with the outer front cover, gently. Then, moving to the back of the book, you take hold of a few pages, lovingly, and press them down. Then you move to the front and press a few more pages down. You work your way from back to front, a few pages at a time, until you reach the center of the book with two or three pages left between your fingers: the heart of the book. You smooth the last pages down into place and close the book. It's ready to read. You don't peek at the ending, because that spoils the story and isn't fair to the writer. You probably peek at the first sentence so you can let your excitement build toward the moment when you will start the book. And once you begin reading, you must always give the writer 100 pages before you decide to quit, if you quit, which you usually don't; but it's allowed if the book is really bad. Most books you choose to read are good. You have that faith. But some are truly bad. A bad book doesn't draw you in, can't keep you awake when you get in, or ends poorly, without reverberating in your heart and soul and without referring in any way back to where it started. A bad book is a selfish book, where the writer was so concerned with his or her elaborate (ever so shallow) style that he or she forgot what the book was supposed to say. A bad book is where the writer hasn't found a voice, and sounds like anyone or everyone or something you read in the newspapers, only not as bald or as succinct or as close to life as a newspaper. A bad book shows off, pretends to have invented a new style, a new genre, or a story not already hinted at somewhere in the Bible or Shakespeare or Emily Dickinson. A bad book has characters who do not come alive and greet you as if they were made of flesh and bone; or a plot that a Yankton Sioux scout couldn't follow; or a theme that shouts itself from every page and drowns out the power and the glory, the underlying melody which will sing to you for weeks and months and years after you finish the book. There are a lot of bad books, more every year, and it's good to avoid them, but if you haven't given each and every writer 100 pages to get your attention, you haven't done the fair thing. You already know this if you've ever tried to write a book yourself.

*****

Dad believes that deep down most readers can be trusted to know what's good. No matter what their work or how smart they are, they'll like a good story, the way they like a warm fire in winter. Some critics can also be trusted to know what's good, but most of them are "almost useless" frustrated writers and you "can't count on them to get you up a hill in a snowstorm." You're proud of what some of them write and you want to kill others, but they're mostly an "unhappy unfulfilled caterwauling bunch," and there are only a few good ones: Malcolm Cowley, Edmund Wilson, Allen Tate, and maybe John Milton from the University of South Dakota, in his youth. "We're short of good critics in the 1980s and 90s, so I hope some come along soon."

Dad has tremendous respect for the daily work of other people (with the possible exception of insurance agents and divorce lawyers). Genuinely curious and humble, he asks hundreds of questions of doctors, nurses, stonecutters, carpenters, plumbers, farmers, businessmen, teachers, and students, and gratefully uses the detailed information they provide in his books. And yet, when we discuss the potential occupations of his own children—the way Dad tells it, most jobs are worthless next to writing. Or, if not worthless, less magnificent. It takes so much hard work and luck and true guts to even become a writer when you have a father who cannot read and a mother who reads mostly religious tracts and the Bible, and when you come from a Calvinistic community which frowns on any kind of artistic truth if it flies in the face of Our Lord. It takes so much pain and fear and years of TB, and slaving as a farm hand, factory worker, short order cook, newspaper reporter, bodyguard, sparring partner, semi-professional basketball player, etc., to keep to the task you were truly called for: novelist and storyteller. There is so much pressure to quit and earn more money doing something more sensible and profitable. Pressure from your struggling wife, your family, distant relatives, the church, the community, the state. So that once you "become" a writer, you can't help but feel it is the luckiest and most kingly of occupations. There is nothing better to be, with the possible exception of composer or musician.

January 24, 1967

My Dear Freya,

What a lovely and thoughtful letter you sent me for my birthday. Not too many people are aware of the trials of authorship . . . .

One of the reasons I rejected teaching too, except for the short stint at Macalester, was that it got in the way (of) dreaming and projecting and imagining. And Hawthorne is right that the very toughness a man needs to keep fighting is almost in complete variance with poetic burst. Except that when you take a job and try and forget that side of you, you know an unhappiness so deep that you must either kill yourself or go back to imagining no matter what the cost. Perhaps this is a good thing. Maybe the best flowers appear on the most durable of trees. God knows, and now you, that I've had to be gnarly tough to keep on writing with all the money troubles and fights we've had in our house. Your mother almost daily keeps taunting me with the fact that I can't pay my way, that I don't even have a pot to pee in, and yet she expects me to do well enough to make the money with which to buy the pot. (I'd rather pee outdoors in the grass.) I must be a true writer because when I go to bed I think of the lovely breakfast I'll have in the morning just before I climb up to my beloved work at the desk.

My love, Dad

*****

A writer who nearly dies from tuberculosis when he's in his twenties and spends two years in a tuberculosis sanitorium where he watches thirteen room-mates die has to develop and keep strong habits to get his writing done. Here are a few of his rules:

1. Don't party or drink alcohol on week nights. Your work will suffer the next day.

July 19, 1968

I, personally, do frown on the use of any narcotics, drugs, etc., unless medically prescribed. There is just no excuse, none at all, for any use of pot, nicotine, LSD, the like, and only goddam fools indulge in it. Liquor there might be some excuse for, as it has food value. The others have no value of any kind, and they probably damage one. In my house there will never be any pot parties; and I don't like it when any one smokes in it. Copulation, yes. Swearing, yes. Truth-telling, yes. Hearing voices, yes. Loud smacking over food, my god yes. Burping, maybe. Cries of joy, oh dear sweet father yes.

Dad

2. Resist visitors on week days, except Friday. Talk is great fun, but it takes energy, which must be saved for writing.

3. Stop writing after three hours, or sooner if you get tired, so you'll have something left for the next day.

4. Nap every day.

5. Answer letters and do errands on Saturday.

6. Rest on Sunday. This means no church except the great outdoors, lots of sleep, the Sunday paper, waffles or pancakes, and maybe a visit with a friend.

7. Keep your meals simple: cereal for breakfast, a slice of bread and an apple for lunch, a slab of meat and some vegetables for dinner. After dinner, try ice cream or bread with jam piled on it an inch thick. Candy's okay on Sundays, but you better cache it in some high place only you can reach or one of your kids will ferret it out and eat it.

8. Keep your weight down. It's better for your knees, and besides, your body is the greatest miracle you'll ever possess.

9. Exercise every day: walk, or use a ski machine, dig a garden, clean house, keep moving.

10. Don't keep a dog or a cat. Dogs demand too much attention, and cats belong in barns where they can catch mice. If the neighbor's cat comes over to eat your mice, that's a gift. It's a pleasure to watch a good mouser work, and maybe have her sit in your lap too, if you're outside reading in the sun.

11. Don't get into an argument with a close relative. If someone starts up, it's best to fall silent.

12. There's no king or queen worth crossing the street to see. Writers and thinkers are the true aristocracy.

13. Find time to be quiet, and alone.

And the most important thing on Dad's list would be: don't whine about how hard it is to write. Several of my talented friends were the children of well-known authors who grumbled and complained endlessly about the tribulations of writing. As a consequence, my friends made up their minds never to write a word themselves. But Dad never complained about how hard writing was. He left for work excited. He returned tired, but happy. Writing was a gift and a blessing, and he was lucky.

"Each day was a gift. Each day came wrapped in sparkling morning sunlight.

> For most people, days are all alike. They forget that they are presents from the unknown.
> But Eric knew they were gifts, all of them. One by one they came, and he knew they would not come again; that this day he was having, this one short spurt of time, this one was the last of its kind; that once it vanished into evening's melancholy sunfall, it was gone forever.
> He caressed them and called them each a name.
> This one, this day, he named 'a golden drop.'
> The next one, this day, he named 'a water drop.'
> The next one, this day, he named, 'a golden drop.'
> They were all new and different names, they were, because when a day had died at sunfall he forgot it sleeping; and waking, found a new one and named it the best name he knew, "a golden drop, a water drop."
>
> *Boy Almighty*, 1945

*****

Dad gave speeches to make extra money, but the older he became the more he hated it, unless he could visit an exotic place like Hawaii or Banff, Canada, and take an extra day or two to explore. He couldn't afford a longer visit, though he didn't say so. Instead he said, "I want to stay home and finish my novel, but this speech is a necessary nuisance."

October 12, 1988

Dear Freya,
    Three weeks ago last Sunday I became very ill with the flu. Spent a week in bed— interrupted twice by talks I had to give which I'd agreed to do and for which I got needed good money. Each time I rose from the sludge and phlegm like a Neptune rising from the sea to give the talk and then collapsed again. I'm still sniffing a little. But the temperature and pulse are normal again.
                                              Love, Dad

He enjoyed workshops and writing festivals more than speeches, because he could meet and talk with his literary friends. He enjoyed the P.E.N. meetings in New York so much that he'd describe them in detail: setting, atmosphere, speeches, parties, food, and especially the people. He'd leap to his feet to imitate how this or that writer stood, or spoke, or walked, and quote what he or she said. After his imitation of John Updike, it was easy for me to instantly recognize that author in a crowd of people in New York—something about the way he inclined his head and moved his face and hands, though the last time I'd "met" him he was six feet nine inches tall and was wearing size 16 buckskin boots with fringes.

Acknowledgments

This collection has been a long time coming. In fact, the idea for it originated at the 1983 meeting of the Western Literature Association in Minneapolis-St.Paul. From the original panel, only the essays by Lawrence Berkove and Barbara Meldrum appear in this volume. The other participants have either submitted different pieces or have disappeared from my parameters of contact. However, the impulse which drove the project has remained constant to break ground in the research on Manfred's work.

Indeed, this is the first collection of its kind to be produced about Fred's writings. To be sure, essays about his work have been published in such journals as *Western American Literaure* and *The South Dakota Review*, and in his later years Manfred himself published essays about his writings (*Duke's Mixture*) and about male influences (*Prime Fathers*). But I believe that this book fills a void in the critical work on Manfred. I hope this is the first of many.

My personal thanks go to a number of people who have continued to remind me through the years of commitment to complete this project: Lawrence Berkove, whose good-natured "thoughts" have remained a constant; Mick McAllister, who knew Fred Manfred better than many of us and whose fine work on the Buckskin Man tales validates the seriousness of Manfred's writing; Art Huseboe, Fred's spiritual brother and my friend, colleague and co-editor of *The Selected Letters of Frederick Manfred*, who has always turned a cheerful and energetic face to our projects; in more recent years, Rick Bailey, Forest "Mickey" Byrd, and Olga Klekner, who joined me at the 1994 Dakota History Conference in Sioux Falls to present their essays (and Larry Juchartz, whose essay I read at that same occasion) and to celebrate the life and writings of Frederick Manfred only months before his death.

I must also thank the editors of *Western American Literature*, who allowed reprinting of the Nelson and McAllister pieces, the University of Iowa Libraries for the Wylder essay (*Books at Iowa*), and the South Dakota Humanities Foundation, which has allowed the reprinting of the Huseboe and Milton essays from their fine 50th anniversary edition of *The Golden Bowl*. Finally Mrs. John R. Milton, in a kind note to me, graciously permitted me to reprint her husband's groundbreaking essay on *Bowl*.

Thanks also to friends and colleagues who have sustained their interest in Manfred's work through the years and in so doing, have sustained mine: Larry Juchartz, Mary Lund, Ed Demerly, and many others too numerous to name.

Nancy Owen Nelson, editor

Publisher's Ackowledgments

The Center for Western Studies gratefully acknowledges the following: Dr. Peter Bischoff and *Studies in the Western* for permission to publish a shorter version of Sanford Marovitz's essay; Robert C. Steensma (University of Utah) and Ronald Robinson (Augustana College) for reviewing an early draft of the collection; and especially Mr. Al Schock for his financial support of this project. He, in turn, wishes to thank Frederick Manfred's former wife Maryanna for her assistance in the editing of Mr. Schock's recently published autobiography.

Books by Frederick Manfred

The Golden Bowl 1944
Boy Almighty 1945
This is the Year 1947
The Chokecherry Tree 1948
The Primitive 1949
The Brother 1950
The Giant* 1951
Lord Grizzly 1954
Morning Red 1956
Riders of Judgment 1957
Conquering Horse 1959
Arrow of Love (stories) 1961
Wanderlust (trilogy)** 1962
Scarlet Plume 1964
The Man Who Looked Like the Prince of Wales*** 1965
Winter Count (poems) 1966
King of Spades 1966
Apples of Paradise (stories) 1968
Eden Prairie 1968
Conversations 1974
Milk of Wolves 1976
The Manly-Hearted Woman 1976
Green Earth 1977
The Wind Blows Free (reminiscence) 1979
Sons of Adam 1980
Winter Count II (poems) 1987
Prime Fathers (portraits) 1989
The Selected Letters of Frederick Manfred (1932-1954) 1989
Flowers of Desire 1989
No Fun on Sunday 1990
Of Lizards and Angels 1992
Duke's Mixture (miscellany) 1994

*Mr. Manfred wrote under the name of Feike Feikema from 1944 through 1951.
**A new revised version of three novels, *The Primitive, The Brother, The Giant*, and published in one volume.
*** Reprinted in paperback as *The Secret Place*.

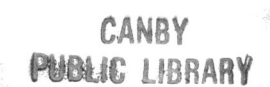

813.54 LIZ

36601007243648 (11)

The lizard speaks